Lexical Gram...

Cambridge Handbooks for Language Teachers

This series, now with over 50 titles, offers practical ideas, techniques and activities for the teaching of English and other languages, providing inspiration for both teachers and trainers.

Recent titles in this series:

Lexical Grammar

Activities for teaching chunks and exploring patterns

Leo Selivan

Consultant and editor: Scott Thornbury

CAMBRIDGE
UNIVERSITY PRESS

CAMBRIDGE
UNIVERSITY PRESS

University Printing House, Cambridge CB2 8BS, United Kingdom

One Liberty Plaza, 20th Floor, New York, NY 10006, USA

477 Williamstown Road, Port Melbourne, VIC 3207, Australia

314–321, 3rd Floor, Plot 3, Splendor Forum, Jasola District Centre, New Delhi – 110025, India

79 Anson Road, #06–04/06, Singapore 079906

Cambridge University Press is part of the University of Cambridge.

It furthers the University's mission by disseminating knowledge in the pursuit of education, learning and research at the highest international levels of excellence.

www.cambridge.org
Information on this title: www.cambridge.org/9781316644751

© Cambridge University Press 2018

First published 2018

20 19 18 17 16 15 14 13 12 11 10 9 8 7 6 5 4 3 2 1

A catalogue record for this publication is available from the British Library

ISBN 978-1-316-64475-1 Paperback
ISBN 978-1-316-64477-5 Apple iBook
ISBN 978-1-316-64478-2 Google eBook
ISBN 978-1-316-64480-5 Kindle eBook
ISBN 978-1-316-64479-9 ebooks.com eBook

Contents

Thanks

What does one do when approached by Scott Thornbury himself about writing a book? **Jump at the offer**, don't you? **Oddly enough,** that **wasn't the case with** me: I hesitated, **citing a number of** | silly excuses. **It took me some time** | **to come to my senses** and realize that this was **a once-in-a-lifetime opportunity.** Therefore, I'm **deeply indebted to** Scott Thornbury for believing in me, **entrusting me with this project** and guiding me through **every step of the way,** which was not always **plain sailing.**

There are many people to thank for **making this book happen.** Jo Timerick and Karen Momber of Cambridge University Press, for **overseeing the project** | **from start to finish** and particularly for bringing in Ros Henderson as editor, who, with her **keen eye** and **expert knowledge,** ensured clarity and consistency while staying **on the same wavelength as** me. The British Council, for giving me years of **valuable experience** and **letting me go** | **at the right time, just as I was about to** | **embark on this journey.** My 'lexical' **kindred spirits,** Ken Lackman and Lindsey Steinberg-Shapiro, discussions with whom have **enriched me professionally** | **in many ways. And not least importantly,** Tzvi Meller, for supporting me mentally.

A number of people have **offered me valuable advice** | **along the way** and helped me – directly or indirectly – with various aspects of the manuscript. **In no particular order,** these include Chris Miller (https://chrismlanguage.wordpress.com/), Todd Beuckens (ELLLO), Laura Patsko, Steffen Wolf and, of course, all my students on whom I **tried out the activities.**

Last but not least, this book **wouldn't have come about** | **if it weren't for** three people: Michael Lewis, Hugh Dellar and Andrew Walkley, who have profoundly **opened my eyes to** | **what really matters** in language teaching. For that, I'll **be forever grateful.**

Acknowledgements

The authors and publishers acknowledge the following sources of copyright material and are grateful for the permissions granted. While every effort has been made, it has not always been possible to identify the sources of all the material used, or to trace all copyright holders. If any omissions are brought to our notice, we will be happy to include the appropriate acknowledgements on reprinting and in the next update to the digital edition, as applicable.

Text:

British National Corpus for the text on p. 2 from British National Corpus website, http://www.natcorp.ox.ac.uk. Copyright © British National Corpus. Reproduced with kind permission; Guardian News and Media Limited for the text on p. 16 adapted from 'Babysitting apps boom as parents bid to reclaim free time' by Tess Reidy, *The Guardian*, 25.02.2017. Copyright © 2017 Guardian News and Media Limited. Reproduced with permission; The Hong Kong University of Science and Technology for the screenshots on pp. 18–19 from Word Neighbors website, http://wordneighbors.ust.hk/help/index.html. Copyright © Hong Kong University of Science and Technology. Reproduced with kind permission; Just The Word for the screenshot on p. 21 from just-the-word website, http://www.just-the-word.com/. Copyright © Just The Word. Reproduced with kind permission; Corpus of Contemporary American English for the screenshots on pp. 26–27 from Corpus of Contemporary American English website, https://corpus.byu.edu/coca/. Copyright © Corpus of Contemporary American English. Reproduced with kind permission; Cambridge University Press for the screenshot on p. 30 from *Cambridge Dictionary* website, https://dictionary.cambridge.org/dictionary/english/charity. Copyright © Cambridge University Press. Reproduced with kind permission; Lexical Computing Ltd. for the screenshot on p. 33 from Skell Engine for Language Learning website, http://skell.sketchengine.co.uk/run.cgi/skell. Copyright © Lexical Computing Ltd. Reproduced with kind permission of Lexical Computing Ltd., vendor of the SKELL and Sketch Engine Corpus Management Systems; Bauhaus-Universität Weimar for the screenshot on p. 69 from Netspeak website, http://www.netspeak.org/#publisher. Copyright © Bauhaus-Universität Weimar. Reproduced with kind permission of Martin Potthast; Elllo Productions for the text on p. 71–72 adapted from 'What is your favourite season?', http://www.elllo.org/english/Mixer126/T148-Season.htm. Copyright © 2016 Elllo Productions. Reproduced with permission; YouGlish for the screenshots on pp. 82–83 from YouGlish website, https://youglish.com/. Copyright © YouGlish. Reproduced with kind permission; Cambridge University Press for text on p. 112 and p. 114 from *English Grammar in Use, 4th edition* by Raymond Murphy. Copyright © 2012 Cambridge University Press; Corpus of Contemporary American English for the screenshot on p. 125 from the Corpus of Contemporary American English website, https://corpus.byu.edu/coca/. Copyright © Corpus of Contemporary American English. Reproduced with kind permission; Pelcra Group for the screenshots on p. 150 from 'Graph-Based Analysis of Collocational Profiles. In Phraseologie Im Wörterbuch Und Korpus (Phraseology in Dictionaries and Corpora), edited by Vida Jesenšek and

Photos:

Introduction

Traditionally, language is viewed as consisting of words, on the one hand, and of grammatical structures, on the other. But what if we got rid of this dichotomy and focused on both at the same time? The activities in this book attempt to do just that: to focus on units of language, such as chunks and patterns, that straddle the border between vocabulary and grammar. The idea of merging vocabulary with grammar is not new in itself and has been convincingly argued by the likes of Dave Willis and Michael Lewis. Drawing on recent research in both corpus linguistics and second language acquisition, this book reinforces the important role that chunks play not only in textual cohesion and fluency, but also in forming the raw material for grammar acquisition. The practical part of the book includes classroom suggestions and activities for making grammar teaching more lexical, and for making vocabulary practice more grammatical.

1 Chunks in language

What is a 'chunk'?

A chunk is a group of words customarily found together. Some chunks are fixed expressions, for example *as a matter of fact*, while others are combinations of words that allow variation such as *see you later/soon/tomorrow.*

Is a chunk the same as collocation?

Some chunks can indeed be described as collocations. Collocation is a kind of chunk which consists of two lexical (content) words:

pursue a career (verb + noun)
a scenic route (adjective + noun)
a chance encounter (noun + noun)
ridiculously expensive (adverb + adjective)
examine carefully (verb + adverb)

However, many frequent multi-word combinations do not fall neatly into the above categories with two identifiable parts of speech (verb + noun, adjective + noun, etc.). Chunks also comprise other types of multi-word units such as:

see you later (speech formula)
come to think of it (discourse marker)
as the study suggests (linking phrase)
at all costs (prepositional phrase)

Chunks can also be structures which have traditionally been associated with grammar. They can include stems that can be used to build various sentences in English:

If I were you
It's been a while since
It took me a long time to

Finally, some full sentences can also be considered chunks:

It's none of your business.
There's no doubt about it.
What are you gonna do?

Is everything chunks, then?

Yes, to a large extent. Evidence suggests that our mental lexicon does not consist of individual words but chunks. Chunks can vary greatly in length (some consist of two words while others, as seen above, can be full sentences) but what makes them chunks is the fact that they are stored in the brain as single units. Research shows that about 50–80% of native-speaker discourse consists of recurring multi-word combinations (Altenberg, 1987; Erman and Warren, 2000).

Is the idea of chunks new?

Linguists, second language acquisition (SLA) researchers and lexicographers have used different terms to describe multi-word units throughout the years: multi-word strings, prefabricated routines, ready-made expressions, lexicalized stems, and so on. However, the terms all mean essentially the same thing. Although their existence was pointed out a long time ago, chunks came to the fore with the advent of **corpus linguistics**. A corpus (from Latin: body; plural = corpora) is a searchable database containing samples of text. Text is referred to here in its broader sense and includes fiction, newspapers, magazines and academic journals, as well as transcripts of TV shows, radio interviews, business meetings and informal conversations. Once the domain of linguists, many corpora are now openly available on the internet, with the British National Corpus (BNC) and Corpus of Contemporary American English (COCA) being probably the most popular resources. For example, this is what random lines – known as concordances – taken from the BNC reveal about how the word *matter* is used:

Figure 0.1: Search result for *matter* from the British National Corpus

Studying these real-life text samples has helped corpus linguists to discover common patterns of use for particular words: *no matter how*, *what's the matter with*, etc.

Although the first corpus of authentic English texts was compiled in the 1960s, corpus linguistics didn't begin in earnest until computers had become powerful enough to hold vast amounts of data and to enable much more rigorous analysis, that is, the 1980s. That is when a joint venture between the University of Birmingham and Collins publishers, known as COBUILD (Collins Birmingham University Language Database) saw the creation of the Bank of English, at that time the largest electronic corpus of contemporary English texts. The project was founded and led by the renowned linguist John Sinclair (1933–2007). Corpus research, and particularly the COBUILD project, has provided some fascinating insights into how real language works and led Sinclair to conclude that language is largely formulaic, i.e. it consists of ready-made chunks. As Sinclair argued in his seminal work *Corpus Concordance Collocation*:

> *A language user has available to him a large number of semi-preconstructed phrases* [chunks] *that constitute single choices, even though they might appear to be analyzable into segments.* (1991: 110)

If the language we use is comprised of ready-made lexico-grammatical units, the boundary between what we have traditionally called 'grammar' and 'vocabulary' is somewhat blurred.

How do chunks blur the boundary between vocabulary and grammar?

The blurred boundary between vocabulary and grammar refers to the tendency of certain words to occur with certain grammatical structures and vice versa. For example, the verb *to found* is likely to be used in the passive (e.g. *The company was founded in 1957*) and the verb *to mind* is normally used in questions and negative statements (e.g. *Do you mind if I, I don't mind*).

This close link between grammar and vocabulary means that while there may be many possible ways of correctly combining grammar with words to make sentences, we tend to go for conventionalized combinations. For example, all the sentences below are grammatically correct and some of them exhibit a very advanced control of English grammar:

Could I make a call using your phone?
Could I call from your phone?
May I place a call by means of your phone?
Could I use your phone?

Yet most competent speakers would choose the last example when talking to a friend. The other examples may sound awkward and unnatural, even though they are grammatically possible. This demonstrates how pieces of language are stored in the brain as whole units, i.e. chunks. Even if language learners possess full control of grammar and can produce correct sentences, they may not always opt for the most natural-sounding – and often, most concise – way of saying something. This is one of the reasons why chunks need to be taught explicitly – see more on this below.

Is there more to knowing a language than just reproducing chunks we have encountered?

Traditional language descriptions tend to treat grammar rules separately from vocabulary, giving the impression that any word can be inserted into any grammatical structure. For example, you could produce a sentence like this: *Colourless green ideas sleep furiously*. Although the sentence does not make sense, it conforms perfectly to the rules of English grammar.

A new theory of language acquisition known as **lexical priming** (advanced by Professor Michael Hoey, University of Liverpool) poses a radical challenge to this 'words-and-rules' view of language. Hoey (2005) argues that as we acquire new words we take a subconscious note of words that occur alongside (collocation) and of any associated grammatical patterns (colligation). Through multiple encounters with a new word, we become primed to associate it with these recurring elements. According to Hoey's theory, our brain is like a giant corpus where each word is accompanied by mental usage notes. Language production is not a matter of simply combining words and rules but rather a retrieval of the language we are primed for, i.e. the patterns and combinations we have previously seen or heard. This accounts for why some sentences that are perfectly grammatical may not sound natural: the words in these awkward sentences do not conform to their primings.

The theory explains why, when producing language, our first port of call is our mental store of pre-fabricated chunks. However, this does not completely negate the role of generative grammar. Knowledge of grammar rules is still important to fine-tune chunks so that they fit new contexts. Because we are only primed to repeat language we have encountered in particular contexts, if we find ourselves in a new communicative situation, we might not have any ready-made language to draw on. This is when grammar knowledge can help us produce completely new sentences. Hoey argues, however, that even when we create completely new language we still follow general primings.

How do chunks promote fluency?

If by fluency we mean fast processing, knowledge of chunks is essential: it is much quicker to process a few larger units (chunks) than a lot of smaller ones (words). For example, without having the chunk *I haven't seen you for ages* at your disposal, you would have to go through a series of lexical and grammatical choices every time you bumped into an old friend. You would have to gather the right words, then apply the appropriate grammar rules. Instead, fluent speakers recall *I haven't seen you for ages* as a unit, rather than assembling the phrase word by word. Freeing up processing energy allows more time for speakers to plan what to say next.

Fluent speakers possess a large bank of memorized chunks ready to be used in various communicative situations and contexts. When it comes to receptive skills (reading or listening), recognizing frequently recurring strings of words allows us to process linguistic input more quickly. It has been shown that a listener recognizes a word more quickly when provided with a word that collocates with it. Likewise, it's quicker to read strings of words which consist of familiar chunks, as shown by studies tracking readers' eye-ball movements (Siyanova-Chanturia et al, 2011).

In summary, chunks are fundamental to language processing and production: they allow us to produce language naturally and fluently and they aid reading and listening comprehension. In recent years, however, there is growing evidence that chunks memorized as whole units of language can also actually drive the process of grammar acquisition. This is the topic of the next section.

2 Chunks in language acquisition

How can chunks promote grammar acquisition?

Memorized chunks can be used by learners to produce situationally appropriate and well-formed language, such as *I haven't seen you for ages*, when their own grammatical competence doesn't yet allow them to generate new sentences in the present perfect. This boosts learners' motivation and allows them to be communicative in the earlier stages of learning a second language (L2). But the role of chunks doesn't end there. Holistically stored chunks gradually evolve into more productive patterns as learners begin to experiment with them, teasing them apart and using them as templates to create new sentences:

I haven't seen you for ages.
I haven't seen her for ages.
I haven't seen him since high school.
I haven't heard from her for ages.

Is it similar to how children acquire their first language?

Very much so. According to contemporary cognitive theories of language acquisition, children acquiring their first language (L1) start out by recording pieces of language encountered during their day-to-day interaction. Early language production starts with repetition of this previously heard language, i.e. words (e.g. *dog*) or multi-word phrases (e.g. *Let me do it, Where's the ball?*). Children then slightly modify the encountered language to suit various communicative needs:

Where's the ball?
Where's the dog?
Where's Daddy?

Only later do abstract categories and schemas, such as the subject–verb–object word order or inversion in interrogatives, begin to form from these specific instances of language use. Michael Tomasello, author of *Constructing a Language: A Usage-Based Theory of Language Acquisition*, is clear on this point:

> … *children's comprehension and production of relatively complex utterances are based on a simple retrieval of stored expressions, whereas in other cases they are based on the cutting and pasting together of stored linguistic schemas and constructions of various kinds and degrees of abstraction. This would seem to be the way that people master a variety of cognitive skills, and there is no reason to think that language is any different in this regard.* (2005: 327–328)

This view, known as a **usage-based** approach to language acquisition, rests on the idea that language knowledge comes from actual language use – listening, reading, speaking and writing – with grammar being the result of the process of acquisition rather than a precondition for it.

Is there evidence that L2 learners go through the same process?

Evidence that L2 learners can extrapolate rules from naturally occurring language is less plentiful, yet fairly convincing. Second language acquisition (SLA) studies have shown that new grammatical structures are often learned initially as unanalysed wholes and later on broken down for analysis. For example, a study conducted at Southampton University (Myles, Hooper & Mitchell, 1998) showed that secondary school learners of French learned *Je m'appelle* (*My name is*) as a chunk and used it in early production without understanding all of its constituent parts. Gradually, as learners became aware of all the elements it consists of (*Je / m' / appelle*) they began to build new sentences using the chunk as a prototype:

Elle s'appelle
Il s'appelle

Or, to give an example from English, learners may learn the *going to* future form as a chunk, such as *I am going to write about* for writing essays (Bardovi-Harlig, 2002), before adapting the structure to include other verbs: *I am going to take/try/make,* etc.

   Drawing on various SLA studies investigating the role of chunks in grammar acquisition, Rod Ellis (2006) advocates delaying the teaching of abstract grammar rules until learners have acquired a stock of ready-made chunks which they can use in various communicative situations. This also echoes an appeal made by one of the founding fathers of the communicative approach to language teaching, Henry Widdowson:

> *The more natural and more effective approach would be to […] begin with lexical items and show how they need to be grammatically modified to be communicatively effective.* (1990: 95)

Can learners acquire L2 from a rich diet of chunks alone?

Children effortlessly acquire their mother tongue from examples using their pattern-finding ability. So why is the process of L2 acquisition sometimes so laborious with many learners never reaching native-like performance? One of the main reasons is quite simply a lack of exposure. L1 proficiency comes as a result of thousands of hours of exposure to incredibly rich language input. The exposure L2 learners receive is often not sufficient to enable them to identify patterns from specific examples.

   Even when there is plenty of input there are additional factors which may hinder the process of L2 acquisition. For example, although it is one of the most frequent words in English, the contracted form of the verb *have* – *'ve* – is not always easily identifiable in spoken phrases like these:

I've been busy.
I've finished.
How long've you been waiting?

Without hearing *'ve*, the learner may not consciously register its presence and therefore presume that these sentences do not contain *have/'ve* at all:

I been busy.
I finished.
How long you been waiting?

An item may appear frequently in the input but it will not be readily acquired by the L2 learner if it is not **salient**, i.e. if it is not noticeable and prominent in relation to its surrounding words. Salience – or the lack of it – may explain why certain grammatical forms are notoriously difficult for learners to acquire. Many grammatical cues in English (for example tense marking, the third person singular -*s* and articles) are not salient. Grammatical words tend to be unstressed in English, making them more difficult to perceive aurally. We stress *know* in *I don't know*, not *don't*, which results in something sounding like *I dunno* in spoken English. We stress *taken* in *You should have taken an umbrella*, which is reduced to *You should've taken an umbrella*, or even *You shoulda taken an umbrella*.

Studies show (see Bybee, 2002 for overview) that extremely frequent chunks, like *Lemme see, I wanna do it* or *Whatcha gonna do,* are subject to more articulatory reduction. For example, the first person pronoun *I* is the most common pronoun occurring with *don't* and reduction of *don't* to *dun* occurs almost exclusively when it is used in conjunction with *I* and followed by verbs that occur most frequently after *don't*, such as *know*, *think*, *have*, *want* and *care*. In a similar fashion, the sequences *did you*, *would you*, *that you*, *last year* are prone to palatalization because their high frequency makes them highly automatized.

So are chunks new grammar?

To be precise, chunks themselves are not grammar but it has been argued that they provide raw data for the development of grammatical competence. This insight is supported by converging evidence from two disciplines: corpus linguistics (discussed earlier) and psycholinguistics (discussed in this section). Each discipline uses different research methods, different thinking approaches and has its own object of enquiry: corpus linguistics investigates language use through the study of samples of real language while psycholinguistics examines the processes of the human mind responsible for language acquisition and proficiency. However, the latest insights from each field dovetail perfectly with each other and point to the experiential, data-driven nature of language learning. Both disciplines place more premium on holistic memory than on the ability to put words together using content-less grammar rules. They also reject the traditional grammar/vocabulary dichotomy.

More recently, the convergence of these two viewpoints has found support in what is called **complexity theory,** which views language as an emergent system. First proposed in the field of physics and mathematics, complexity (or 'chaos') theory studies complex systems that emerge as a result of the interactions of their components. This theory has been used to study, among other things, the weather, the human brain or consumer behaviour in a market. When applied to linguistics and language acquisition, complexity theory can explain why language evolves over time and how the learner's grammar develops and organizes itself from the bottom up. According to this view, complex grammar and grammatical systems arise from the learner's exposure to language data – specifically, frequently recurring chunks – in the course of social interaction and simple cognitive processes, such as pattern detection. In this sense, the grammar is said to be 'emergent'.

Keeping in mind the 'chunky' nature of language and the role chunks potentially play in language acquisition, we shall now turn to the practical implications of the theories we have discussed.

3 Chunks in language teaching

Why don't chunks feature more prominently in ELT methodology?

Coursebooks tend to separate grammar and vocabulary, with occasional pages devoted to functional language (suggesting, apologizing, inviting, etc.). It may seem that ELT methodology has not taken into account the corpus research findings outlined earlier – but this is not entirely true. There have been a few notable attempts to bridge the gap between vocabulary and grammar in recent ELT publications. The first major pedagogical development based on corpus research was the publication of the *Collins Cobuild English Course* in the late 1980s. Instead of focusing on a specific grammar structure (e.g. present simple or past continuous), each unit in the coursebook presented several frequent English words and highlighted common patterns associated with them. The decision to abandon a traditional grammar syllabus in favour of an entirely lexical syllabus was groundbreaking. One of the authors, Dave Willis, later wrote this in the introduction to *The Lexical Syllabus*:

> *Teachers and researchers have been aware for many years that 'input' does not equal 'intake', that what teachers claim to be teaching bears only a tenuous relationship to what learners are actually learning. But in spite of this, coursebook writers continue to act on the assumption that language can be broken down into a series of patterns* [Willis means here grammatical structures] *which can then be presented to learners and assimilated by them in a predictable sequence. It does not seem to worry people a great deal that this assumption flies in the face of our experience as teachers.* (1990)

The next two developments in the field emerged in the early 1990s. On one side of the Atlantic, Nattinger and DeCarrico attempted to organize conventionalized lexical phrases (the term they used to describe chunks) according to the functions they perform and suggested ways of teaching them. On the other side of the Atlantic, Michael Lewis (probably the most influential figure in promoting the importance of chunks in language teaching) developed his Lexical Approach, which can be summarized by this key quote: 'Language consists of grammaticalised lexis, not lexicalised grammar' (Lewis, 1993). Lewis derived many of his ideas directly from the corpus linguistics insights outlined above, particularly John Sinclair's work.

While Lewis argued for a syllabus based on chunks, his detractors criticized the lack of clear specification of which chunks should be taught and in what order. Another shortcoming often pointed out in Lewis's approach is the sheer number of chunks – hundreds of thousands – which learners need to commit to memory. Opponents of the Lexical Approach argue that equipping learners with generic grammar rules requires less time and effort and therefore ensures faster progress. However, critics may be missing a crucial point in Lewis's work: Lewis convincingly argued for 'chunking' as a primary pedagogical activity, where students are explicitly taught to divide language into meaningful units, paying attention to which words occur with other words and their associated grammatical patterns. This aspect of language learning fosters independent learning, provided students are adequately trained to identify and record chunks. Regarding the cognitive load, learning complex grammatical structures, for example the third conditional (*if* + past perfect + *would have* + past participle), is arguably more demanding than memorizing a typical expression containing the target structure such as *If I'd had the time I would've helped you* (Jones, 2015). These principles were effectively put into practice in the *Innovations* series of coursebooks by Hugh Dellar and Andrew Walkley (Heinle-Cengage, 2004–8).

What is missing in current teaching practice?

Effective language teaching should reflect the nature of language and be the best possible match for the process of natural language acquisition. As we have seen, language acquisition is much more holistic than was traditionally believed: modern usage-based theories of language acquisition and corpus research convincingly argue that breaking language down into discrete grammar items is at odds with accounts of how language is stored, acquired and produced. Of course, some itemization of language is inevitable for teaching purposes but chunks seem to be the most likely candidates for items of learning, rather than individual words or discrete grammar rules.

The learning of new structures should ideally start off as gradual exposure to and accumulation of chunks containing the target structures. As the number of stored chunks grows, chunks exhibiting the same pattern will gradually feed into the grammar system. This is when grammatical competence with a particular structure begins to emerge. For some learners this 'tipping point' will occur earlier, for others later. However, no amount of incidental exposure can come close to the amount of linguistic data that native speakers are exposed to – about 7,000 utterances per day (Sheffler, 2015). To speed up the process of chunk accumulation and pattern detection – and therefore create favourable conditions for the tipping point to occur sooner – chunks need to be taught explicitly.

Since chunks can provide raw material for grammar development, it may be worthwhile directing learners' attention to chunks containing certain grammatical structures. Learners can practise and learn the chunks lexically before moving on to any kind of grammar explanation, i.e. they should be encouraged to memorize before they analyse. This does not suggest a return to behaviourist models of instruction (where no explicit analysis of grammar takes place at all) but rather that teachers use memorization as a useful additional tool before introducing any grammar analysis.

The teaching and learning of chunks can be approached in much the same way as the teaching of grammatical structures: clarifying meaning and form, checking understanding, practising in meaningful contexts (Jones, 2015). For example, we can explicitly teach a range of chunks (e.g. *I don't know, I don't believe it, I don't care*) and only later focus on the role of *don't* in the formation of negative sentences in the present simple.

Should single words be banished completely when teaching vocabulary?

Recently, vocabulary has gained greater significance in ELT, evidenced by the amount of research into L2 vocabulary acquisition which has been published in the last twenty years. Much of this research agrees that vocabulary learning is a daunting task: learners require knowledge of around 9,000 word families – not to mention tens of thousands of chunks – to understand texts. New items also need to be frequently re-encountered for learning to take place.

The sheer number of new words learners need has led L2 vocabulary acquisition researchers to reassess whether picking up words from input (e.g. from extensive reading) is sufficient for vocabulary learning. Learning vocabulary out of context – characteristic of earlier language-learning approaches – fell out of favour when more communicative teaching approaches became popular. However, in recent years many researchers concur that learning decontextualized lists of words can in fact be a useful strategy, particularly for learning the basic vocabulary of English. The problem is that basic vocabulary items – the 2,000 most frequent words of English, including *any, by, get, there, way*, etc. – also carry the most common grammatical patterns. There is clearly a contradiction here. On the one hand, learners quickly need to get to a level where they can engage in simple communication and comprehend texts – and any means will do to reach this threshold, including decontextualized vocabulary learning using flashcards or word lists. On the other hand, these basic words are essential for acquiring grammatical competence. So, quick gains in learning individual, decontextualized words may actually inhibit grammar development. This book takes the view that vocabulary should be taught in chunks because exposure to surrounding language (co-text) is of such great importance. This way learners can pick up not only collocations – essential for appropriate and natural use of vocabulary – but also the grammatical patterns those new words occur in. For example, when teaching *look for* it is worth pointing out that it often appears in the present continuous:

He's looking for a job.
What are you looking for?
I'm looking for my glasses/keys. Have you seen them?

What are the central principles underlying this book?

This book aims to bridge the gap between vocabulary and grammar by teaching both elements alongside each other. It contains several chapters of practical activities for teachers of all levels of experience. Below are some general principles underlying the activities provided:

Learners need a lot of linguistically rich and meaningful input (reading and listening)
A lot of input doesn't mean that learners should only be given long texts. Intensive listening and reading of short texts (for example the ones on http://tinytexts.wordpress.com/) has a high pedagogical value. This is not to detract from the benefit of extensive listening and reading: graded readers, for example, provide exposure to new items in context and help learners to consolidate language learned in class.

Draw learners' attention to lexical and grammatical patterns
Many classroom activities should focus on highlighting chunks in reading and listening input. Such receptive, awareness-raising activities can be gradually combined with more productive ones, where learners manipulate the chunks they have encountered to fit different communicative situations and scenarios. However, before learners are expected to produce correct grammar, they should be trained to recognize new grammatical structures in their input. A lot of priming needs to take place before learners can produce more abstract forms like the present perfect continuous (*have + been + v + -ing*), for example.

Chunks before grammar
Ease learners into new grammar areas through chunks. For example, *Have you ever been to* can be presented in the context of travel or holidays, without delving into a grammatical analysis of the present perfect. Similarly, *Have you seen* can be presented when discussing films in class. Start by getting learners to practise and memorize chunks containing a new grammatical structure, resisting the temptation to move too quickly into any grammar explanation. Remember, grammar rules are best learned when learners can already draw on a stock of accumulated samples: memorized chunks can guide the learners into the grammar.

Learners need opportunities to produce language in meaningful contexts
Getting learners to produce new language – as opposed to just encountering it in input and recording it – is an essential pedagogical activity. Using new grammatical structures, however partially or provisionally understood, promotes fluency and acquisition of these structures. It also allows learners to produce language which is structurally beyond their present level of competence. It is, therefore, the teacher's role to encourage learners to incorporate new structures in their output and 'push' them beyond their comfort zone.

Chunks help activate passive vocabulary
Coursebook exercises such as matching words and definitions, matching parts of collocations, gapfills and clozes are all important in helping learners understand various aspects of new vocabulary. However, they are not enough to activate passive knowledge. Although coursebooks help students practise new lexical items, it is still up to the teacher to create opportunities for meaningful output and push learners towards integrating new items into their active lexicons.

Chunks play a crucial role in helping learners to activate new and partially learned vocabulary. For example, learners don't need to fully understand the meaning of *stiff* in *I was scared stiff*. It's enough for them to know that that the expression means to be very scared. Lengthy explanations of what *stiff* means can actually divert learners' attention and mental resources from remembering the new form. Time could be better be spent by drawing learners' attention, for example, to the alliterative pattern in s*cared stiff*, helping learners to remember and use the expression. Similarly, the chunk *I agree to some extent* can be used in writing without fully understanding the meaning of *extent*. Indeed, many successful language learners report that they often know how and when to use a certain phrase or expression but may not know exactly what it means or understand all its elements.

Grammar rules as priming

As the research this book draws on suggests, learning grammar is primarily an implicit process – but this does not completely invalidate the role of explicit grammar instruction. Grammar teaching is still effective because it directs learners' attention to specific structures and points out salient features. This is one way of compensating for lack of exposure to the L2. Providing grammar rules may help learners to notice new and partially learned structures and aid pattern-registration. Learning the rules might not immediately lead to correct production but it has a priming effect because it prepares learners for future encounters with input containing the new structure. Indeed, research shows that students who receive explicit grammar instruction alongside exposure to rich input 'seem to have the best of both worlds' (MacWhinney, 1997, as cited in Scheffler, 2015:95).

How can this book help me?

Unlike learning a first language, learners of second languages usually need more than simple exposure to the target language to become competent speakers. Since classroom time is often very limited, it is important to manipulate exposure so that learners meet new pieces of language – or chunks – over and over again. Helping learners to notice underlying patterns in the chunks they encounter may speed up the process of accumulation, which L1 acquirers are lucky to get from exposure alone. This book aims to help with this process of noticing patterns to aid accumulation of chunks.

The principles of language description and acquisition that underpin this book may be different from a traditional grammar syllabus but the activities presented are still compatible with one – so don't rush to throw out your coursebook! By using the activities in this book, you will be providing your learners with a rich diet of language chunks, helping them with pattern-recognition which promotes implicit grammar learning. Your coursebook may still be useful for more explicit grammar teaching – particularly for more analytical learners who find that learning grammar rules boosts confidence and provides the safety of the familiar.

In the following chapters, you will find activities and ideas for:

- identifying, highlighting and recording chunks of language
- drawing attention to vocabulary which frequently occurs with certain grammar structures
- drawing attention to grammar structures that attract certain items of vocabulary
- 'unpacking' texts
- sensitizing learners to formulaic features in language
- pushing learners to incorporate chunks into their active repertoire
- pattern drills
- reviewing and recycling language.

References

Aitchison, J. (1994) *Words in the Mind: An Introduction to the Mental Lexicon*, Oxford: Blackwell.

Altenberg, B. (1998) 'On the phraseology of spoken English: the evidence of recurrent word-combinations', In A. P. Cowie (Ed.), *Phraseology: theory, analysis and application* (pp. 101–122), Oxford: Oxford University Press.

Bardovi-Harlig, K. (2002.) 'A new starting point?', Studies in Second Language Acquisition, 24(2), 189–198.

Bybee, J. (2002) 'Phonological Evidence for Exemplar Storage of Multiword Sequences', Studies in Second Language Acquisition, 24(2), 215–221.

Dellar, H. & Walkley, A. (2004–8) *Innovations*, Heinle-Cengage Learning.

Ellis, R. (2006) 'Current Issues in the Teaching of Grammar: An SLA Perspective', TESOL Quarterly Vol. 40(1), 83–107.

Erman, B. & Warren, B. (2000) 'The idiom principle and the open choice principle', Text, 20(1), 29–62.

Jones, C. (2015) 'In defence of teaching and acquiring formulaic sequences', ELT Journal, 69(3), 319–322.

Lewis, M. (1993) *The Lexical Approach: The State of ELT and a Way Forward*, Hove: Language Teaching Publications.

Myles, F., Hooper, J. & Mitchell, R. (1998) 'Rote or rule? Exploring the role of formulaic language in classroom foreign language learning', Language Learning, 48(3), 323–363.

Nattinger, J. & DeCarrico, J. (1989) *Lexical Phrases and Language Teaching*, Oxford: Oxford University Press.

Sinclair, J. (1991) *Corpus Concordance Collocation*, Oxford: Oxford University Press.

Siyanova-Chanturia, A., Conklin, K. & Schmitt, N. (2011) 'Adding more fuel to the fire: An eye-tracking study of idiom processing by native and nonnative speakers', Second Language Research, 27(2), 1–22.

Scheffler, P. (2015) 'Lexical priming and explicit grammar in foreign language instruction', ELT Journal, 69(1), 93–6.

Tomasello, M. (2005) *Constructing a Language: A Usage-Based Theory of Language Acquisition*, Cambridge, MA: Harvard University Press.

Widdowson, H. G. (1990) *Aspects of Language Teaching*, Oxford: Oxford University Press.

Willis, D. (1990) *The Lexical Syllabus*, London: Collins.

1 Defining and identifying chunks

As Hanna Kryszewska noted in her article 'Why I won't say goodbye to the lexical approach', a chunk is what it is: a bit of language. As seen in the Introduction, this book takes a broad view of chunks, i.e. that they can be big (e.g. *There's no getting away from the fact that …*) or small (e.g. *At first*) but they always make sense. So how can teachers identify what constitutes a chunk and what does not? And how are chunks different to collocations, patterns or any other terms proposed by different authors? This section contains practical activities which aim to help identify and define chunks, as well as make sense of the terminological minefield associated with this area of language learning.

Defining a chunk

Many different terms are associated with the area of formulaic language: lexical phrases, lexicalized routines, pre-fabs, formulae and ready-made utterances, to name just a few! In her book *Formulaic Language and the Lexicon*, Alison Wray counted at least 40 different terms referring to the same phenomenon. Given the terminological profusion, I have chosen 'chunk' as the all-purpose term to be used throughout the book. Not only do I feel that it is important to use existing, teacher-friendly terminology, but 'chunk' has also become a catch-all term for all kinds of multi-word units in ELT. Nevertheless, I wasn't happy with existing definitions of either 'chunk' or 'formulaic language' – the term normally used by applied linguists. Most available definitions refer to chunks as holistic units stored in the brain. This is certainly true as far as native speakers are concerned, but a bit premature for L2 learners. They do not have any chunks stored (yet!), so a different pedagogical definition is needed. To capture all the different features of chunks and the view taken in this book, I propose the following definition:

> *A chunk is a frequently recurring, meaningful string of two or more words – either fixed or with variable slots – which can be learned as a single unit, without the need to analyse its elements. Once committed to (long-term) memory, a chunk can be retrieved and used 'as is' or with modifications, if necessary, bypassing the need to generate it from individual words and grammatical rules.*

A 'string of two or more words' covers all manner of multi-word units such as collocations (*do homework*), discourse markers (*to begin with*), social formulae (*Nice to meet you*), sentence frames (*As far as _____ is concerned*) and idioms (*No news is good news*). 'Frequently recurring' implies that a string can be searched for in a corpus and results will show that it is indeed common in the English language. However, a corpus-based estimate of frequency cannot be the sole criterion in the identification of a chunk, especially since different researchers propose different thresholds of frequency. The string also has to be 'meaningful', i.e. have a clearly identifiable meaning or perform a distinct function in communication. Lastly, my proposed definition refers to chunks of varying degrees of fixedness. Some chunks are 'frozen', such as idioms (*There's no smoke without fire*) or fixed expressions (*as a matter of fact*). However, some chunks allow variation in a particular slot, for example *as far as I know,* in which *know* can be replaced by *understand* or *remember.*

Some chunks allow variability in more than one slot, for example:

	30 minutes		to work
It takes me	one hour	to get	to school
	ages		home

Chunks and chunking

Lexical grammar is not only about chunks of language but also about chunking language – grouping individual words into meaningful wholes. Many frequent strings of words can be brought to learners' attention as whole chunks. Take, for example, *I didn't have time to do it.* It can be generated from the individual words *have*, *time* and *do* and pieced together with the rules of grammar (past simple negative). On the other hand, it can be presented, practised and memorized as a chunk without analysing its individual elements. So, why would teachers want to do that? Learners' grammatical competence may not yet be at the level where they can create a sentence using the past simple – let alone produce it fluently – but if the phrase is taught and practised as a chunk, learners can use it in their speaking, for example when answering the question *Have you done your homework?.* Knowing the chunk gives them a sense of being able to produce language which is beyond their level of grammatical competence and, arguably, provides raw data for grammar acquisition (see more on this in the Introduction).

Most teachers already present a lot of grammar as chunks, for example *Let's go, How are you?* and *I was born.* Phrases like these are taught as chunks in early lessons, long before learners understand contractions, inversion or passives.

Chunks and patterns

Knowledge of many grammatical structures may start out as exposure to fixed chunks. *What's your name?* may be first learned as a single unit, used when you start a conversation with a stranger. Later, learners may notice some variability after being exposed to sentences such as *What's your address?* and *What's your phone number?.* That is the process of segmentation: the learner becomes aware that *What's your name?* contains a variable slot which can be filled by other noun phrases (*address, phone number*) and the chunk becomes a pattern.

A similar route from a chunk to a pattern can occur with *as far as I know.* At first it can be represented as a holistic unit, and later 'unpacked' and used as a blueprint for creating similar phrases like *as far as I remember* and *as far as I can see.*

Identifying chunks

In pre-corpus approaches to phraseology, the main criteria for identifying and classifying multi-word units were 1) transparency – whether a phrase had a literal or non-literal meaning, and 2) restrictedness – whether or not one of its elements could be substituted by another word.

Literal meaning: *blow your nose*
Non-literal meaning: *blow your own trumpet*
Very restricted: *shrug your shoulders*
Less restricted: *bend (the) knees/elbows/arms/back*

In this view, chunks can be seen on a continuum ranging from free combinations (*pay money*) to collocations (*pay attention*) to figurative idioms (*pay an arm and a leg*). However, this approach overlooks frequent combinations which are not in any way restricted such as *research has shown that, it has been argued that* or *I didn't have time*. Many recent corpus studies have shown that the most frequent three-, four- and five-word strings are not idioms or restricted collocations, but perfectly transparent word combinations such as *in the middle of, I was wondering if* or *do you want me to*. However, frequency cannot be the sole determiner because a 'frequency-based' approach, which measures how frequently words co-occur in a corpus, has its own drawbacks and should be used with caution. Although generally reliable, this approach tends to favour statistically frequent combinations, which do not always meet the pedagogical criteria of being meaningful units, such as *and it was, a bit of a* or *one of the*. Conversely, idiomatic chunks that are not very frequent but are nevertheless important for learners (e.g. *would you be so kind*) might not be captured by corpus analysis software.

Today most experts on formulaic language, such as Alison Wray (2008) or David Wood (2016), agree that a blended approach is better than purely statistical measures of frequency. They do not rule out intuitive judgment either. Another important pedagogic consideration is relevance to the learner. For example, according to the Corpus of Contemporary American English (COCA), the most common noun collocates of *reckless*, in order of frequency, are:

> *behaviour*   *disregard*   *endangerment*   *driving*

Secondary school teachers would be well advised to ignore *disregard* and *endangerment* and focus on *reckless behaviour* and *reckless driving*. Corpus data provides information about frequency but it should always be balanced by considerations of usefulness to the learner at a given level and teachability. This is where our role as the teacher comes into play.

To sum up, there are various criteria and procedures for identifying chunks. However, for pedagogical purposes the most valid approach seems to be a combination of intuition and consultation with a reference source, such as a corpus or a corpus-based tool. Start by identifying strings of words in a text that look familiar. Check the strings against reference corpora in order to establish whether they are indeed frequent. Even internet search engines such as Google can be used to validate your intuitive choices. The activities in this chapter can be used with learners but can also serve as useful practice for teachers preparing to teach lexical grammar.

References

Kryszewska, H. (2003) 'Why I won't say goodbye to the Lexical Approach', Humanising Language Teaching, 5(2). Retrieved from: www.hltmag.co.uk/mar03/mart.htm

Wood, D. (2016) *Fundamentals of Formulaic Language: An Introduction*, Bloomsbury Publishing, London.

Wray, A. (2005) *Formulaic Language and the Lexicon*, Cambridge: Cambridge University Press.

1.1 Identifying chunks

Outline	This activity guides teachers through the process of identifying useful chunks in a short text.
Level	Intermediate and above (B1+)
Time	10 minutes
Preparation	None

Procedure

1   Look at the text in Figure 1.1 below. In the first paragraph, <u>underline</u> any verb + noun collocations. (Hint: There are four of them.)

2   In the second and third paragraphs, highlight a few chunks containing two nouns. (Hint: Some of them start with a preposition or an article.)

3   In the second paragraph, circle chunks containing these specific grammatical structures: present perfect, present continuous, passive.

4   Go through the whole text again and see if there are any other chunks worth focusing on, for example discourse markers (see *Glossary* on p. 223).

5   Compare your answers with the annotated text in Figure 1.2. (Other chunks worth noting are in **bold**.)

We can order cabs, reserve a table in restaurant or book a holiday through social media. But surely, some things are too important to seek online? Apparently not. These days, many parents are turning to the Internet to find a babysitter.

Word of mouth and noticeboards in community centres are being replaced by babysitting apps such as Bambino, UrbanSitter or RockMyBaby, and the industry is booming. The number of people using Sitters has grown by 65% in the last three years.

Bookings are becoming more flexible than ever and can be made at two hours' notice. Parents put in a request, the app notifies local babysitters and the booking can be confirmed in a matter of minutes.

Apps are particularly popular for late-night requests, but early morning sitters for parents who want to have a lie-in at the weekend are also on the rise.

Adapted from 'Babysitting apps boom as parents bid to reclaim free time' by Tess Reidy, the Guardian:

www.theguardian.com/lifeandstyle/2017/feb/25/parents-babysitting-apps-boom-childcare

---

Figure 1.1: Babysitting apps text

We can <u>order cabs</u>, <u>reserve a table</u> in restaurant or <u>book a holiday</u> through social media. **But surely**, some things are too important to seek online? **Apparently not**. These days, many parents are <u>turning to the Internet</u> to find a babysitter.

Word of mouth and noticeboards in community centres are being replaced by babysitting apps such as Bambino, UrbanSitter or RockMyBaby, and the industry is booming. The number of people using Sitters has grown by 65% in the last three years.

Bookings are becoming more flexible than ever and can be made at two hours' notice. Parents put in a request, the app notifies local babysitters and the booking can be confirmed in a matter of minutes.

Apps are **particularly popular** for late-night requests, but early morning sitters for parents who want **to have a lie-in at the weekend** are also **on the rise**.

Figure 1.2: Annotated babysitting apps text

Note
Find a babysitter can also be considered a collocation but is not included in the answers because *find* is a very frequent verb which combines freely with a large number of nouns.

For more activities exploring and reviewing chunks in texts, see Chapter 3: *Exploring text*.

Rationale
As mentioned in the introduction to this chapter, chunks are a somewhat fuzzy concept and cannot always be clearly defined. However, when it comes to identifying chunks, the more the merrier. If you – or your learners – have found more chunks in this text than I intended, this activity has achieved its aim and successfully set you off chunking.

1.2 Collocation cards with Word Neighbors

Outline Learners record new and partially known vocabulary on word cards using Word Neighbors.
Level Elementary and above (A2+)
Time 10 minutes
Preparation Cut up several pieces of A4 card into postcard-sized pieces. These will be used as word cards during the activity. Make sure you have access to the internet and a projector during the session.

Procedure

1 Distribute a few word cards to each learner – see *Preparation*.

2 Navigate to wordneighbors.ust.hk in your browser and project the webpage so the class can see it. (Alternatively, ask learners to navigate to the website on their own devices.)

3 Type in the target word, e.g. *advice*. Select **Noun** from the drop-down menu under the search box. Select **Show 1 word(s) before** from the drop-down menu on the left.

4 Click **Find it!**, then **Show results** for ADJ + NOUN.

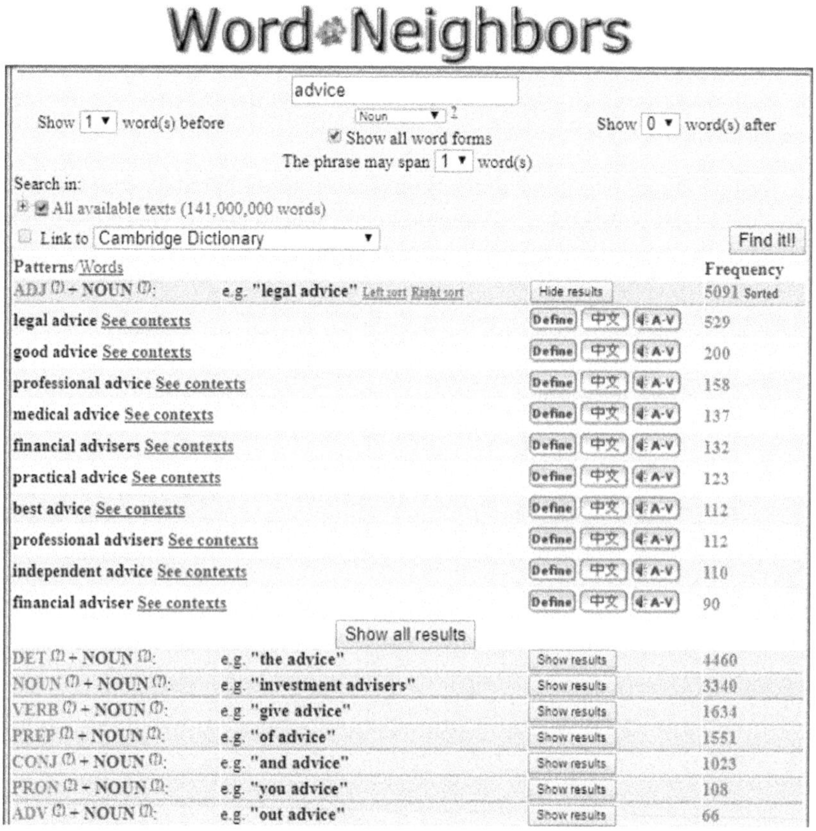

Figure 1.3: Screenshot from wordneighbors.ust.hk

5 Ask learners to record three or four adjectives that go with *advice* on the back of a word card, in the right-hand column – see the example in Figure 1.5 below.

6 Now select **Show 2 word(s) before**. Ask learners to scan the results and note down three or four common verbs that collocate with *advice*. They should write them in the left-hand column on the back of their word card. (The search span needs to be expanded to two words because there may be a determiner between the verb and the noun, e.g. *give some advice, take my advice*.)

7 Next, expand the search to three words before and three words after, using the drop-down menus. (You may want to untick/uncheck **Show all word forms** to eliminate derivative words like *adviser*.) Ask learners to study the patterns and record at least one chunk at the bottom of their word card.

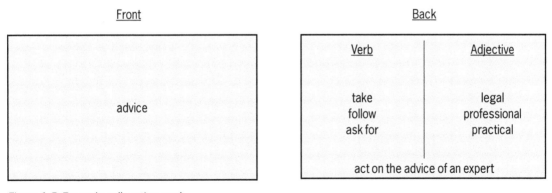

Figure 1.4: Screenshot from wordneighbors.ust.hk

Front	Back

	Verb	Adjective
advice	take follow ask for	legal professional practical
	act on the advice of an expert	

Figure 1.5: Example collocation card

Note

Word Neighbors is a user-friendly corpus tool developed by the Hong Kong University of Science and Technology: http://wordneighbors.ust.hk/help/index.html There is a useful tutorial here: http://mws.ust.hk/mmw/full/Word_Neighbors.htm

Students can be encouraged to follow this activity to record vocabulary during the rest of their course, either individually or in small groups.

See also Activity 9.10: *From word box to chunk box*.

Follow-up

When learners have accumulated enough cards, organize them into groups of four. Each group should have 15–20 cards and each group member is dealt four or five cards. In turn, group members read the collocations on the back (adjectives and nouns), making sure to cover up the front of the card with their hand so that others cannot see the key word. Other students try to guess the key word. The correct guesser keeps the card. The group member with the most cards at the end of the round is the winner.

Rationale

Although learners may understand the importance of recording vocabulary, the idea of recording it with co-text (see *Glossary* on p. 223) may be new. Word Neighbors is a useful tool for learners who are less familiar with a lexical approach to learning language. While the concept of collocation or chunk might take a while to grasp, it is fairly easy to get across the idea that words 'live' in the vicinity of other words, as the name of the tool suggests – especially when teaching younger learners.

1.3 Expanding word knowledge

Outline	Learners use an online dictionary of collocations to identify collocates for a key adjective.
Level	Elementary and above (A2+) (the example is at B1/B2 level)
Time	10 minutes
Preparation	Select five to seven adjectives learners have recently studied or seen in their coursebook. Ensure learners have access to a device with internet connection (one per small group).

Procedure

1 Divide the class into small groups and assign each group one adjective. With smaller classes, each group can be assigned two or three adjectives.

2 Tell groups to navigate to www.just-the-word.com and type their target adjectives into the search box. They should then click **combinations**.

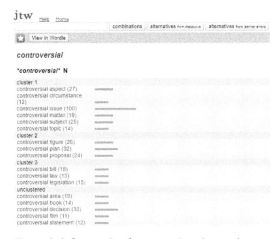

Figure 1.6: Screenshot from www.just-the-word.com

3 The frequency of each collocation is illustrated by a green bar – the longer the bar, the more frequent the collocation. Clicking on the chosen collocation brings up concordance lines (see *Glossary* on p. 223), showing how it is used in context.

4 Learners choose three or four of the most frequent collocations and come up to the board to record them as follows:

Figure 1.7: Collocation fork on the board

Variation

If students don't have access to devices in class, the activity can be done at home. Students can present their findings in the next lesson or share them online using a tool like Google Docs. (Results can be presented in 'collocation forks', which are easy to create using the Table function in Google Docs.)

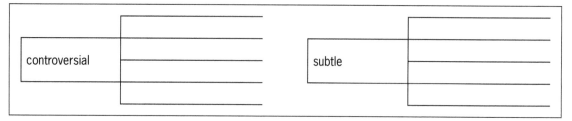

Figure 1.8: Example collocation forks

Note

www.just-the-word.com is an online dictionary of collocations based on the British National Corpus (BNC).

Follow-up

In a subsequent lesson, provide the same forks (in a handout or displayed on the board) without their key adjectives. Students try to remember what the key adjectives are.

	village		scenery
	island		views
	part		firework display
	possibility		success

	history		award
	civilization		law school
	city		job
	monument		firm

Figure 1.9: Collocation forks for *remote, spectacular, ancient, prestigious*

If you are using the board, you can then erase the collocates (leaving the first letter of each one) and get students to try and recall them.

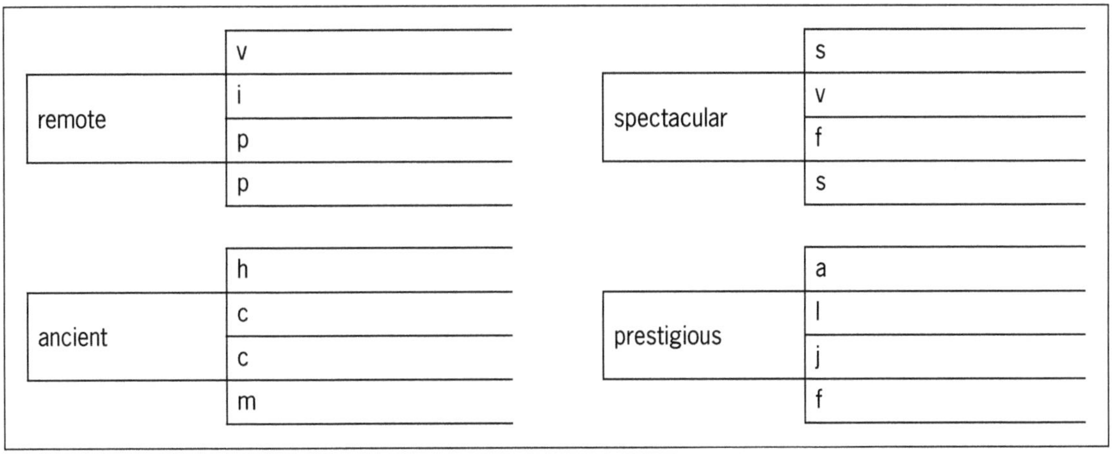

remote	v		spectacular	s
	i			v
	p			f
	p			s

ancient	h		prestigious	a
	c			l
	c			j
	m			f

Figure 1.10: Collocation forks with partial collocates

Rationale

Collocation is a crucial aspect of word knowledge. Even when an English word has a direct equivalent in the learners' L1, the two words may differ in collocational behaviour. Therefore full mastery of a new word is not complete without knowledge of its collocational range: which words the target word collocates with and which words it avoids.

1.4 Making mini-stories with collocation forks

Outline	Learners use pre-prepared collocation forks to create mini-stories.
Level	Elementary and above (A2+) (the example is at B1 level)
Time	10 minutes
Preparation	Prepare collocation forks for eight to ten nouns using information from www.just-the-word.com (see Activity 1.3: *Expanding word knowledge*). Put the key nouns on the right and the collocates on the prongs on the left – see Figure 1.11 below.

Procedure

1 Write up eight to ten nouns that learners are familiar with on the board, e.g. *money, business, problem*. Ask learners to think of verbs that go with them (e.g. *solve a problem*).

2 Distribute or display your pre-prepared collocation forks – see *Preparation*. Check whether the learners' ideas match the collocations on the collocation forks.

3 Ask students to create mini-stories for each key noun, trying to incorporate all the verb collocates, for example:

*The **business** was **set up** by his father who **ran it** for almost 35 years. He successfully **did business** with China and the USA. After he retired, his son **took over the business** and is now the boss.*

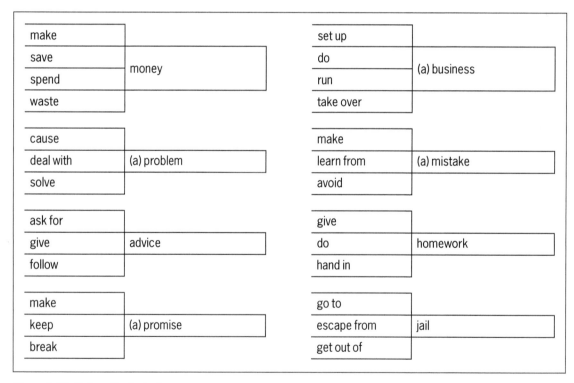

Figure 1.11: Collocation forks for nouns

Variation

Give students a handout with blank collocation forks and look up the collocates for the nouns together with the class, using www.just-the-word.com
Agree on the most important collocates and get students to enter them into the forks.

Follow-up

Collect in the learners' mini-stories. After the lesson, edit them by blanking out the key nouns. In a subsequent lesson, distribute the blanked-out mini-stories and ask learners to try and remember all of the missing key nouns.

Rationale

Research shows that the more learners engage with new words by manipulating and playing with them, the more likely they are to retain them. The same principle can be extended to collocations.

1.5 Revisiting delexicalized verbs with COCA

Outline The Corpus of Contemporary American English (COCA) is a large, up-to-date corpus available online. Learners use COCA to revisit delexicalized verbs (see *Glossary* on p. 223).

Level Upper intermediate and above (B2+)

Time 15 minutes

Preparation Ensure learners have access to a device with internet connection (one per small group).

Procedure

1 Divide the class into small groups and assign each group one delexicalized verb such as *do, make, take, get, set, put,* etc.

2 Tell each group to navigate to corpus.byu.edu/coca, click on **Collocates** and type their target verb in the search field as shown in Figure 1.12 below. (Writing the target word in CAPITAL LETTERS ensures that all the forms of the word are included (*make, makes, making, made*) while _v limits the search to verbs only.)

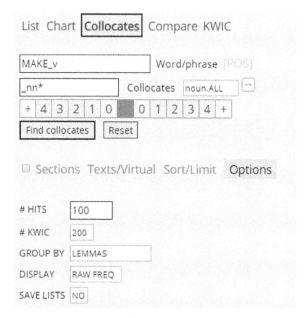

Figure 1.12: Screenshot from corpus.byu.edu/coca

3 From the **Collocates** drop-down menu, learners select **noun.ALL**.

4 Learners click **Options**. In the **GROUP BY** drop-down menu, they change **WORDS** (default setting) to **LEMMAS**. (The WORDS option will treat different word forms separately, e.g. *step* and *steps*; the LEMMAS option groups all forms containing *step* together.)

5 Learners change the search span to two words on either side of the node, i.e. two words before and after the key word (highlighted in green in Figure 1.12 above).

6 Learners click **Find collocates**. The results are displayed in order of frequency.

		CONTEXT	FREQ	
1		[DECISION]	39471	
2		[SENSE]	25629	
3		[WAY]	23808	
4		[PEOPLE]	20771	
5		[MONEY]	17839	
6		[DIFFERENCE]	17368	
7		[MISTAKE]	15881	
8		[TIME]	14414	
9		[THING]	13980	
10		[POINT]	13053	
11		[CHOICE]	10921	
12		[YEAR]	10578	
13		[CHANGE]	10541	
14		[EFFORT]	9423	

Figure 1.13: Screenshot from corpus.byu.edu/coca

7 Students choose five verb + noun collocations and try to use them to write down questions for other groups – see Figure 1.14 below. (Not all the collocations will lend themselves to personal questions, therefore students should scroll down and choose the ones that do.)

8 When the questions are prepared, groups swap papers and have a discussion based on the questions they have received.

9 After the group discussions, conduct whole-class feedback. Ask groups to report on interesting things they learned about their classmates and find out which collocations were new for them.

Questions using collocations with SET

Do you often **set goals** for yourself?

Have you ever **set** a **record**?

When did you last **set foot** in a gym?

Do you like to watch the **sun set** over the ocean?

Do you think celebrities should **set** an **example** for children?

Figure 1.14: Example questions using collocations with *set*

Classroom management tip

For this activity, it is a good idea to group students of similar ability together – otherwise stronger ones may take charge of writing and discussing the questions, with weaker learners being more passive. Stronger groups can be asked to write extra questions if they finish quickly.

Note

After making around ten queries on the COCA website, you might be prompted to register. Registration is free and fairly straightforward – and advisable!

Have and *go* are also considered delexicalized verbs but searching for their collocates is trickier. It's best to avoid these verbs for the purpose of this activity.

Variation

Traditional learner dictionaries or the tools featured in Activities 1.2 and 1.3 can also be used to find common collocates of delexicalized verbs.

Rationale

Delexicalized verbs have a large number of meanings as evidenced by the long entries that accompany them in dictionaries. For instance, http://dictionary.cambridge.org lists 17 meaning senses for *get* and 23 for *do* (and that's excluding its use as an auxiliary verb)! Each of these senses is associated with different collocations, for example *get* =*RECEIVE a grade / a phone call (from) / some time off work*; *get* =*REACH home / to work / far*. Therefore, the only way to master delexicalised verbs is to learn them with their collocations.

On the whole, delexicalized verbs are a good way of introducing the concept of collocation to learners of any L1 background. I usually start with *make/do* and show how one goes with *homework* while the other goes with *mistake* (*I did my homework*; *I made a lot of mistakes*). Why is it this way and not the other way around? Because words have collocations – they prefer the company of certain other words.

For more ideas on teaching delexicalized verbs, see Activity 10.6: *Seemingly easy verbs.*

1.6 Using multiple sources to find chunks

Outline	Learners look up the same items using different resources and pool their findings.
Level	Elementary and above (A2+) (the example is at B1/B2 level)
Time	Variable, depending on the number of items
Preparation	Ensure learners have access to a device with internet connection (one per small group). Alternatively, provided groups with a range of paper learners' dictionaries, for example *Cambridge Learner's Dictionary*, *Longman Dictionary of Contemporary English* or *Oxford Learner's Dictionary*.

Procedure

1   Write up a list of words on the board. These can be words students already partially know (which came up earlier on in a reading text) or new words – see the following suggestions:

A2/B1	B2
train (n.)	*budge*
accident	*clinch*
scenery	*streak*
bargain (n.)	*courtesy*
watch out	*bleak*
charity	*gloomy*

Depending on their level, ESP students can be given some further items, as follows:

Business English	EAP
proceeds	*basis*
resources	*unprecedented*
domestic	*perspective*
recession	*draw on*
target	*sufficient*
impose	*occupy*

2   Divide the class into small groups. Provide each group with a copy of a paper dictionary or a link to an online dictionary such as http://dictionary.cambridge.org or http://ldoceonline.com – see *Useful resources* on p. 227. Different groups should access different dictionaries to look up the target words.

3   Encourage learners to look for interesting or unusual (not obvious) chunks. Very often useful chunks are in **bold**.

4   Pool the groups' findings. Write four or five chunks or whole sentences on the board. Encourage students to copy them into their notebooks or onto vocabulary cards (see Activity 1.2: *Collocation cards with Word Neighbors*).

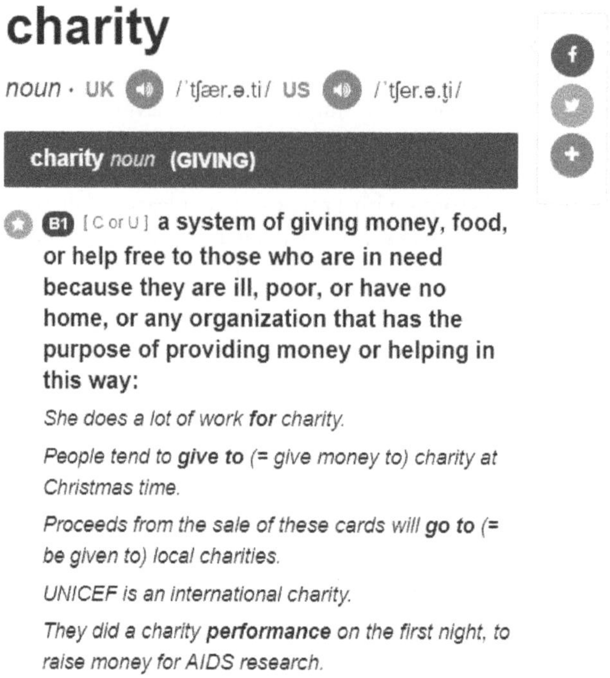

charity

noun · UK 🔊 /ˈtʃær.ə.ti/ US 🔊 /ˈtʃer.ə.t̬i/

charity *noun* **(GIVING)**

⭐ **B1** [C or U] **a system of giving money, food, or help free to those who are in need because they are ill, poor, or have no home, or any organization that has the purpose of providing money or helping in this way:**

She does a lot of work **for** *charity.*

People tend to **give to** *(= give money to) charity at Christmas time.*

Proceeds from the sale of these cards will **go to** *(= be given to) local charities.*

UNICEF is an international charity.

They did a charity **performance** *on the first night, to raise money for AIDS research.*

Figure 1.15: Screenshot from Cambridge Dictionary Online

Rationale

Learners will be surprised at how examples are often similar across different dictionaries. Language is used in predictable patterns and modern corpus-based dictionaries are an excellent language-learning tool because they show how a word is most commonly used. Take, for example, the word *skyline* which appears in *Manhattan skyline* or *New York skyline* in at least five learners' dictionaries! Learners' dictionaries also expose learners to grammar commonly associated with the target words, therefore it's a good idea to encourage learners to copy out whole example sentences.

1.7 Using Contrastive Analysis

Outline	Learners in monolingual classes compare chunks in L1 with English.
Level	Intermediate and above (B1+)
Time	10–15 minutes
Preparation	Ensure learners have access to a device with internet connection (one device per small group). Prepare a three-column handout. In the left-hand column, add around ten chunks in the learners' L1. The other columns are for word-for-word translations and English equivalents – see an example in Figure 1.16 below.

Procedure

1   Give learners the handout containing the list of chunks in their L1 – see *Preparation* and Figure 1.16. (Note that Figure 1.16 contains example answers in Columns 2 and 3, but your handout will only contain L1 chunks in Column 1.)

2   Learners work in pairs and decide if the chunks are directly translatable into English. They can write some word-for-word translations in the middle column of their handout and some English equivalents in the right-hand column.

3   To check their intuitions, learners use a dictionary or corpus tools such as COCA (see Activity 1.5) or Word Neighbors (see Activity 1.2).

German	Literal/word-for-word translation	English equivalent
1 keine Angst	no fear	don't worry
2 eine knappe Sache	a close/scant thing/matter	a near miss / a close call
3 eine Theorie vorschlagen	suggest/propose a theory	propose / put forward a theory ✓
4 den Zug verpassen	to miss the train	to miss the train ✓
5 den Anschluss verpassen	to miss the connection	to miss the bus/boat
6 Schlüss ziehen	to draw/pull conclusion	to draw conclusions ✓
7 Es sagt mir einfach nicht zu	It simply doesn't say to me	It just doesn't do anything for me
8 ein tropfen im Ozean	a drop in the ocean	a drop in the ocean ✓
9 Aufmerksamkeit schenken	give attention	pay attention
10 Kannst Du mich zum Flughafen bringen?	Can you bring me to the airport?	Can you give me a lift to the airport?
11 er unterbrach meinen Gedankengang	He interrupted my train of thought	He interrupted my train of thought ✓
12 Wo sich die Füchse gute Nacht sagen	where the foxes say goodnight	in the middle of nowhere

✓ = chunk is directly translatable from German

Figure 1.16: Examples of idiomatic chunks in German and English

Note

For other activities drawing learners' attention to inter-lingual differences, see Activity 10.8: *Lost in translation*.

Rationale

Contrastive Analysis (CA) gained prominence in the 1950s. Its proponents recommended comparing structural patterns of L1 and the target language before creating materials for learners of the target language. In recent years, CA has made a comeback in the field of L2 vocabulary research. Many applied linguists, for example Batia Laufer and Nadja Nesselhauf, argue for a CA-driven approach to teaching collocations. They say it's essential to focus on collocations that have no direction L1 translation and pedagogical intervention is needed to clarify such collocations. For example, *ask a question* needs to be explicitly taught to Spanish speakers because the Spanish equivalent – *hacer una pregunta* – translates literally as *make a question*. Similarly, *deliver/make a speech* needs to be taught to French learners because the French equivalent – *prononcer un discours* – translates directly as *pronounce a speech*. Assuming you know your learners' L1, you can use CA to anticipate collocational errors.

However, even if English collocations are congruent with L1, it is still worthwhile focusing on them. For example, the English equivalent of the French expression *Tout est bien qui finit bien* is *All's well that ends well*, which is perfectly congruent. Nevertheless, you can still draw learners' attention to the use of *all* in *all's well* (and not *everything*), and point out that we say *ends well* and not *finishes well*.

1.8 Chunks everywhere

Outline	Learners collect chunks containing a key word, compare them with a corpus and share them in class.
Level	Intermediate and above (B1+)
Time	Variable
Preparation	Ensure learners have access to a device with internet connection (one per small group).

Procedure

1   Elicit some of the most frequent words in English and/or provide a list based on corpus data. For example, you could provide this list of the most frequent verbs in English:

be	*make*	*come*	*give*
have	*know*	*want*	*tell*
do	*think*	*look*	*work*
say	*see*	*use*	*call*
go	*take*	*find*	*try*

2   Assign each word to a learner.

3   Set a homework task asking learners to collect examples (e.g. from the coursebook, from texts they read or hear, from songs, films, signs, etc.) that include these words.

4   Learners bring their findings to the next class and check them against the SkELL (Sketch Engine for Language Learning) corpus tool: skell.sketchengine.co.uk

5   They type their target word into SkELL, click on **Word sketch** and turn the **Context** toggle on. Clicking on the collocations will bring up examples from the corpus.

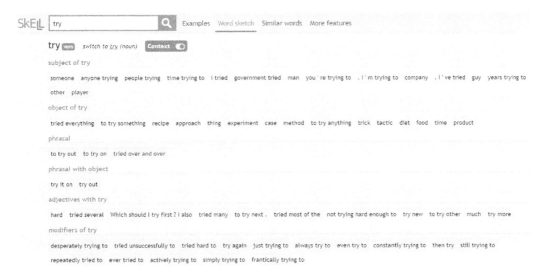

Figure 1.17: Screenshot from skell.sketchengine.co.uk

Note

Learners might end up with different phrases containing the target verbs, not all of which would count as chunks. For example, they may come up with the following phrases containing the verb *try*:

I decided to **try my luck**
try your hand at
don't **try my patience**
'We **try harder***'* (from a car rental advert)
Let's **try a different tack**
Try sleeping *with the windows open.*

Although the last one contains a useful pattern that learners need to know (*try* + verb + *-ing*), *try sleeping* is not a chunk as such because *try* can potentially take any verb in this pattern.

Rationale

As stated in the introduction to this chapter, a combination of a few corpus-based tools – together with intuitive judgment – is possibly the best way of identifying chunks. Therefore, even with generally reliable tools such as SkELL, it's a good idea to check the examples across multiple platforms, if possible. For example, a search on SkELL will confirm that *try your luck* and *try your hand at* are indeed frequent chunks but *try your patience* is inexplicably absent from the results. However, a quick check in a learners' dictionary will confirm that it is indeed a collocation.

---

2 Revising and recycling chunks

This chapter outlines a number of activities which can be used for revising and recycling chunks, in order to provide further practice and consolidation of the language learners have already encountered in class. Most of the activities are kinaesthetic, i.e. they involve movement, and therefore are great for warmers at the beginning of a lesson or for filler activities in the middle. It's a good idea to start every lesson with some kind of language review, covering vocabulary from previous lessons as well as some grammar items presented as chunks, for example *I've never been to China* in Activity 2.3 or *We've known each other for years* in Activity 2.4.

The activities are presented in a cumulative order, with each subsequent activity containing a greater number of target items. This reflects the learners' process of accumulation of new vocabulary throughout their course. By continuously revisiting previously encountered items and integrating relatively new items, teachers can assess exactly what students have already mastered and find out which items require further review and practice.

2.1 Walkabout cloze

Outline Students walk around the classroom looking for missing words from a text they read in a previous lesson.

Level Intermediate and above (B1+)

Time 20 minutes

Preparation Blank out parts of chunks in a text which students have read in a previous lesson – see an example in Figure 2.1 below. Prepare small cards containing the blanked out parts and stick them on the walls all around the room.

Procedure

1 Distribute blanked out versions of your selected text – see *Preparation* and Figure 2.1. Give learners a couple of minutes to try and remember the missing words in each chunk.

2 Tell learners to get up and walk around the room to find the missing words. They can do this in pairs and you may want to play some background music during this part of the activity.

3 Check answers by displaying or writing the missing words on the board.
Answers for the text in Figure 2.1:
1 *true*, 2 *offer*, 3 *ridiculously*, 4 *catch*, 5 *terms*, 6 *launched*,
7 *achieved*, 8 *attracted*, 9 *taken off*, 10 *flooded*, 11 *over*, 12 *expressed*

4 Now tell learners to turn over their text. Ask them to try and recall the chunks which appeared in the text by looking at the list of missing words on the board.

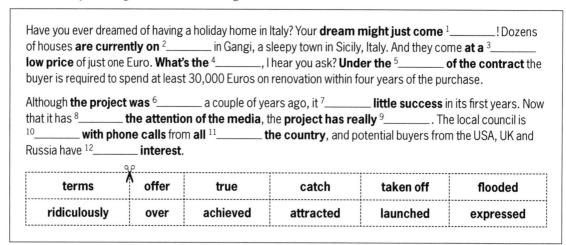

Have you ever dreamed of having a holiday home in Italy? Your **dream might just come** [1]_____! Dozens of houses **are currently on** [2]_____ in Gangi, a sleepy town in Sicily, Italy. And they come **at a** [3]_____ **low price** of just one Euro. **What's the** [4]_____, I hear you ask? **Under the** [5]_____ **of the contract** the buyer is required to spend at least 30,000 Euros on renovation within four years of the purchase.

Although **the project was** [6]_____ a couple of years ago, it [7]_____ **little success** in its first years. Now that it has [8]_____ **the attention of the media**, the **project has really** [9]_____. The local council is [10]_____ **with phone calls** from all [11]_____ **the country**, and potential buyers from the USA, UK and Russia have [12]_____ **interest**.

terms	offer	true	catch	taken off	flooded
ridiculously	over	achieved	attracted	launched	expressed

Figure 2.1: Blanked out text and accompanying cards

Rationale

Classroom walls are a readily available, yet underused, classroom aid. They can be used not only for exhibiting learners' work (for example, pieces of writing) or classroom posters (see Activity 9.8: *Classroom language posters*), but also for displaying all kinds of vocabulary items in revision activities like this one. By using classroom walls, you will get learners out of their seats and infuse some variety into your classroom routine.

2.2 Word – Collocation – Example

Outline Learners form groups of three by matching a word with its common collocates and a gapped example sentence. This grouping activity is suitable for larger classes.

Level Elementary and above (A2+) (the example is at C1 level)

Time 20 minutes

Preparation Select a number of target words, one for every three learners, or 10 items for 30 students. Prepare a three-column table and add target items to the left-hand column, three common collocates to the middle column and an example sentence to the right-hand column – see an example in Figure 2.2 below, suitable for C1-level learners. Print the table and cut it up to make small cards.

Procedure

1 Distribute the cards – see *Preparation* and Figure 2.2 – one per learner. Learners should not show their card to anyone.

2 After you give a signal (for example, start playing music), learners get up and start moving around the classroom. The aim is to form groups of three so that each group consists of the target word + its collocates + an example sentence. To do this, learners should not show each other their cards, but instead say the words on the cards. If their card has a gapped sentence, they can hum the gap, for example: *I was in for a hmmm surprise when I got my mobile phone bill.*

3 Once they've formed a group, learners should sit down in threes. While others continue looking for their missing group members, early finishers can make additional sentences with the collocations they have.

4 Display answers on the board or hand out a complete version of the collocation table.

curb	… your enthusiasm … the rise in temperature … inflation	The new law is aimed at _____-ing harmful gas emissions.
rig	… the results of the election … the competition … the tests	Big banks allegedly tried to _____ the market.
seek	… advice … asylum … a solution	The flow of refugees _____-ing shelter from the war has increased considerably.
discovery	major … startling … grim …	NASA's research led to a surprising _____.
evidence	convincing … compelling … hard …	Despite the discovery of water on Mars, there is still no conclusive _____ that there was once life on the planet.
nasty	… fall … shock … taste in the mouth	I was in for a _____ surprise when I got my mobile phone bill.

Figure 2.2: Table of words, collocations and examples

37

Note

If the number of students in your class is not divisible by three, join in to make up the desired number of groups or ask two students to share one card.

With lower levels, you may want to base the activity on target words belonging to the same part of speech, i.e. all nouns or all verbs.

Follow-up

In their new groups, you could give learners a full set of the cut-up cards to match together. This way they will be exposed to all the chunks, not only the ones you gave them at the beginning of the mingling activity.

Rationale

This easy-to-prepare activity can be done with the help of a learners' dictionary (see *Useful resources* on p. 227). Most learners' dictionaries provide natural examples and highlight common collocations.

2.3 Memory quiz

Outline Students mingle to recall chunks they have learned in previous lessons.
Level Any
Time 20 minutes
Preparation Prepare a document with around 12 chunks you have covered previously. Make sure you include a couple of items containing grammatical structures which learners have not mastered yet. These can be from an exercise or correction activity you did with the whole class in a previous lesson, for example *I was born in, How long have you been* – see Figure 2.3 below for more examples. Ensure you have a computer and projector to display your document in class. (Alternatively, you can simply write the chunks up on the board but make sure it's possible to conceal them when necessary – see *Procedure*.)

Procedure

1 Make sure learners cannot see your selected chunks – see *Preparation* – at the start of the activity. Tell the class you are going to display some language they learned in a previous lesson. Explain that learners have one minute to memorize as many chunks and phrases as they can, clarifying that they probably won't remember all of them and they shouldn't worry about it at this stage.

2 Show the chunks for one minute (or a bit longer for lower-level learners) then remove them from view. Ask students to quickly write down as many chunks as they can remember.

3 Ask them how many they could remember. The number will vary but usually students will remember between four and seven items. Tell learners exactly how many chunks were written on the board.

4 The learners' task now is to complete their lists. To do that, they mingle and compare their lists with classmates. However, they are not allowed to show their lists to each other. They have to help each other complete their lists by speaking.

5 Stop the activity when most students have completed their lists.

6 Display the chunks on the board again (one by one, if possible), eliciting the contexts in which learners first saw them (or how they can be used in other contexts). Draw attention to pronunciation where necessary.

Note

Use different fonts and/or colours when you prepare your list of chunks. This makes each item more visual and adds interest.

Preventing learners from showing each other their lists in Step 4 will encourage them to communicate and say the target items several times. You could teach some helpful phrases to scaffold the activity such as *How many do you have?*, *I don't have that one*, *How do you spell it?*, *Are you sure it's ___ and not ___ ?*, etc.

She's got good people skills   antisocial behaviour

go on a diet   *extremely fast learner*   **tell lies**

every other day   keep a diary   impossible to deal with

leisure activity   *I couldn't get any work done*

Figure 2.3: Memory quiz chunks

Rationale

Learners should approach chunks containing 'grammar' (such as *I couldn't get any work done*) in the same way they approach chunks containing just vocabulary. Encourage learners to commit to memory prototypical examples of a certain grammar structure before delving into any analysis.

2.4 Prompted recall

Outline This activity aims to activate chunks learners have previously studied or been exposed to. Students try to remember and write whole chunks in response to the teacher's oral prompts.

Level Elementary and above (A2+)

Time 20 minutes

Preparation Prepare a document with around 12 chunks you have covered previously. Try to use chunks with clear interactional functions such as *I have an early start*, *Don't beat around the bush* and *Let me give you a hand* (chunks like *leisure activity* or *tell lies*, as in the previous activity, would not work as well). Also include a couple of items containing grammatical structures which learners have not fully mastered yet – see Figure 2.4 below for examples.

Ensure you have a computer and projector to display your document in class. (Alternatively, you can simply write the chunks up on the board but make sure it's possible to conceal them when necessary – see *Procedure*.)

In addition, think of and script some oral prompts to describe situations in which some of your selected chunks can be used – see Figure 2.5 below for examples.

Procedure

1 Display or write your selected chunks on the board – see *Preparation* and Figure 2.4.

2 Show the chunks for one minute (or a bit longer for lower-level learners) then remove them from view.

3 Begin to read out your oral prompts – see *Preparation* and Figure 2.5. Give six to eight prompts only. Learners should think of the corresponding chunk for each prompt and write it down. They should also number their responses to help with Steps 4 and 5.

4 After learners have written their responses, tell them to stand up, mingle and compare answers. As in Activity 2.3: *Memory quiz*, they should not show their lists to each other; they should compare answers orally.

5 When most students have compared lists, conduct whole-class feedback. (See *Note* below about differing answers.) Focus on any areas of difficulty such as auxiliary verbs, word stress, etc.

Note

It doesn't matter if learners' responses differ from what you intended or if they disagree with each other when comparing answers. In fact, differing answers will lead to discussion and, as a result, students will end up using and reusing the target chunks, which will aid retention.

come to terms with	takes after his mother
That'll **come in handy.**	It's becoming increasingly common
You'd be better off… + ing	I've got _____ lined up.
There's nothing decent on	I have an early start tomorrow.
There's been a lot of controversy about …	blend in with the crowd
Oh no, I couldn't possibly.	**Don't beat about the bush.**

Figure 2.4: Prompted recall chunks

1   There are more and more single parents today. What do you think about this phenomenon? (*It's becoming increasingly common.*)

2   I got a lot of money when my grandfather died. I don't know whether I should put it all in a bank or invest it in the stock market. What do you think? (*You'd be better off investing …*)

3   Do you want to go out tonight or just stay in and watch TV? (*There's nothing decent on.*)

4   Do you want to go clubbing tonight? (*No, I have an early start tomorrow.*)

5   Should I throw this wrapping away? (*No, that'll come in handy.*)

6   His sister died a few years ago but he is still depressed. (*He still hasn't come to terms with it.*)

7   Many people are unhappy about the government's latest decision. I saw another angry article about it this morning (*There's been a lot of controversy about it.*)

8   Here's a gold watch I got you for your birthday. (*Oh no, I couldn't possibly.*)

Figure 2.5: Oral prompts for prompted recall

Follow-up (suitable for B1+)

Learners repeat the activity in pairs. One reads the prompts and the other responds with suitable chunks. Then they switch roles. (More advanced learners could give the original prompts from memory, or even script their own new prompts.)

Variations

If this activity becomes a regular part of your language-review repertoire, you can vary it by giving more diverse instructions, for example:

'Disagree with this sentence: *He always gets to the point straight away.*'
(= *No, he doesn't. He always beats about the bush.*)
'Agree with this sentence: *You've planned a lot of activities, haven't you?*'
(= *Yes, I've got a lot of things lined up.*)
'Find another way to say that this glue will be useful.'
(= *This glue will come in handy.*)

A more challenging option is NOT to write the target chunks on the board at all but get students to recall them from a previous lesson or from a text they have read.

Rationale

This activity helps to create meaningful contexts in which new language can be used. Some of the example chunks (e.g. *there's been a lot of controversy about ...*) are particularly difficult to produce by combining vocabulary and grammar – even for higher-level students. They'd have to think about the correct verb form (past simple or present perfect) and then figure out whether the sentence should begin with *it* or *there,* and so on. Learning the chunk as a single unit saves processing effort and creates a mental template for similar phrases such as *there's been a lot of debate/talk/speculation about ....*

2.5 Chunk match

Outline	Learners find a partner with the missing part of a collocation/chunk. This review activity can be used for regrouping students.
Level	Any (the example is at B1 level)
Time	5 minutes
Preparation	Select a number of chunks, one for every other learner, or 15 items for 30 students. Prepare a two-column table and add the beginnings of the target chunks to the left-hand column and the endings to the right-hand column. Use ellipses (…) to clarify whether the parts are endings or beginnings (see Figure 2.6 for examples suitable for B1 level). Print the table and cut it up to make small cards.
	Alternatively, the set can be prepared on www.quizlet.com. Make sure you enter the first part in the right-hand column (under **Definition**) and the second part in the left-hand column (under **Term**). In the **Print** sub-menu, select **Small Cards**. After the set opens in a PDF, you can print it and cut it up.

Procedure

1 Give one card to each learner. They should not show it to anyone until you give a signal.

2 When you give the cue (for example, you can start playing music), learners get up, move around the classroom and find a partner with the matching half of their collocation.

3 Once pairs have found each other, they should sit down together. While others are still looking for their missing partners, early finishers try to make two sentences with the chunk (see Activity 9.7: *Two sentence contextualization*).

4 To check answers, display the chunks on the board or hand out a complete version of the table containing the target chunks.

5 Ask a few pairs to read out the sentences they came up with in Step 3. Clarify any collocations that pose any difficulty.

Follow-up

1 In their new pairs, you could give learners a full set of the cut-up cards to match together. This way they will be exposed to all the chunks, not only the ones you gave them at the beginning of the mingling activity.

2 Each pair is given a printed page with all the chunks practised in the activity. The page should be cut up the middle – Student A gets the first column and Student B the second. Student A calls out the beginnings of the chunks in random order, while Student B looks at their list and responds with the correct match.

Note

Although it is not always easy, try to avoid including more than one possible match in the set for each target item. In any case, tell students that they should try to find the most likely combinations, or specifically the ones they learned in previous lessons.

a great sense …	… of humour
a sharp …	… eye (for)
pick up …	… languages easily
offered her …	… a lift
designer …	… boutique
make …	… a decision
was run …	… over (by a car)
They went …	… to school together
We've known each …	… other for years

Figure 2.6: Beginnings and endings of chunks

Rationale

You will see from the examples above that the mix of items suggested for this activity is quite diverse. There are:

- individual words that might be genuinely new at this level, e.g. *sense*
- new chunks containing familiar words, e.g. *a sharp eye*
- chunks containing seemingly easy words that students tend to make mistakes with, e.g. learners often say *They learned at the same school* instead of *They went to school together*
- fully grammaticalized sentences, e.g. *We've known each other for years* (you can include chunks like this regardless of whether the present perfect has been 'covered' on the course or not).

2.6 Chunks on chairs

Outline	Learners find their chair using chunks as prompts.
Level	Any
Time	5 minutes
Preparation	Select a number of chunks, one for every learner. Prepare a two-column table and add the beginnings of the target chunks to the left-hand column and the endings to the right-hand column. Use ellipses (…) to clarify whether the parts are endings or beginnings (see Figure 2.6 in Activity 2.5: *Chunk match* for examples suitable for B1 level). Print the table and cut it up to make small cards. Before the lesson, stick one chunk ending to the back of each learner's chair. Alternatively, the set can be prepared on www.quizlet.com. Make sure you enter the first part in the right-hand column (under **Definition**) and the second part in the left-hand column (under **Term**). In the **Print** sub-menu, select **Small Cards**. After the set opens in a PDF, you can print it and cut it up.

Procedure

1   Distribute the beginnings of the chunks – see *Preparation* – to learners.

2   When you give the cue (for example, you can start playing music), learners get up, walk around the room and find a chair with the second half of their chunk on it.

3   Once learners have found their chairs, they should sit down and think of two sentences with their chunk (see Activity 9.7: *Two sentence contextualization*).

4   To check answers, display the chunks on the board or hand out a complete version of the table containing the target chunks.

5   Ask some learners to read out the sentences they came up with in Step 3. Clarify any collocations that pose any difficulty.

Variation

This activity can also work with words and their corresponding definitions (see Activity 9.5: *Matching words and definitions*). Stick the words to the chairs and hand out the definitions to learners.

Rationale

This activity can be done as a warmer at the beginning of a lesson or as a filler in the middle. It helps not only to review vocabulary but also to break up the routine a little and regroup learners.

2.7 Chunk swap

Outline	Students move around the room looking for the second parts of chunks.
Level	Any
Time	10 minutes
Preparation	Select a number of chunks, one for every learner. Prepare a two-column table and add the beginnings of the target chunks to the left-hand column and the endings to the right-hand column. Use ellipses (…) to clarify whether the parts are endings or beginnings (see Figure 2.6 in Activity 2.5: *Chunk match* for examples suitable for B1 level). Print the table and cut it up to make small cards.
	Alternatively, the set can be prepared on www.quizlet.com. Make sure you enter the first part in the right-hand column (under **Definition**) and the second part in the left-hand column (under **Term**). In the **Print** sub-menu, select **Small Cards**. After the set opens in a PDF, you can print it and cut it up.

Procedure

1   Hand out two cards to each learner: a beginning and an ending of a chunk. Make sure you have shuffled the cards before distributing them. Learners should not show their cards to anyone.

2   Ask learners to look at their cards and see if they match. (They probably won't, but if they do, retrieve them – as well as those from a couple of other students – and redistribute.)

3   The aim is to find the matching endings for the beginnings that learners have in their hands. Endings should be handed over to whoever needs them so that each student ends up with only two cards that match.

4   When you give the cue (for example, you can start playing music), learners get up, move around the classroom and look for the second half of their chunk. After they find it, they should NOT sit down, but should continue trying to get rid of the second half they don't need (the one they originally received from you).

5   After all students have matched their cards and sat down, check answers by displaying the chunks on the board or handing out a complete version of the table containing the target chunks.

Variation

If you have more target items than the number of learners, you can give stronger learners more than two cards. For example, they can have two beginnings and one ending (and another student will then have more endings to get rid of). In much smaller groups, all students can be given more than two cards.

Rationale

Like Activity 2.5: *Chunk match*, this activity particularly lends itself to two-word collocations e.g. *draw a conclusion, casual clothes*, but with a little imagination it can be extended to longer chunks such as *to make matters worse, I wouldn't be seen dead wearing that*, etc.

2.8 Get the chunk off my back

Outline	Learners move around the room with chunks attached to their backs. They listen to descriptions and try to figure out what their chunk is.
Level	Intermediate and above (B1+)
Time	Minimum 15 mins
Preparation	Write a selection of known chunks on self-adhesive pieces of paper, like Post-it® notes, one chunk per piece of paper. (Alternatively, you can use ordinary pieces of paper and paper clips). You may want to underline key words in some longer chunks – these will indicate the words other learners cannot use when describing the chunk. See Figure 2.7 below for examples at B1 and C1 levels. You will need many more items than learners in your class.

Procedure

1   Stick one pre-filled Post-it® note on the back of each learner – see *Preparation* (or attach papers with paper clips). When all students have a chunk on their backs, they can mill around and give each other clues to the meaning of the chunks, e.g. *It's what you do in football, you kick the ball and the whole stadium goes Hooray! (score a goal)*.

2   For longer chunks with underlined words (see Figure 2.7 below), learners cannot use the words that are underlined when giving clues but CAN use the other words., e.g. *It's when the police ignore a problem; they know it's a crime, it's prohibited by law, but they pretend not to see it* (*The police turn a blind eye*).

3   If a learner struggles to figure out their chunk from the clues given, they should move to another learner to get more clues. After they have identified the chunk, they can take it off their back and keep it.

4   Monitor and attach a new chunk to a learner each time they correctly identify one. Keep sticking until the chunks run out.

5   Ask students to sit down and count the number of chunks they have. The student with the most chunks is the winner.

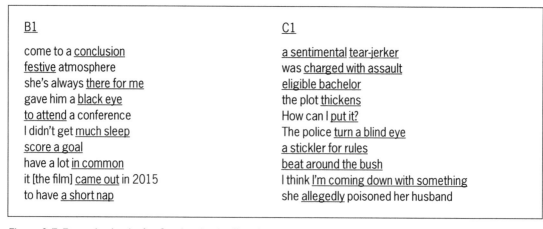

B1	C1
come to a <u>conclusion</u>	a sentimental <u>tear-jerker</u>
<u>festive</u> atmosphere	was <u>charged with assault</u>
she's always <u>there for me</u>	eligible <u>bachelor</u>
gave him a <u>black eye</u>	the plot <u>thickens</u>
<u>to attend</u> a conference	How can I <u>put it?</u>
I didn't get <u>much sleep</u>	The police <u>turn a blind eye</u>
<u>score a goal</u>	a <u>stickler for rules</u>
have a lot <u>in common</u>	<u>beat around the bush</u>
it [the film] <u>came out</u> in 2015	I think <u>I'm coming down with something</u>
to have <u>a short nap</u>	she <u>allegedly</u> poisoned her husband

Figure 2.7: Example chunks for Get the chunk off my back

Cultural awareness tip

In some contexts touching students of the opposite sex might be inappropriate. If that is the case, ask learners of the same gender to stick the chunks on each other's backs. (Do not ask the students to stick them on their own backs – you don't want them to see what's written on the paper!)

Follow-up

After the activity, collect in all the chunks. At the end of the lesson (or in a subsequent lesson) call out each chunk and ask learners to remember who it 'belonged' to.

Rationale

This activity should ideally be done with a large number of known chunks and after you have done other review activities. This activity would be suitable for the final week of a course, for example. Unlike previous activities which focused on recognition of chunks and recall of meaning, this one requires students to recall the form.

2.9 Chunks around the room

Outline	This activity is suitable for an end-of-course review after various topics have been covered. Learners replace descriptions with chunks learned on the course.
Level	Upper intermediate and above (B2+)
Time	Minimum 15 minutes
Preparation	Prepare small cards containing a wide range of chunks studied during the course. Script a few short dialogues (one per small group): each dialogue should focus on a topic covered on the course and should contextualize several of the chunks. However, instead of including the target chunks themselves, use synonymous words and expressions – see Figure 2.8 below for examples. (Make sure the synonymous phrases do not contain words that are more difficult than the chunks they are supposed to define!)

Procedure

1 Put the cards containing the target chunks all around the room (on chairs, on the board, on windowsills, etc.).

2 Divide the class into small groups. Give each group one of your scripted dialogues – see *Preparation*.

3 Groups first try to work out which chunks are being described the dialogue. Then they walk around the room looking for the relevant chunks.

4 Stop the activity after all the chunks have been collected. Confirm answers orally or by giving out new versions of the dialogues with the correct chunks in place.

Follow-up

Groups turn over their dialogue and try to reconstruct it using the chunk cards in front of them.

Rationale

Learners usually get a surprise when they enter the classroom and see it covered in chunks (you can use coloured paper or brightly-coloured Post-it® notes to make them as noticeable as possible). Students are usually keen to look at all the language on the cards before the activity has even begun. It also gives a real sense of how much has been covered and, hopefully, how much has been learned on the course.

Dialogue 1 (Topic: work and health)

A: So why did you leave your previous job? Were you **laid off**?
B: No. I just quit. One of my boys **fell ill with** the flu. So I had to stay at home and **take care of** him.
A: Did you find a new job afterwards?
B: Well … I **didn't have a job** for more than six months. I was doing some **jobs which were not on a permanent basis**.
A: I see. Look, unfortunately you **aren't exactly the person we're looking for**.

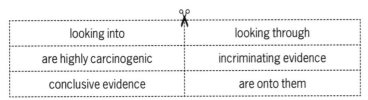

made redundant	came down with
look after	was out of work
don't meet our requirements	casual work

Dialogue 2 (Topic: law)

A: You know, I am **investigating** this case. The other day, I was **quickly reading** the papers and I found that the company was using preservatives that **cause cancer**.
B: Really? So are you going to sue them?
A: Well, we have to find **proof that leaves no doubt** first.
B: Be careful because, you know, **the documents that prove someone's guilt** might disappear once they realize you **are suspicious of them**.

looking into	looking through
are highly carcinogenic	incriminating evidence
conclusive evidence	are onto them

Dialogue 3 (Topic: various)

A: So why won't you go out with him?
B: Oh, come on! He **is not good looking and doesn't have social skills**.
A: You cannot **tell what someone is like by looking only at their appearance**.
B: But he is **only interested in computers and technology**.
A: **Look who's talking.** You've just **spent too much money** on a new smartphone.
B: I don't know **what that is supposed to mean**. What smartphone?

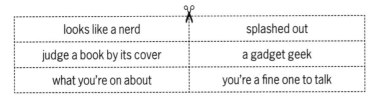

looks like a nerd	splashed out
judge a book by its cover	a gadget geek
what you're on about	you're a fine one to talk

Figure 2.8: Dialogues and cards

3 Exploring text

Texts are most usually used in ELT for the purposes of reading comprehension and teaching reading skills (e.g. skimming and scanning), and less often for teaching grammar. When it comes to vocabulary, students are often pre-taught difficult items before a reading activity or are encouraged to infer the meaning of unfamiliar words as they read (which incidentally does not always result in accurate guessing or necessarily lead to effective vocabulary learning). Consequently, students may get the impression that it's only worth focusing on new and difficult individual words in a text. As a result, they fail to notice useful chunks that texts are packed with. This is especially true of chunks that have transparent meaning, i.e. they can be understood from the individual words. Activities in this chapter are aimed at drawing learners' attention to chunks in reading texts and revisiting texts in order to derive the maximum linguistic benefit.

3.1 Predicting grammar

Outline	Learners predict grammatical structures they are likely to encounter in a text.
Level	Intermediate and above (B1+)
Time	6–7 mins (not including reading a text)
Preparation	None

Procedure

1   Write on the board some words and chunks which appear in a text your learners are going to read. Tell learners what the text is about and ask them to predict which grammar structures may appear in a text of this genre. Accept all ideas and do not give any answers at this stage. For example, a text describing how a town has changed since the author's childhood may contain the items below and may contain passives, present perfect and comparative adjectives:

   converted into a hotel   *knocked down*   *restored to its former glory*   *much safer*

2   Give students five minutes to discuss why/how the items on the board may appear in the text and ask them to write sentences containing them.

3   There is no need to do any error correction at this stage although you may want to elicit from students what they have come up with.

4   After reading the text and doing comprehension checks, a vocabulary focus and other activities, ask learners to compare their sentences from Step 2 with those in the text. (They will probably have noticed them while reading anyway!) In the example text about how a town has changed, the items are likely to appear in the present perfect – mostly in the passive form (a–c) but also active (d).
   a   *The old derelict building **has now been converted into a hotel**.*
   b   *Many old buildings on the waterfront **have been knocked down**.*
   c   *The grand old Post Office, which was badly damaged in a fire in 2001, **has now been restored to its former glory**.*
   d   *The area around the old railway station **has become much safer**.*

Note

For less grammatically inclined learners, it might be helpful to supply a checklist of grammar areas first. Learners can then choose which areas they think are likely (and unlikely) to occur in the text.

Rationale

We often ask students to predict vocabulary before reading a text. Why not do the same for grammar? Getting learners to predict grammar before reading triggers and enhances noticing (see *Glossary* on p. 223). In fact, there are two kinds of noticing at play here: noticing as in paying special attention to the grammatical forms in the input and noticing the gap between learners' output and a target model – when learners compare their own sentences with those in the text.

3.2 Guided discovery of chunks

Outline Learners find chunks in a text they have read using clues from the teacher.
Level Intermediate and above (B1+)
Time 10–15 minutes
Preparation Use a text that learners are familiar with as this is a post-reading activity. Decide which chunks in the text should be pointed out and prepare a definition or paraphrase for each one – see Figure 3.1 for examples.

Procedure

1 Tell learners you are going to read out some clues. Explain that they have to identify and underline chunks in the text that match your clues. They should do this individually. Clarify that the clues will be given in the order in which the chunks appear in the text.

2 With longer texts, it is a good idea to provide paragraph numbers to help learners find the chunks. The idea is to help students locate the chunks in the text without making the activity unnecessarily daunting.

3 Do the first clue as an example.

4 Learners should number the underlined chunks in the margins. This will help later when comparing with others or checking answers.

5 When you have read out all the clues, learners can compare answers, then check with the whole class.

6 Make sure students record the chunks in their vocabulary notebooks.

Variation
For lower levels, clues could be given in L1.

Follow-up
As you go through the answers you can engage learners further with the target items by asking extra questions, for example:

lose some weight:	Find the same collocation used in a different tense. (*I've lost a lot of weight*)
	What's the opposite? (*gain / put on weight*)
go for a run:	What other nouns can be used with *go for*? (*a walk/swim/ride/drive*)
get home:	Find in the text another *get* used in the sense of reaching a place.
	(*get to the office*)

You can also ask learners what other chunks in the text they find useful.

THE TREADMILL

When Manuel Pedro's daughter looked at him one morning and said "Wow, you're fat!", he knew it was time to lose some weight. The trouble was, he didn't have time to do any exercise. "I work in an office all day and when I get home in the evening, I generally just want to sit down and relax. At the weekend I normally do things with my kids, so I just don't have time to go to the gym or go for a run."

However, one day, his wife suggested buying a treadmill and walking on it while he worked. "I thought she was crazy at first," he says. "But then I thought, why not?" So the forty-year-old bought a cheap treadmill and put it in the corner of his office. He fixed his laptop to it and began walking and working at the same time.

"At first, I found it hard to type and walk at the same time. I got really stressed and sometimes only did it once or twice a week. I also looked really stupid in a shirt and tie on a treadmill. My colleagues thought it was really funny." However, soon Manuel got better at working while he walked, and started to feel healthier. After a while he was doing several hours' walking every morning.

"I have a lot more energy now," says the office manager. "When I get to the office, I get straight on the treadmill and check my emails. I do three hours a day at the moment. Every week I do ten minutes' more walking. I've lost a lot of weight. My wife can't stop smiling."

<u>Clues</u>

1   a verb + noun collocation which means *to become less fat* (para. 1)
2   a phrase which means *he was busy with other things* (para. 1)
3   a verb + noun collocation which means *return to the house* (para. 1)
4   a collocation which means more or less the same as *to jog* (para. 1)
5   a two-word combination which means *tell someone to get something from a shop* (para. 2)
6   an expression which means *doing two things together* (para. 2 and 3)
7   an expression which means *I thought it wasn't easy* (para. 3)
8   a collocation which means *became very nervous and worried* (para. 3)
9   a collocation which means *improve* (para. 3)
10 an expression which means *always have a happy face* (para. 4)

<u>Answers</u>

1 *lose some weight*, 2 *He didn't have time*, 3 *get home*, 4 *go for a run*, 5 *suggested buying*,
6 *at the same time*, 7 *I found it hard (to)*, 8 *got really* stressed, 9 *got better (at)*, 10 *can't stop smiling*

Figure 3.1: Text from *English Unlimited Pre-intermediate* with guided discovery clues

Rationale

It's possible to try and get learners to underline useful chunks themselves, without any prompts or clues. However, an eye for spotting chunks takes learners (as well as teachers) a while to develop. This activity not only highlights useful lexis but also sensitizes learners to the kind of language they should be noticing while reading outside the classroom.

3.3 Were you paying attention?

Outline	Learners fill in the gaps in a text they have read.
Level	Elementary and above (A2+)
Time	6–7 minutes
Preparation	This activity should be done after reading, in the same or the following lesson. Make a copy of the text and blank out single words from common collocations or fixed phrases. You can use white correction fluid or a black marker pen to do this. Delexicalized verbs (see *Glossary* on p. 223) and prepositions are good candidates for this. See Figure 3.2 for an example, which uses the same text as in Activity 3.2: *Guided discovery of chunks*. Print enough copies of the gapped text (one for each learner or pair of learners).

Procedure

1 Hand out copies of the blanked-out text – see *Preparation* and Figure 3.2. Learners try to figure out or remember which words go in the gaps. This can be done individually or in pairs.

2 In order to check answers, learners go back to their original text and compare.

3 Discuss with the whole class which words they knew straightaway and which ones they couldn't remember.

THE TREADMILL

When Manuel Pedro's daughter looked at him one morning and said "Wow, you're fat!", he knew it was time to ▮ some weight. The trouble was, he didn't have time to ▮ any exercise. "I work in an office all day and when I ▮ home ▮ the evening, I generally just want to sit down and relax. At the weekend I normally do things with my kids, so I just ▮ have time to go to the gym or go ▮ a run."

However, one day, his wife suggested ▮ a treadmill and walking on it while he worked. "I thought she was crazy ▮ first," he says. "But then I thought, why not?" So the forty-year-old bought a cheap treadmill and put it in the corner of his office. He fixed his laptop to it and began walking and working ▮ the same time.

"At first, I ▮ it hard to type and walk at the same time. I ▮ really stressed and sometimes only did it once or twice a week. I also looked really stupid in a shirt and tie on a treadmill. My colleagues thought it was really funny." However, soon Manuel got better at working while he walked, and started to feel healthier. After a ▮ he was doing several hours' walking every morning.

"I have a lot more energy now," says the office manager. "When I ▮ to the office, I get straight on the treadmill and check my emails. I do three hours a ▮ at the moment. Every week I do ten minutes' more walking. I've ▮ a lot of weight. My wife can't stop smiling."

Figure 3.2: Text from *English Unlimited Pre-intermediate* with blanked out words

Variation

Stick small pieces of paper containing the missing words on the walls of the classroom. After students have tried working out the answers on their own, tell them to walk around the room and find the missing words. See Activity 2.1: *Walkabout cloze*.

 Classroom management tip

> In multi-level classes, two versions of the text could be prepared so that less able students have fewer gaps to fill (e.g. only 10 instead of the 15 in the sample text above). Alternatively, you could pair weaker learners with stronger ones to do the activity together.

Rationale

When learners read, their cognitive resources are used up processing the meaning of the text, so linguistic features can sometimes be ignored. In other words, students focus on the 'what' rather than on 'how'. This activity helps students move from semantic ('what') to syntactic processing ('how'). If you make a habit of using this activity after each reading task, it may encourage students to pay more attention not only to the message but also the medium, i.e. how the message is constructed.

3.4 Text reconstruction

Outline	Using chunks taken from a text, learners try to reconstruct the whole text – orally or in writing.
Level	Intermediate and above (B1+)
Time	15 minutes
Preparation	Prepare a list of around 12 chunks from a text your students have recently read. The example chunks below are from the 'Treadmill' text in Activities 3.2: *Guided discovery of chunks* and 3.3: *Were you paying attention?*. For texts with a clear chronological narrative, the chunks can be provided in random order.

time to lose some weight	*didn't have time*	*get home*
normally do things with my kids	*go for a run*	*suggested buying*
at the same time	*I found it hard (to)*	*got really stressed*
once or twice a week	*got better (at)*	*can't stop smiling*

Procedure

1 Distribute or display your selected chunks – see *Preparation* – and organize learners into pairs.

2 If the chunks appear in a mixed order, pairs should first try and arrange them into the order they appeared in the text.

3 Using the list of chunks, pairs can now practise retelling the story. (For short texts, this step could be done in writing.)

4 Conduct a whole-class reconstruction of the original text, making sure that each pair retells a part of the story which contains at least one target chunk.

5 Learners go back to the text and skim through it to see if they got anything wrong or if any details were left out.

Variation

This activity can also be used in the pre-reading stage: learners use the chunks to try and predict the content of the text they are about to read.

Rationale

Texts can be used not just for reading lessons but for intensive language work. This activity shows how a text studied in a previous lesson can be revisited and reused for lexical enrichment. Deliberately reusing previously encountered chunks in their original context is an important step before the chunks become fully integrated into the learner's lexicon and can be freely used in new, learner-generated contexts.

3.5 What do they stand for?

Outline Learners fill in chunks in a text they have read.

Level Elementary and above (A2+) (the example is at B1+ level)

Time 15 minutes

Preparation You will need an editable copy of the text on a computer or other device. Using word processing software, delete whole chunks but leave the first letter (or two) of each word as a clue – see Figure 3.3 for examples. Load the edited document to a shared drive or email it to learners directly. Ensure learners can access the document during the lesson on their devices. (Alternatively, you can print the edited text and distribute it in class.)

Procedure

1 Ask learners to open the edited document you provided before the lesson – see *Preparation*. (Alternatively, hand out paper copies.)

2 Students complete the gaps individually or in pairs, either on their devices or on the paper copies.

3 To check their answers, learners compare them with the original text in their coursebook.

4 Conduct feedback, asking which chunks students remembered easily and which ones they couldn't recall. Encourage students to think of situations or contexts where they can use the target chunks.

WHY SO CLUMSY?

What makes one person have more accidents than another? Most people would say that it's to do with taking risks. Take fewer risks and you'll have fewer accidents. But is taking risks really a m_____ o_ c_____?

Some experts believe that whether or not you take risks in life has a lot t__ d__ w_____ your up_____ and, some believe, with your birth order. Parents are often stricter and more careful with their first child, and so first-born children tend to grow up taking fewer risks and being more cautious. Parents are often more relaxed with a second and third child, so these children tend to take more risks.

But why do children tend to be more accident-prone than adults? During childhood and adolescence, the body grows very quickly. There seem to be periods in these years when our brain and body are at different stages of development. Our arms are longer than the brain thinks they are, so we k_____ t_____ o_____; our legs are longer than the brain believes, so we trip over easily.

Another ex_____ h__ b___ o_____ by scientists in Spain who have found a possible link between the number of hours a child watches TV and how accident-prone they are. The research suggests that the more time a child spends watching TV, the less they are developing their p_____ co-_____ s_____. If a child doesn't r_____ a_____ a lot, they don't begin to understand that the world is full of physical risk. Watching cartoons and action adventure films d_____ h_____ e_____. It gives the child a false sense of how the world works and of how much danger it contains.

So, what about adults? Some s_____ h_____ s_____ that left-handed people are more accident-prone than right-handed people. Why the difference? N__ o_____ k_____ f_____ s_____. One theory is that we live in a right-handed world. Everything – from cars to door handles, from children's toys to engineering tools and equipment – is made by right-handed people for right-handed people. So left-handed children and adults are m_____ l__ t_ h_____ a_____ because the modern world is not designed for them.

Figure 3.3: Text from *English Unlimited Intermediate* with chunks deleted

WHY SO CLUMSY?

What makes one person have more accidents than another? Most people would say that it's to do with taking risks. Take fewer risks and you'll have fewer accidents. But is taking risks really a matter of choice?

Some experts believe that whether or not you take risks in life has a lot to do with your upbringing and, some believe, with your birth order. Parents are often stricter and more careful with their first child, and so first-born children tend to grow up taking fewer risks and being more cautious. Parents are often more relaxed with a second and third child, so these children tend to take more risks.

But why do children tend to be more accident-prone than adults? During childhood and adolescence, the body grows very quickly. There seem to be periods in these years when our brain and body are at different stages of development. Our arms are longer than the brain thinks they are, so we knock things over; our legs are longer than the brain believes, so we trip over easily.

Another explanation has been offered by scientists in Spain who have found a possible link between the number of hours a child watches TV and how accident-prone they are. The research suggests that the more time a child spends watching TV, the less they are developing their physical co-ordination skills. If a child doesn't run around a lot, they don't begin to understand that the world is full of physical risk. Watching cartoons and action adventure films doesn't help either. It gives the child a false sense of how the world works and of how much danger it contains.

So, what about adults? Some studies have shown that left-handed people are more accident-prone than right-handed people. Why the difference? No one knows for sure. One theory is that we live in a right-handed world. Everything – from cars to door handles, from children's toys to engineering tools and equipment – is made by right-handed people for right-handed people. So left-handed children and adults are more likely to have accidents because the modern world is not designed for them.

Figure 3.4: Complete text from *English Unlimited Intermediate*

Rationale

Because whole chunks are blanked out (rather than individual words, as in Activity 3.3: *Were you paying attention?*), this activity targets productive knowledge in that it encourages retrieval of whole chunks from memory. Like many others in this chapter, this activity encourages learners to go beyond focusing on the message (semantic processing) to paying attention to the form (syntactic processing).

3.6 'You're wrong, teacher!'

Outline	The teacher makes deliberate mistakes with chunks students have been focusing on and learners try to correct them.
Level	Intermediate and above (B1+)
Time	15 minutes
Preparation	None

Procedure

1 Read a recently studied text aloud but deliberately change some chunks that you focused on earlier. Your 'mistakes' can be factual, lexical (e.g. mis-collocations, for example *make a photo* instead of *take a photo*) or grammatical (e.g. *I'm not have time* instead of *I don't have time*). See Figure 3.5 for examples, which relate to the 'Treadmill' text in Activities 3.2: *Guided discovery of chunks* and 3.3: *Were you paying attention?*.

2 Pause after each mistake, allowing students time to think and produce the correct chunk.

3 Learners should shout out 'You're wrong!' every time you make a mistake, followed by the correct chunk. Alternatively, they can make a note of the correction quietly and then compare in pairs.

THE TREADMILL

When Manuel Pedro's daughter looked at him one morning and said "Wow, you're fat!", he knew it was time to **put on some weight**. The trouble was, he didn't have time to **make exercises**. "I work in an office all day and when I get home **in the morning**, I generally just want to sit down and relax. At the weekend I normally **go to visit my parents**, so I just don't have time to go to the gym or **go swimming**."

However, one day, his wife **suggested to buy** a treadmill and walking on it while he worked. "I thought she was crazy at first," he says. "But then I thought, why not?" So the forty-year-old bought a cheap treadmill and put it in the corner of his office. He fixed his laptop to it and began walking and working **one with each other**.

"At first, I found it hard to type and walk at the same time. I **got really excited** and sometimes only did it **one or two times in a week**. I also looked really stupid in a shirt and tie on a treadmill. My colleagues thought it was really funny." However, soon Manuel **became good** at working while he walked, and started to feel healthier. After a while he was doing several hours' walking every morning.

"I have a lot more energy now," says the office manager. "When I **get home**, I get straight on the treadmill and check my emails. I do three hours a day at the moment. Every week I do ten minutes' more walking. I've lost a lot of weight. My wife **can't stop to smile**."

Figure 3.5: Text from *English Unlimited Pre-intermediate* with 'mistakes'

Follow-up
You may want to go through your mistakes and analyse each one, i.e. whether it was genuinely faulty in terms of grammar/collocation (e.g. *one or two times in a week* instead of *once or twice a week*) or merely contained wrong information (e.g. *go to visit my parents* instead of *do things with my kids*). This is particularly important if the 'wrong chunks' in the dictation contained different kinds of mistakes.

Note
You can see the original (correct) chunks for the example text in Activity 3.2: *Guided discovery of chunks*.

Rationale

The teacher is usually the one correcting mistakes, so this fun activity lets students reverse the roles! The activity should be done when students have more or less mastered the target chunks, perhaps after other activities presented in this chapter.

3.7 Input enhancement

Outline After reading a text containing highlighted chunks, students turn over the text and try to recall the chunks.

Level Elementary and above (A2+) (the example is at B1 level, business English)

Time 12–15 minutes (depending on the length of the text)

Preparation Choose a new text from a coursebook or the internet. Try to use short texts like those on tinytexts.wordpress.com or similar websites for teachers. Using word processing software, highlight around 12 chunks in the text – see Figure 3.6 for an example – then print enough copies for the class (one per learner).

Procedure

1 Distribute copies of the highlighted text, asking learners to read it straight away. Set a time limit of around two minutes.

2 Immediately after learners finish reading, ask them to turn the page over and write down as many of the highlighted chunks as they can remember.

3 Learners can compare answers in pairs or move around the room to complete their lists with the help of other students.

4 Conduct feedback, eliciting the contexts in which the target chunks were used.

5 Proceed to other post-reading activities, such as a comprehension check or discussion questions.

United Parcel Service

With the help of UPS, you can have a parcel sent quickly to almost anywhere at any time. The company was founded at the beginning of the twentieth century. It was a time when more and more businesses and private individuals needed to get errands done and messages delivered. UPS founder, James Casey, saw a business opportunity, so he borrowed $100 to set up his own business, Most deliveries were made on foot or by bicycle. Today UPS delivers 16 million packages and documents a day by airplane, ship and truck. One important condition for the new UPS franchise owners is that they have to be good in English and have to pass an exam to prove it.

Figure 3.6: Text from *Business Plus Level 3* with highlighted chunks

---

Rationale

Textual input enhancement is one way of making linguistic input more salient, in order to induce noticing (see *Glossary* on p. 223). You can emphasize certain features of input (e.g. tense markers, word order or chunks, like in this activity) by underlining, highlighting or using bold font. Although not conclusive, research suggests that input enhancement is more effective when accompanied by an explicit instruction to learners to notice the highlighted items. It might therefore be a good idea to tell learners in advance – before reading – to pay attention to the highlighted chunks.

3.8 Gaming language

Outline	Learners collect chunks while playing an online digital game.
Level	Elementary and above (A2+)
Time	Variable
Preparation	Choose an online game suitable for the learners' level and appropriate for their age. The game should have a reasonable amount of written text in it – see suggestions in *Note* below. Play the game briefly yourself and note down 10–20 useful chunks – see examples in Figure 3.7. Prepare a handout with a list of your selected chunks. Ensure learners have access to a device with internet connection (one device per pair) so they can play the game in class.

Procedure

1   Provide learners with a list of your selected chunks – see *Preparation*. Clarify language as necessary.

2   Ask pairs of learners to access the chosen game in their browsers. Pairs play the game and tick (✓) the chunks as they encounter them. (If it's not possible to play the game during class time, this stage can be done as homework.)

3   After playing the game (possibly more than once), pairs compare which chunks they noticed.

4   Conduct feedback with the whole class, eliciting the contexts that the chunks occurred in.

Variation

If students are familiar with the idea of chunking, rather than providing a list ask them to make a note of useful chunks themselves as they play. They can use an online dictionary (see *Useful resources* on p. 227) to look up any language they don't know. In class, ask learners to share the chunks they noted down while playing.

Follow-up

Use some of the ideas in Chapter 2 to revise and recycle the gaming chunks, for example Activity 2.5: *Chunk match*.

Note

There are hundreds of online games but for this activity the game you choose should involve a considerable amount of reading – not just pointing and clicking. Here are some suggestions:

• *Spent* http://playspent.org – an online game about how to survive on a limited budget.
• *Survive* https://live58.org/play.html – a game with similar themes to *Spent*.
• www.practicalmoneyskills.com/play – more games about money and spending.
• *We the Jury* www.icivics.org/games/we-the-jury – a game where learners become members of a jury in a civil trial. They analyse evidence and try to reach a fair verdict.
• *Win the White House* www.icivics.org/games/win-white-house – players manage a presidential campaign, involving debating, raising money and dealing with the media.
• *Ayiti: The Cost of Life* https://ayiti.globalkids.org/game/ – players manage a family in Haiti by making decisions to help them improve their lives.
• For more educational games on different topics (e.g. environment, conflict), visit www.gamesforchange.org/play

take-home pay	let a friend camp out in the living room
sick pay	put up with his/her annoying habits
make ends meet	extracurricular activities
fired on the spot	know your stuff
keep afloat	place a heavy burden on
basic necessities	monthly insurance premiums
live below the poverty line	provide full coverage
pitch in for a co-worker's gift	end up in the street
affordable housing	put a considerable strain on
life throws curveballs	take its toll
effective immediately	stress level is through the roof

Figure 3.7: Example chunks from http://playspent.org

Rationale

Digital games are an important part of many learners' lives, especially those who are often referred to as 'digital natives'. It has been argued that many online games, particularly simulation games, provide learners with a linguistically rich environment. Games specifically designed with L2 learners in mind are few and far between. However, there is no shortage of mass-market games which can be enhanced with supplementary materials to support language learning. See some suggestions in *Note* above.

4 Chunks and listening

The basis for each activity in this chapter can be a listening activity from a coursebook or the internet. There are numerous websites which offer listening activities and podcasts for second language learners. However, most of them focus on listening comprehension with occasional focus on vocabulary – mainly single words.

Noticing chunks in audio texts (as opposed to reading texts) is difficult even for learners who already understand the idea of chunking. When listening, learners tend to grasp the gist or focus on the overall message using what are called top-down listening strategies, paying less attention to the individual words or chunks the message is comprised of. However, reliance on top-down strategies alone may only give a partial understanding of the message. Learners also need to develop bottom-up listening strategies, including paying attention to chunks. In fact, just as in speaking, the ability to recognize and process chunks – as opposed to individual words – can speed overall processing time and significantly increase comprehension. This chapter shows how a focus on chunks can be added to listening activities.

4.1 Are you primed for this?

Outline Learners check their intuitions about frequently occurring chunks using an online tool called Netspeak, then listen to a podcast containing the chunks.
Level Elementary and above (A2+)
Time 20 minutes
Preparation Use a transcript of a listening activity to identify some chunks you would like to focus on. Prepare a handout containing a four-column table with as many rows as the number of target chunks – see Figure 4.1. The first column should contain the target chunks with the last word or two omitted. The remaining three columns will be used to write learners' own guesses, the most frequent combinations suggested by Netspeak and the actual words heard in the audio recording.
Ensure the classroom has a device with internet connection to play the recording.

Procedure

Before listening

1 Give learners your table containing the list of incomplete chunks (with last words omitted) – see *Preparation* and Figure 4.1.

Target chunks	Learner's guesses	netspeak.org results	Chunks on recording
1 the sun goes …			
2 it's cold …			
3 all of a …			
4 crisp autumn …			
5 warm cup of…			
6 hang out with …			
7 it just feels…			
8 covered with …			
9 There's really not that …			
10 love walking …			
The chunks above are taken from a podcast on elllo.org (see *Note* below). Go to elllo.org and find Mixer 148: 'My Favorite Season' (or enter 'ELLLO Mixer Favorite Season' in an internet search engine).			

Figure 4.1: Chunks from a podcast on elllo.org

2 Ask learners to complete each chunk with the first word(s) that comes to mind. They should write their answers in the second column. You might want to establish context here, i.e. tell students that the chunks are taken from an audio clip and explain what the topic is.

3 Tell learners to check their guesses using netspeak.org (see *Note* below). Do one as an example with the whole class, making sure learners enter ellipses (…) after each target string of words – see Figure 4.2. Learners fill in the third column in the table.

4 Ask the class if their intuitions were confirmed or not. Discuss any interesting findings.

Netspeak   One word leads to another.

warm cup of ...		i ×
warm cup of	10,000 100.0%	+
warm cup of coffee	2,600 25.2%	+
warm cup of tea	1,700 16.9%	+
more		

Figure 4.2: Search results on netspeak.org

While listening

5 Play the recording, asking learners to note down the chunks they hear in the fourth column of their tables. Do they match Columns 2 and/or 3?

6 Play the recording again to make sure students have caught all the chunks. Clarify the meaning of any problematic words in the chunks or in other parts of the listening text. See answers for the elllo.org podcast 'My favorite season' in Figure 4.3 below.

Target chunks	Learner's guesses	netspeak.org results	Chunks on recording
1 the sun goes …		down	down
2 it's cold …		outside	outside
3 all of a …		sudden	sudden
4 crisp autumn …		day, air, night	wind / air
5 warm cup of…		tea, coffee	hot chocolate
6 hang out with …		my (best friend), friends	friends
7 it just feels…		like…, good, right, wrong, better	better
8 covered with …		snow, water, blood	snow
9 There's really not that …		much to do	much to do
10 love walking …		in (the rain), around	around

Figure 4.3: Chunks from a podcast on elllo.org, with answers

Follow-up

Hand out the audio script so that learners can check their answers. Ask them to underline the target chunks (as well as any other chunks that are worth noticing). Alternatively, if you have a computer and projector, this can be done with the whole class on the board.

You can also point out interesting or unusual uses of grammar/language. For example, if you use the elllo.org text mentioned above, you could point out how speakers use *would* when something is probable but not completely certain: *My favourite season <u>would</u> probably be autumn.*

Note

Netspeak.org allows you to find any word in a search phrase or, in computational linguistics terms, perform a 'wild card' query. It is particularly handy when you have doubts about how a phrase is formed or cannot find the right word. See Figure 4.2 above for an example of a search result. Netspeak.org is not the only tool which can be used for this activity. A simple query in an internet search engine will trigger predictions for the next word in a string – see Activity 8.10: *Upgrading a text using Google.*

Elllo.org is one of numerous websites which offer listening activities and podcasts for second language learners. It contains thousands of unscripted conversations featuring both native and non-native speakers with a range of accents.

Rationale

Although any listening text can be used for this activity, texts that involve asking the same questions to several people are particularly useful because of their inherent repetition. The 'Mixer' podcasts on elllo.org are good examples of this – see elllo.org/english/Mixer.htm. When the topic is familiar and there is a lot of built-in repetition (e.g. *My favourite season is …, my least favourite season is …*) learners' attention can be drawn to the speakers' linguistic choices rather than the overall understanding of the message. This is sometimes referred to as 'narrow listening' – see Activity 4.8: *Very narrow listening.*

4.2 Reviewing chunks: repeated gapfills

Outline	Learners complete gapfill exercises to review chunks they have encountered in previous listening activities.
Level	Elementary and above (A2+)
Time	Variable
Preparation	You will need an editable transcript from a previously completed listening activity in which learners have focused on some target chunks (for example, an activity like 4.1: *Are you primed for this?*). Using word processing software, prepare a gapfill exercise for the class. You can do one or more of the following:

EITHER: Blank out single words from previously studied chunks (e.g. if you use the elllo.org text from Activity 4.1, you could blank out *covered* in *covered with snow* – see Figure 4.4).
OR: Blank out single words from the previously studied chunks and from some new chunks – see Figure 4.5. In mixed-ability classes, this version could be given to stronger students.
OR: Blank out bigger portions of the target chunks (two or three words).
OR: Delete whole chunks but leave the first letter (or two) of each word as a clue.

Procedure

1 Distribute the gapfill activity to learners – see *Preparation* – asking them to complete the gaps in the transcripts.

2 Ask learners to check answers in pairs (ensuring each pair has the same version of the gapfill, if you prepare more than one version).

3 Play the audio so learners can check answers.

Lindsay from the United States

My favorite season is summer. I love summer. There is no school. It's warm. The sun sets late. You can sit on your balcony and drink a beer and barbecue. I just think it's fabulous. My least favorite then obviously is winter, because the sun goes [1] _____ early, you can't go on your balcony and relax, it's freezing cold, and it's just not an enjoyable season at all.

Kat from Germany

My favorite season is winter, because there's a lot of snow, and it's cold [2] _____, and it's just beautiful. When the countryside is [3] _____ with snow, it's just perfectly white, and I think that's amazing. Also, I love to build a snowman, have snowball fights with my friends, so that is definitely my favorite season. My least favorite season is summer, because it's too hot. I really don't like the heat.

Figure 4.4: Transcript from elllo.org with gapped chunks (previously studied)

<u>Lindsay from United States</u>

My favorite season is summer. I love summer. There is no school. It's warm. The sun [1]_____ late. You can sit on your balcony and drink a beer and barbecue. I just think it's fabulous. My least favorite then obviously is winter, because the sun goes [2]_____ early, you can't go on your balcony and relax, it's [3]_____ cold, and it's just not an enjoyable season at all.

<u>Kat from Germany</u>

My favorite season is winter, because there's a lot of snow, and it's cold [3]_____, and it's just beautiful. When the countryside is covered with [4]_____, it's just perfectly white, and I think that's amazing. Also, I love to build a snowman, have snowball fights with my friends, so that is definitely my favorite season. My least favorite season is summer, because it's too hot. I really [5]_____ like the heat.

Figure 4.5: Transcript from elllo.org with gapped chunks (previously studied and new)

Note

Since none of the gapfill suggestions here include a list of missing words (i.e. a 'word bank'), you should take care to blank out only words in previously studied chunks or in fairly predictable, fixed chunks such as *sudden* in *all of a sudden*. A word bank is not recommended because the aim here is to aid recall from memory; providing a word bank turns this into a receptive matching activity rather than productive retrieval. (You may still, however, wish to provide a word bank for weaker learners.)

Rationale

Although gapfills have sometimes been criticized for being superficial, unoriginal and overused in ELT, these tried-and-tested vocabulary practice techniques are excellent tools for reviewing chunks. In fact, their greatest value is achieved when they are used repeatedly. This is supported by Keith Folse's study (2006) which found that a gapfill exercise repeated a number of times led to better learning of the new items than more creative exercises such as writing sentences with target words.

4.3 Live listening

Outline	Learners listen to the teacher speaking 'live' and note down useful chunks.
Level	Intermediate and above (B1+)
Time	20 minutes
Preparation	Think of a topic you can talk about to the class for a few minutes. It is advisable to pre-plan what you're going to say to make sure your narrative (e.g. a story you're going to tell) is adequately enriched with chunks. You could prepare a list of target chunks as prompts for your talk.

Procedure

1 Tell learners you are going to give a short talk about a particular topic – see an example in Figure 4.6. As you speak, learners should note down useful chunks you use.

2 If it's the first time you have done a live listening, you can signal every time you use a chunk with the help of 'air quotes', i.e. making virtual quotation marks with your index and middle fingers on both hands. This helps ease the way into the activity.

3 When you finish speaking, give learners a couple of minutes to check in pairs how many chunks they spotted while you were talking.

4 Elicit the chunks and put them on the board. If learners come up with more chunks than you originally 'planted', accept all responses; the more, the better!

My favourite season

My favourite season is autumn. It's neither very hot nor **cold outside. It just feels right**. Everything is **covered with leaves**. I love **walking around** in the **crisp autumn air.**

Some people don't like autumn because **the sun goes down** early and some days you can't tell if it's going to be cold or hot. When it is warm, it can **turn cold all of a sudden**. But I think autumn is the best time to **hang out with friends** and walk around the city.

If there is a season **I really don't like** it is winter. It's freezing cold. And **there's not really that much to do**, except stay at home, watch TV with a **warm cup of tea** or hot chocolate.

Figure 4.6: Script for live listening with target chunks in bold

Note

To confirm your intuitions about your choice of chunks you can check them using various resources – see Chapter 1. In the example above, *covered with leaves* and *warm cup of tea* both have a high MI score (see *Glossary* on p. 223) according to COCA and the string *there's not really that much to do* returned almost two million hits on Google.

Variation

As an alternative to signalling each chunk with air quotes, you can provide a list containing key words for each chunk. Learners listen for the word and identify the chunk.

    With weaker learners, you can provide a list of complete chunks in advance and ask them to tick off the ones they hear.

Rationale

In a live listening, a person (a teacher or guest) speaks 'live' to students, i.e. there is no recording. Live-listening activities provide a welcome change from pre-recorded material. They are also more authentic as learners can ask questions, seek clarification and signal to the speaker when they don't understand something.

4.4 Live listening extra

Outline	This is an extended version of a live listening suitable for higher levels. Learners first ask the teacher questions, then listen and identify chunks, then incorporate the chunks into a speaking activity.
Level	Upper intermediate and above (B2+)
Time	20 minutes
Preparation	Think of a topic you can talk about to the class for a few minutes. It is advisable to semi-prepare what you're going to say to make sure your narrative (e.g. a story you're going to tell) is adequately enriched with chunks. You could prepare a list of target chunks as prompts for your talk. However, this activity requires some flexibility as you also need to answer learners' question as you talk – see *Procedure* and Figure 4.7.
	You will also need some self-adhesive pieces of paper such as Post-it® notes.

Procedure

1 Tell students you're going to give a short talk about a particular topic, for example you've just come back from a trip and want to tell them about your experience. Before you talk, ask each learner to write down one or two questions to ask you. Each question should go on piece of paper or Post-it® note. Circulate and help with grammar as learners write their questions.

2 Collect the Post-it® notes, telling learners you will try to answer most questions during your talk.

3 Give your (semi-prepared) talk, answering learners' questions as you speak. If learners are already experienced at identifying lexis, they should note down any useful chunks as they listen. Otherwise, you can use 'air quotes' to signal some chunks, i.e. make virtual quotation marks with your index and middle fingers on both hands.

4 When you finish speaking, give learners a couple of minutes to check in pairs how many chunks they spotted while you were talking. Elicit the chunks and board them.

5 Ask learners to talk about the same topic with their partners. They should try to use as many chunks from your talk / the board as they can.

Variation

You can do a pre-listening activity where students first talk about the selected topic (e.g. their last trip or favourite book) with their partners. After the live listening, learners can repeat this task with a new partner, this time incorporating the chunks they noted down.

My trip to Rome

Most of my friends **fall into two categories**: those who love Paris and those who love London and **can't stand** Paris. I could never understand that; I've always liked both capitals. But my recent trip to Rome completely **changed my mind**. Its beauty is just stunning. I was **absolutely blown away**. Honestly, **when it comes to** European capitals, **from a purely aesthetic point of view**, Rome **wins hands down**.

So, when did I visit Rome [*referring to a learner's question*]? In October.

Just to give you an idea, I arrived in Rome after travelling around the south of Italy. So it was towards the end of a long trip and I'd already seen a lot, and done a lot. So Rome was, in a way, **the climax of the trip**. In fact, it was a bit of a **sensory overload**: the churches, the temples, medieval churches, little piazzas everywhere and art **on every corner**.

And the food. Oh the food. The best pizza I've ever had. **Mind you**, you don't have to go to a **posh restaurant** to try good Italian food. **Cheap and nasty joints** that you can find everywhere had pizza **to die for** – way **better than back home**.

What did I like most [*referring to a learner's question*]? What I particularly liked about Rome is that it's quite a **compact city**: you can **easily get around** on foot …

Figure 4.7: Script for live listening with useful chunks in bold

Note

The aim is for learners to include as many chunks as possible in the speaking stage – but what if some target chunks don't immediately seem suitable, e.g. *conveniently located* doesn't describe the students' hotel accommodation, or their favourite film is not heavy on *spectacular visual effects*? Encourage learners to find other ways to incorporate the chunks such as using negative forms:
This film's not for you if you love spectacular visual effects but it's got an intriguing plot.
The hotel wasn't conveniently located – it was miles from the centre.
The same adaptations can also be made in writing – see Activity 8.6: *Writing frame*.

Rationale

The addition of a question-writing stage arouses learners' interest in the topic (and possibly their teacher's life) and makes the live listening even more 'live', in the sense that the teacher is genuinely answering learners' questions.

4.5 Intonation contours

Outline	The teacher 'sings' the intonation of different chunks and learners identify them.
Level	Any
Time	6 minutes
Preparation	None

Procedure

1 Write on the board a list of chunks. For example:

   a *I don't know.*
   b *Where are you from?*
   c *Don't worry.*
   d *There you go.*
   e *Have a nice day!*
   f *What a nice day!*
   g *Can I help you?*
   h *Have a good trip!*
   i *I'll let you know.*
   j *Shall we wait?*
   k *Is this a joke?*
   l *Good for you!*
   m *Be careful!*

2 Hum (=sing with the mouth closed) *I don't know*, in a slightly defensive way: **^Mm/M**
   Ask students to guess what the chunk is.

3 Explain that you're going to hum each chunk in the list while students try to guess it. They can do it by either writing down the whole chunk or writing the letter a, b, c, etc. next to the corresponding number in a list.

a	*I don't know.* (said defensively)	^Mm/M
b	*Where are you from?*	^Mmm\M
c	*Don't worry.*	^M_M/m
d	*There you go.*	^Mm/M
e	*Have a nice day!*	^MmM\M
f	*What a nice day!*	^mm/M\M
g	*Can I help you?*	mm/Mm
h	*Have a good trip!*	^MmM\M
i	*I'll let you know.*	mMm\M
j	*Shall we wait?*	mm/M
k	*Is this a joke?*	^mMm/M
l	*Good for you!*	Mm\M
m	*Be careful!*	^M_M/m

Key:

M = stressed syllable	**m** = unstressed syllable
/ = rising intonation	**** = falling intonation

4   Alternatively, learners can group the chunks according to their intonation patterns. Hand out the following table or draw it on the board:

↘	↘	↗↘
↺	↗	↗
I don't know.		

5   Go through the answers with the whole class. Practise humming the chunks together. Answers:

↘	↘	↗↘
Have a nice day! *Have a good trip!*	*I'll let you know.* *Where are you from?* *Good for you!*	*What a nice day!*
↺	↗	↗
I don't know. *There you go.*	*Don't worry.* *Be careful!*	*Shall we wait?* *Can I help you?* *Is this a joke?*

Note

This activity is perhaps better suited to teachers who have some experience of dealing with intonation in class.

Rationale

The slightly defensive intonation of *I dunno* (*I don't know*) – or even *I'unno*, often accompanied by a shrug – is a clear example of how intonation helps convey the message. The speaker doesn't even need to open the mouth and can just hum *MmM* as a three-syllable grunt (partially made popular by Homer Simpson from the television show 'The Simpsons'!) for the listener to understand. Although other chunks suggested in the activity have not evolved into non-verbal mumbles, understanding melodic cues in a stream of sounds contributes to listening comprehension. In English, intonation and sentence stress play a particularly important role in decoding aural input. This might be different to learners' L1 where speech may be decoded mainly on the basis of word stress.

4.6 Tease 'em apart

Outline	As a pre-listening activity, learners focus on some chunks which might be difficult to comprehend because of connected speech.
Level	Elementary and above (A2+)
Time	5 minutes (not including the listening activity)
Preparation	Choose some chunks from an audio or video text which contain connected speech, i.e. where speakers run words together and possibly deviate from pronunciation given in dictionaries – see examples in Step 1 below. A transcript may come in handy.

Procedure

1   Before students listen to the audio or watch the video, say your selected chunks – see *Preparation*. Make sure you pronounce them as quickly and naturally as possible, using connected speech. Examples a–g below are from a scene in the film *The Freedom Writers*, where the main character (played by Hilary Swank) confiscates a drawing from one of her students. The parts in brackets give an indication of how the connected speech might sound:

   a   *What's going on?*　　　　　　　　*[Whassgoin ON?]*
   b   *Just leave it alone.*　　　　　　　*[Jus LEAVEitaLONE.]*
   c   *Don't you think?*　　　　　　　　*[Dontcha THINK?]*
   d   *You want to know how?*　　　　　*[Yawanna KNOW HOW?]*
   e   *What you're saying is …*　　　　　*[Whach-yr SAYin IS …]*
   f   *Can I please get out of here?*　　*[CAN I please get OUTTA HERE?]*
   g   *Do you think it's going to matter?*　*[D'yaTHINK isgonna MATTER?]*

2   Learners listen and count the number of words in each chunk.

3   Write the chunks on the board and discuss why learners' word counts for each chunk may have been different. Draw attention to various aspects of connected speech, such as elision (*just → [jus]*) or assimilation/reduction (*want to → [wanna]*).

4   Allow learners some time to practise saying the target chunks in pairs.

5   Proceed to the listening/video activity.

Rationale

Students often struggle to understand aural input, even if they know all the words. The reason is their inability to process connected speech. This activity helps learners improve decoding skills by dividing chunks into word segments.

4.7 Rhythmic chunks

Outline Higher-level learners categorize chunks according to their rhythm.
Level Upper intermediate and above (B2+)
Time 12 minutes
Preparation Make a list of 15–20 chunks with different rhythms – see examples in Figure 4.8 below. They don't have to be only chunks your learners are familiar with or have already encountered. Any new chunks can be clarified during the activity.

Procedure

1 Draw the table and example chunks below on the board, asking learners to copy it down. Clarify that the black boxes indicate the stress pattern – or rhythm – of each chunk.

■▪■	■■▪	▪■▪■	■▪▪■	▪▪■▪▪■
by the way	not really	a piece of cake	see you tonight	if you see what I mean

2 Give each learner a handout containing your selected chunks – see *Preparation* – or display them on the board.

3 Tell learners to group the chunks according to their rhythm and place them in the correct columns in their tables.

4 After students have completed the table and you have checked answers, challenge them to add two more chunks to each column.

■▪■	■■▪	▪■▪■	■▪▪■	▪▪■▪▪■
after you	here's hoping	it's hard to say	out of the way	do you know what I mean
here and there	I'm sorry	it's quite alright	something like that	at the click of a mouse
not at all	no problem	the way ahead	speak for yourself	at the drop of a hat
there you go	nice going	I tell you what	haven't a clue	at the end of the day
wait and see	quite frankly		how do you know	

Figure 4.8: Chunks categorized by rhythm

Follow-up

You can draw learners' attention to some recurring patterns in the table, for example *at the X of a X*. Ask learners to think of other chunks which follow the same pattern, then look it up on the Corpus of Contemporary American English (COCA) as follows: the [n*] of a [n*]

Ask learners to find out which preposition precedes the following chunks found on COCA:

the edge of a cliff
the crest of a wave
the back of a truck
the course of a day
the touch of a button

Alternatively, give learners the endings of these noun + *of* + noun chunks and ask them to think of the beginnings. They can check their intuitions using a corpus tool – see Activities 1.5: *Revisiting delexicalized verbs with COCA* and 4.1: *Are you primed for this?*

_____ *of a cliff*
_____ *of a wave*
_____ *of a truck*
_____ *of a day*
_____ *of a button*

Note

To activate some of the chunks in this activity, try Activity 2.4: *Prompted recall*.
The ideas in this activity are adapted from *About Language* by Scott Thornbury (2017).

Rationale

English is a stress-timed language with more or less equal intervals between stressed syllables, irrespective of how many unstressed syllables come in between. This makes English sound very rhythmical. In stress-timed languages, stress is essential to meaning because content words tend to be stressed, while words that are less important, such as auxiliaries, conjunctions, prepositions and other function words, tend to be unstressed and may seem 'swallowed'. This often creates comprehension problems, particularly for learners whose L1 is syllable-timed. For that reason, learners struggling with understanding spoken English would benefit from more work on pronunciation, particularly practising to pronounce chunks of language with an appropriate rhythm.

4.8 Very narrow listening

Outline Learners listen to very short YouTube clips containing the same chunk, and identify the chunk.
Level Elementary and above (A2+)
Time Variable
Preparation Select some chunks you want your learners to listen to. Search for each target chunk on youglish.com, a pronunciation tool which searches thousands of YouTube video transcripts to find clips containing a target word/phrase. Use inverted commas to find videos containing an exact string of words, for example "get it over with", then click **Say it!** The search engine will find several YouTube videos containing the target chunk. It's a good idea to open a new tab in your browser for each target chunk – this will make it easier to navigate during the lesson. In Figure 4.9 below you can see three tabs, each with results for a different chunk.

Ensure you have access to a device with internet connection, and a projector and speakers, so you can play your selected chunks/clips in class.

Procedure

1 Make sure learners can hear the sound but can't see the video/screen (this technique is known as 'vision off'). Play several clips on youglish.com containing the same target chunk – see *Preparation*. Learners listen and note down the chunk that repeats itself in each clip.

2 As each clip on youglish.com usually starts with a sentence containing the target chunk, you don't have to play more than 10–15 seconds of each clip, some of which can be almost an hour long! Click the right arrow button to move on to the next video. Play around five snippets for each chunk. Do not close the tabs containing videos you have already played.

3 Allow learners time to compare their answers.

4 To check answers, play the clips again. This time students should see the screen – 'vision on'. Pause the videos where necessary or replay the same snippets to focus on any pronunciation or features of connected speech which posed problems.

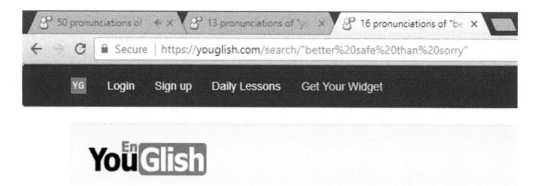

Figure 4.9: Tabs with search results from youglish.com

Variation

If the audio-visual set up of your classroom doesn't allow for vision off, you can show the video in Steps 1–3, but make sure students cannot see the accompanying subtitles. To achieve this on youglish.com, you need to do two things:

1 Turn off the Closed Captions button in the bottom-right corner of the actual YouTube clip. This is usually indicated by a red line under a CC logo.

2 Play with the **Toggle UI** button, a youglish.com feature. Clicking on it allows you to control where you want the captions to appear – below, on or above the screen. Try Toggle UI1 or UI4, which show the navigation arrows on the video itself and the captions above or below it.

Figure 4.10: Screenshot from youglish.com, showing a YouTube clip

Note

This activity will work well with partially known chunks or new chunks consisting of known words. See also Activities 3.3: *Were you paying attention?* and 9.1 *Chunks as a way into a song activity.*

Rationale

'Narrow listening' is an extension of Stephen Krashen's concept of 'narrow reading': exposing learners to similar input over and over again. Repeated exposure to the same sample of language is beneficial for learners' listening comprehension. The added value here is that the same chunks are reused by speakers with different accents, thus exposing students to a wide range of samples of real-life speech. The abundance of YouTube videos today makes access to authentic speech samples easier than ever.

---

5   From words to grammar

The idea that language learning starts with learning words, combining them with other words and then grammaticalizing underpins all activities in this book, therefore the whole book could perhaps have been called *From Words to Grammar*. Nevertheless, this chapter in particular focuses on how vocabulary can be used as a starting point and extended to include grammar practice. This is achieved by taking activities that are traditionally used for teaching vocabulary and giving them a light grammatical focus. These activities range from getting students to notice the grammatical content of vocabulary exercises to recognizing how different words have different grammatical preferences and patterns. There are also some ideas for encouraging beginners to move from learning isolated words to making basic but meaningful sentences.

If you adopt the approach these activities exemplify, you may actually end up teaching **more** grammar than you would with a traditional language-learning method. Instead of giving short, condensed bursts of grammar explanation and practice you will be focusing and re-focusing on many different grammar points as they arise. This emergent, distributed approach to grammar teaching not only provides students with more opportunity to study grammar in meaningful contexts, it is also probably the best match for how learners' grammatical competence develops naturally. Equally importantly, using lexical items as a springboard for grammar exploration shows learners how grammar and vocabulary go hand in hand, and how grammar is used to manipulate and mediate meaning.

5.1 Tricky word families

Outline Learners use dictionaries or corpus tools to research words, then write sentences.

Level Upper intermediate and above (B2+)

Time 15 minutes

Preparation Choose (or create) a word-formation exercise where learners have to first complete a table with missing nouns or verbs, then complete sentences with the correct forms, for example:

NOUN	VERB
advice	_____
_____	describe
_____	enjoy
exhibition	
_____	pay
pollution	_____
success	_____

She gets a lot of _____ from playing the piano. (enjoy)
His book is full of wonderful _____ of the countryside. (describe)

Procedure

1   After students have completed your selected word-formation exercise – see *Preparation* – ask them to rewrite their sentences using the other word from the same word family. For example, if a sentence in the exercise calls for a verb, they should rewrite it using the corresponding noun, or vice versa. The meaning should stay (more or less) the same.

2   To do this, they should first consult a learner's dictionary or a corpus-based tool (see Activities 1.3 and 1.6) to find out how the word is used: its collocations, grammatical patterns, etc.

3   Do one sentence as an example with the whole class. It is important to show that occasionally students might have to rephrase the whole sentence, for example:

*You have to work hard to **succeed**. → **Success depends on** hard work. / You have to work hard to **achieve success**.*

4   After students have rewritten their sentences – individually or in pairs – conduct whole-class feedback. Write examples of good sentences on the board, highlighting useful collocations or grammatical patterns – see Figure 5.1 below.

Variation

Instead of completing gapped sentences from a coursebook exercise, pairs of learners can write their own sentences using half of the target verbs. Pairs then swap sentences with learners who were assigned the other half. All pairs rewrite the sentences they have received, using nouns instead of verbs.

Alternatively, this activity can be used with Cambridge exam-style word-formation exercises, in which learners use the correct form of a given word to complete a sentence. In this case, after completing the exercise you can ask learners to rewrite the sentences using the given words.

Original sentences

a   You have to work hard to **succeed**.
b   The factory has been **polluting** the river for 20 years.
c   I wasn't **impressed** with his performance.
d   Your lawyer should be able to **advise** you on the best course of action.
e   I'm doing an English course in order to **improve** my English.
f   His efforts were rewarded when he was **promoted**.
g   She has **exhibited** her works all over the world.

Rewritten sentences

a   You have to work hard to **achieve success. / Success depends on** hard work
b   The factory has been **(responsible for) causing pollution** in the river for 20 years.
c   His performance didn't **make an impression on** me.
d   Your lawyer should be able to **give you advice** on the best course of action.
e   I'm doing an English course but I haven't seen any **improvement**.
f   His efforts were rewarded when he **got/was given a promotion**.
g   She has **had / taken part in exhibitions** all over the world.

Figure 5.1: Example word-formation practice exercises

Note

Sometimes one form cannot be substituted by the other without a change of meaning. Look at this example sentence:

*She prefers to **entertain** at home rather than go out to an expensive restaurant.*

It cannot be rewritten using the noun *entertainment*, because *home entertainment* refers to an audio-visual system used at home for having a cinema-like experience. Some other 'tricky' words like this are:

confide / confidence
express / expression
free / freedom
imagine / imagination
receive / reception, receipt

Rationale

This activity goes beyond word formation and gets learners to focus on syntactic transformation, brought about by a change in the word form. It shows that learners need to think about collocation and grammar to use the new word form. It also highlights how meaning may change between different parts of speech belonging to the same word family.

5.2 Connecting words and grammar

Outline	This activity raises learners' awareness of grammar patterns associated with different words.
Level	Intermediate and above (B1+)
Time	15 minutes
Preparation	None

Procedure

1 Draw learners' attention to the following common ways of answering the question *What do you do?*:

*I **work in** a bank / **for** Vodafone.*
*I'm **studying** to be a doctor.*

2 Ask them why the two different forms are used to answer the question. (Answer: When we talk about work we tend to use the present simple if we see it as a permanent thing. Being a student, on the contrary, implies a temporary state of limited duration, so we use the present continuous.)

3 Discuss the difference in the following pairs of verbs. In the first person singular, which verb in each pair is more likely to take the simple form (in the past or present) and which one the continuous form? Ask students to make sentences or short dialogues to demonstrate the difference.

live / stay
rent / own (a flat)
look for / find (my keys)
speak / talk
hear / listen
sit / sit down

4 Do whole-class feedback, asking some learners to share their example sentences. The following verbs are more likely to occur in the continuous form (past or present):

stay, rent, look for, talk, listen, sit

Variations

1 To add an extra element of challenge, higher-level students (B2+) can try and include both verbs from each pair in the same sentence, e.g. *I don't own a flat so I'm renting one.*

2 The same sorting activity can be done specifically with verbs that often occur in past tenses – simple or continuous.

Past simple	Past continuous
fall off (the chair)	*walk*
fall over	*swim*
knock over (a glass)	*dance*
trip over (a cable on the floor / a rock)	*run*

Follow-up
Students can use online corpus tools to see which combinations are the most frequent – see *Useful resources* on p. 227.

Rationale
Although each word has slightly different reasons for 'liking' either the simple or continuous form, it is important to understand how grammar and vocabulary work together and are interdependent. For example:

- *own* seldom takes the continuous form because it is a stative verb, i.e. it describes a state rather than an action
- *find (my keys)* is a verb which implies a result or end state, known as telic verb (see *Glossary* on p. 223), so it does not usually take the continuous form
- *knock over / fall off / trip over* denote isolated acts and are referred to as punctual verbs. Using them in the continuous form would imply repetition rather than a single event, so they usually take the simple form
- *walk, swim* or *dance* are durative verbs which go on for extended periods, so they often take continuous forms.

Whatever the reason in each case, students should be made aware that different verbs tend to go with different forms. According to the Longman Grammar of Spoken and Written English (Bieber et al, 1999), the verbs *bleed, chase, chat, joke, kid, moan, shop* and *starve* are strongly associated with the continuous aspect. On the contrary, the verbs *accuse, agree, conclude, convince, invent, hear, know, like, see, shrug, smash* and *swallow* are almost never used in the continuous form (less than 2% of the time).

5.3 Collocation Concentration

Outline	Young learners play Concentration (also known in the UK as Pelmanism): matching collocations with pictures.
Level	Beginner and elementary (A1–A2); particularly suitable for young learners
Time	15 minutes
Preparation	Prepare several sets of 12–14 cards – one set for every three learners. Half of each set should contain a range of adjective + noun collocations, the other half should contain pictures – see Figure 5.2. Pre-teach the collocations over the course of one or two lessons before you do the activity. Examples are:

blue sky
red dress/flower
black coffee
green grass/hills
yellow sand
white snow
brown bear
orange sun
purple fruit
grey clouds

Procedure

1 Divide the class into groups of three and give each group a set of cards – see *Preparation*.

2 Ask groups to shuffle the cards and spread them face down on the table or floor.

3 The first player turns two cards face up. If they get a matching collocation card and picture card, the student keeps the two cards. If they don't match, the student turns them back over, taking care not to move them from their original places.

4 Students continue in turn, until all the cards have been picked up as matched pairs. The student with most pairs is the winner.

Note

The images in Figure 5.2 are in black and white for illustration purposes but obviously the activity will work much better if you are able to make and use colour images!

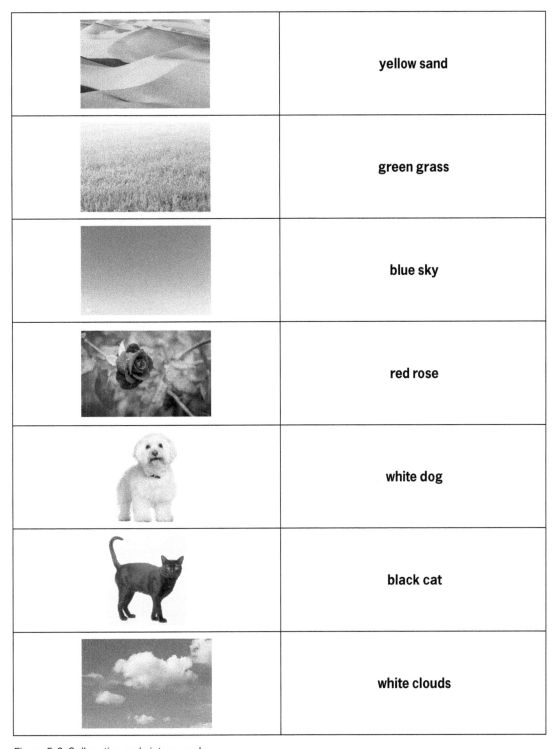

Figure 5.2: Collocation and picture cards

Follow-up

Groups play the game again, but this time you can add a few extra cards which combine the target collocations into longer phrases – see Figure 5.3.

	**white dog on yellow sand**
	**black cat on green grass**
	**white clouds in the blue sky**

Figure 5.3: Collocation cards with longer phrases

Arrange the flashcards on the floor face up, as a winding trail of 'stepping stones'. Explain that each flashcard is a stepping stone and learners need to get to the end, i.e. to 'cross the stream'. Pupils should say the chunk correctly before stepping on the stone. If they get it wrong, they go one step back.

Rationale

Several studies have shown that students learn new vocabulary items better when they are not grouped in semantic sets (e.g. all colours or items of clothing together). These studies suggest that it would be more productive instead – at least at first encounter – to present unrelated words or words with their co-text (see *Glossary* on p. 223). This is why the *Preparation* section above suggests pre-teaching colours alongside the nouns they can go with, rather than simply teaching a list of colours as discrete items in one go.

Admittedly, the collocations practised here are rudimentary but the activity allows learners to make simple phrases out of the few words they know. This would not be possible if words were taught in semantic sets where every word belongs to the same part of speech: all nouns (e.g. animals) or all adjectives (e.g. colours). This arguably boosts learners' confidence and draws attention to the importance of syntagmatic relations – see *Glossary* on p. 223.

Note also how the alliterative patterns in *red rose* and *green grass* can serve as mnemonic devices, which have been shown to facilitate retention (Boers & Lindstromberg, 2005). See also Activity 10.5: *Alliterative chunks*.

5.4 From word lists to patterns

Outline Learners match selected items from semantic sets (see *Glossary* on p. 223) with corresponding grammatical patterns.

Level Beginners and above (A1+); particularly suitable for young learners

Time Variable

Preparation Choose a coursebook unit where vocabulary is generally presented in semantic sets, for example adjectives for colours (*red*, *blue*, etc.) or nouns for items of furniture (*sofa*, *bed*, etc.). Do not teach whole sets at once; choose only three or four items from each set and think of words they are likely to collocate with or grammatical patterns they can go in, i.e. what learners might actually say with the words, for example:

Transport
bus
train
car   →   *fly a plane, drive a car, go to school by bus*
bike
taxi
plane

See Figure 5.4 for some suggestions of other grammatical patterns which can be taught with semantic sets.

Prepare and cut up a set of cards containing the target items from the semantic set you want to focus on – see Figure 5.5 for examples. Make sure learners have access to some self-adhesive putty such as Blu Tack® during the lesson.

Procedure

1 Write some grammatical patterns on the board which go with items from your selected semantic set. Include gaps for the target words – see *Preparation* and the examples below.

____	____	____
____	____	____
My mum/dad goes to work by ____	*Do you have* ____ *?*	*She plays the* ____
____	____	____

2 Distribute the cut-up cards between the learners – see *Preparation*. (It's not necessary for everyone to have a card.)

3 Ask learners to come up to the board and stick their word cards in the appropriate slots according to the patterns. They can use Blu Tack® for this.

4 After all the cards have been stuck on the board, go through the answers with the whole class. Elicit one more word which can be added to each list.

Semantic set	List of words	Suggested patterns
Transport	bus train car bike taxi boat	I come/go to school by _____. S(he) comes/goes to school by _____. My mum/dad goes to work by _____. (S)he always takes the _____ to school. Also: get on/off the bus/train/plane drive a car/van/taxi, ride a bike
Classroom objects	pen pencil eraser scissors	Have you got / Do you have a(n) _____? Can I use your _____? Can I borrow your _____?
Musical instruments	guitar piano drums violin	(S)he plays the _____. (S)he would like to learn to play the _____.
Food	juice chicken ice cream fish	I like _____. I don't like _____.

Figure 5.4: Grammatical patterns to introduce with semantic sets

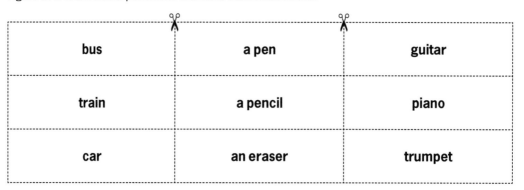

Figure 5.5: Cards containing selected items from semantic sets

Note

It's better to teach a few words from a semantic set along with their co-text (see *Glossary* on p. 223), rather than teach a larger number of items from a semantic set on their own. Using the example set in *Preparation* above, instead of teaching six words from the semantic set of transport, you'll be teaching three words from the set plus three other words that can form syntagmatic relations: two collocations (*fly + plane, drive + car*) and one grammatical pattern (*go + to + place + by + means of transport*). The remaining words in your selected semantic set can be taught later on with other collocations/patterns or inserted into a pattern which has already been presented: *I go to school by bus/train/car / on foot.*

Variations

1 If your students can already write, the activity can be done as a relay race – see Activity 7.5.

2 Semantic sets can also be used in combination with each other: animals can be combined with action verbs or habitats; countries can be taught alongside their traditional foods; food can be taught together with names of meals; colours can be combined with just about anything. Generally, the more random the combinations are when first presented, the more likely learners are to retain them. See some possible combinations in Figure 5.6.

Semantic field	List of words	Suggested patterns	Examples
Animals	cat kangaroo turtle dolphin lion fox	The [ANIMAL] likes to [ACTION VERB] The [ANIMAL] lives in the [HABITAT]	The cat likes to play. The dolphin likes to swim. The kangaroo likes to jump. The lion lives in the jungle. The fox lives in the forest. The turtle lives in the ocean.
Clothes	a shirt a skirt a hat shoes a T-shirt	[PERSON] is wearing a(n) [COLOUR] + [ITEM OF CLOTHING]	Jessica is wearing a blue skirt. Tomas is wearing a black T-shirt.
Family members	mother father sister brother grandmother friend	Where's your [FAMILY MEMBER]? She's in the [ROOM IN A HOUSE] + [ACTION VERB + -ing]	A: Where's your mother? B: She's in the kitchen, making dinner. A: Where's your brother? B: He's in the bedroom, playing computer games. A: Where's your grandma? B: She's in the living room, watching TV.

Figure 5.6: Cards containing selected items from semantic sets

Rationale

Like Activity 5.3: *Collocation Concentration*, this activity draws on research which suggests that, because of the similarity between items, presenting new vocabulary in semantic sets does not always facilitate learning. Nevertheless, this is how vocabulary in elementary coursebooks tends to be organized. Some coursebook authors have defended this method of organization by saying that it would not be feasible to group new vocabulary any other way in order to have meaningful learning units built around a theme. The activity outlined above shows how you can move away from presenting new vocabulary in discrete semantic sets yet still cover the vocabulary in the coursebook – especially when faced with external demands to adhere to a school syllabus.

5.5 Look left, look right

Outline	Learners are encouraged to notice surrounding language (co-text) in a vocabulary exercise.
Level	Intermediate and above (B1+)
Preparation	Choose a vocabulary exercise, such as gapfill, where the target words appear in context – either in discrete sentences or longer pieces of text.

Procedure

1 After learners have done your selected vocabulary exercise and you've checked answers, tell them to 1) look to the left of the target word and 2) look to the right of it. If learners are already in pairs, assign the left/ride side according to how they are sitting: the student sitting on the left looks to the left and the one on the right looks to the right.

2 Students go through the sentences in the exercise and underline what they find.

3 If there is nothing worth noting on one side of some words, tell learners to increase the 'span' and look slightly further to the left/right.

4 Collect learners' findings.

5 Pick out a selection of the most useful or interesting chunks and write them on the board.

Note

You can train your learners to do this activity after any vocabulary exercise. Just say 'remember, look left and look right' and remind students to add any useful findings to their notebooks.

Follow-up

Ask learners to do the same vocabulary exercise again but shift the gaps to the left or right of the original target words (depending on the learners' and your findings) – see Figure 5.7. Sometimes both words – to the right and to the left – can be gapped. Students try to recall the missing words, then turn back to the original exercise to check their answers.

Original exercise

| fascinating | grief | fit | benefit | put down | showers | abandon |

She keeps _____ by jogging every morning.

I've read Carlos Ruiz Zafón's latest book and I found it _____.

I couldn't _____ the book until I'd read the last chapter.

Her _____ at her son's death was terrible.

As a baby he was _____ by his mother.

Heavy _____ are expected in the mountains tomorrow.

Millions of people have _____ from biotechnology.

Reworked exercise

She ____ **fit** ____ jogging every morning.

I've read Carlos Ruiz Zafón's latest book and I _____ it **fascinating**.

I _____ **put down** the book until I'd read the last chapter.

Her **grief** _____ her son's death was terrible.

As a baby he _____ **abandoned** _____ his mother.

_____ **showers** are _____ in the mountains tomorrow.

Millions of people _____ **benefited** _____ biotechnology.

Figure 5.7: Original and reworked gapfills

Rationale
The exercise encourages learners to pay attention not only to the meaning of new words but also to the surrounding co-text (see *Glossary* on p. 223).

5.6 Four circle introductions

Outline Beginners make basic sentences about themselves using four sentence starters.
Level Beginner (A1)
Time Variable, depending on class size
Preparation Prepare a worksheet for each learner containing four sentence starters in circles, as shown in Figure 5.8 below.

Procedure

1 Distribute the handout – see *Preparation*. Make sure students know the meaning of the verbs in each of the four circles.

2 Introduce yourself using the four sentence starters to provide a model for students:
I am a teacher.
I live in Barcelona.
I have a cat.
I like pop music.

3 Now it's the learners' turn. If they can write, ask them to write one sentence next to each circle. If they can't write, they should say their sentences to a partner.

4 Call on each learner and ask them to read out or say their sentences.

5 Now encourage learners to think of two more sentences for each circle, for example:
I am tall / 38 years old.
I live in a flat / with my parents.
I have a car / two sisters.
I like sushi / going skiing.

Encourage learners to incorporate as many words as they know. Monitor and help by feeding in any vocabulary they may lack.

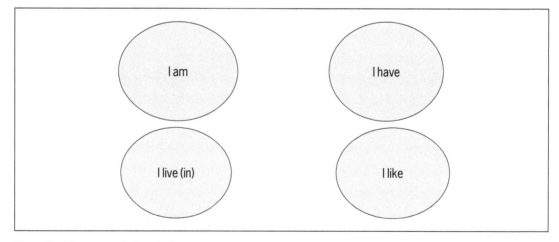

Figure 5.8: Sentence starter circles

Note
In some languages (for example Spanish or French), age is expressed with *I have*, often resulting in the error *I have nine years old* instead of *I'm nine years old*.

Variations
1   For adult beginners, you can add a fifth circle with *I work as a*, although this can also be expressed with *I am a*. You can also add *I don't like* presented as a chunk, even if the rules of the present simple have not been 'covered' yet.

2   The activity can be adapted for higher-level learners. You can put the following kinds of chunks in the circles:
    I wouldn't mind
    It normally takes me
    What I don't like about _____ is
    If there's one thing I've learned

Follow-up
The activity can be repeated using the same worksheet a few lessons later. Ask students to make as many sentences as they can. This shows them how much they have learned in a short span of time and gives a confidence boost.

Rationale
Beginners' grammatical competence is not yet at the level where they can build their own utterances by combining words with grammar. Learning useful chunks such as these allows beginner learners to communicate using appropriate grammar and creates templates which can be used later on.
See pages 5 and 6 (*Is there evidence that L2 learners go through the same process?*).

5.7 Verbs that go both ways

Outline Learners swap round parts of collocations to learn about the behaviour of certain verbs.
Level Intermediate and up (B1+)
Time 25 minutes
Preparation Prepare a handout containing the five pairs of sentences in Step 1 below. Alternatively, you can display the sentences on the board. Prepare sets of cards containing the items in Figure 5.9 – one set for every third learner, or 10 sets for a class of 30.

Procedure

1 Provide the following sentences, either in a handout or on the board. Ask learners to add missing words to the second sentence in each pair, clarifying that the meaning of each pair of sentences should remain the same. Explain that learners can use the same words as in the first sentence but they should NOT use the passive voice when rewriting; however, this instruction can be omitted if you want to play a trick on your students.

   a *The manager himself opens the shop every day at 9 am.*
      The shop _____ every day at 9 am.
   b *I looked at her; there was sadness in her eyes.*
      Her eyes _____.
   c *They have changed their approach.*
      Their approach _____.
   d *I could hear stress in her voice.*
      She _____ stressed on the phone.
   e *They've closed down the tourist attraction.*
      The tourist attraction has _____.

2 Go over the answers. Point out that except for d the same verbs can be used in the rewritten sentences:

   a *The shop **opens** every day at 9 am.*
   b *Her eyes **looked** sad.*
   c *Their approach **has changed**.*
   d *She **sounded** stressed on the phone.*
   e *The tourist attraction has **closed down**.*

3 Explain that the verbs in a–c and e can be both transitive and intransitive, and that the direct object of the transitive form (original sentences) can become the subject of the intransitive form (rewritten sentences). If your students are not familiar with the terms transitive/intransitive, you can refer to them as verbs that can go 'both ways'.

 Tip

You can also show learners how transitivity is indicated in learners' dictionaries (usually using I/T). The Cambridge Learner's Dictionary also uses the word 'cause' in brackets to show 1) that a verb can communicate a change of state or position and 2) that somebody causes this change in state or position: *Defrost = to (cause to) become free of ice or no longer frozen*

---

4 Distribute a set of cards to each group of three learners – see *Preparation*. Ask groups to match verbs and nouns (in a similar way to Activity 2.5: *Chunk match*). Make sure that learners lay the cards next to each other when matching (and not, for example, one on top of another). Verbs should be on the left and nouns on the right, as in Figure 5.9 – this is important for the next stage.

5 After all the cards are matched, learners should swap round each pair of cards so that verb + noun collocations become noun + verb collocations.

6 Ask learners to make two sentences for each pair of words, one with a verb + noun collocation and one with a noun + verb collocation. Do all the verbs work both ways? Learners may have to change the form of the verbs to make natural sentences, for example:
She grows plants in her garden.
Look! The plants are growing really quickly

The captain sailed the boat to the other side of the island.
That boat sailed long ago.

7 Clarify that all the verbs apart from one are ergative, i.e. they go both ways. The exception is *raise* which is only transitive; its intransitive counterpart is *rise:*
They've raised the gas prices.
The gas price has risen.

Explain that *shake* goes both ways, but the meaning is not always the same:
We shook hands.
His hands were shaking (because he was nervous).

Also, *download* is listed in most dictionaries as transitive but intransitive use is becoming increasingly common:
The file is still downloading.
Wait for the video file to download before playing it.

💡 **Classroom management tip**

To keep early finishers busy, ask them to sort the collocations into meaningful categories. There are four distinct groups: cooking (*defrost, melt, boil*), verbs related to vehicles/transport (*fly, sail, crash*), changes of state (*spill, break, grow*) and 'other/miscellaneous' (all the exceptions – *raise, download, shake*). Learners might, of course, come up with their own categories, for example: accidents (*spill, break, crash*).

Variation
If students are familiar with transitive/intransitive verbs, skip Steps 1–3. Steps 1–3 can also be done on the board to provide examples before Step 6 (swapping verbs and nouns).

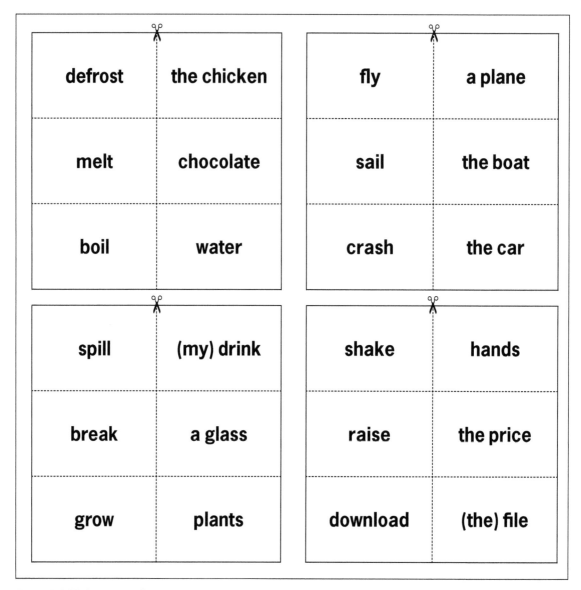

Figure 5.9: Verb + noun collocation cards

Rationale

Learners might not be aware that some verbs are transitive and may opt for the passive voice when it is uncalled for. For example, they may use *It has been changed* when *It has changed* would be perfectly alright. Not being aware of transitivity can also lead to other errors such as saying *the cost of living was increased* when it would be more appropriate to say *the cost of living has increased*. This is usually a result of overgeneralization – applying the rules of grammar to cases where they do not apply – and incomplete word knowledge, when learners have only partially mastered the verbs involved.

5.8 Get the last word in

Outline	Learners think of noun phrases to follow verb + adjective combinations, check their predictions with a corpus tool, then write sentences.
Level	Intermediate and above (B1+); particularly suitable for EAP/ESP students
Time	20 minutes
Preparation	Ensure learners have access to a device with internet connection (one per small group).

Procedure

1 Write around six verb + adjective combinations on the board – see some examples for different levels in Figure 5.10 below.

2 Ask learners to think of a noun phrase that can follow each of the combinations.

3 Learners can check their predictions on netspeak.org – see Activity 4.1: *Are you primed for this?*. (Alternatively, check the results with the whole class yourself, using a computer and projector.) See possible answers in Figure 5.11.

4 Learners then write two sentences for each of the complete verb + adjective + noun phrase combinations – see Activity 9.7: *Two sentence contextualization*.

B1/B2	B2 +
a find a suitable …	a avoid direct …
b cause serious …	b maintain high …
c launch a new …	c promote economic …
d play a crucial …	d protect human …
e release a new …	e cause severe …
f receive appropriate …	f pose a significant …
Business English	**EAP / Exam preparation**
a achieve maximum …	a adopt new …
b avoid potential …	b offer financial …
c hold a special …	c place great …
d identify potential …	d provide a brief …
e perform specific …	e pursue further …
f require further …	f produce the desired …

Figure 5.10: Verb + adjective combinations

B1/B2	B2 +
a find a suitable candidate/job/place	a avoid direct contact/confrontation
b cause serious damage/problems/pain/harm	b maintain high standards/levels
c launch a new product / line of products / service	c promote economic growth/development
d play a crucial role/part	d protect human health/rights
e release a new version/album	e cause severe damage/problems/pain /injury
f receive appropriate training/treatment/care	f pose a significant threat/risk
Business English	**EAP / Exam preparation**
a achieve maximum effectiveness/results	a adopt new ways/technologies/strategies
b avoid potential problems / conflicts of interest	b offer financial assistance/support/aid/ incentives
c hold a special session/meeting	c place great emphasis/importance on
d identify potential problems / market sources	d provide a brief overview/review/summary/ description
e perform specific tasks/functions/duties/ actions	e pursue further education/studies/research
f require further information/assistance	f produce the desired results/effects

Figure 5.11: Verb + adjective + noun phrase combinations

Variation

If you don't have internet access in class, you can give students cards with possible noun phrases – see examples for B2+ in Figure 5.12. Students should find two matching noun phrases for each verb + adjective combination.

contact	**confrontation**
standards	**levels**
growth	**development**
health	**rights**
damage	**injury**
threat	**risks**

Figure 5.12: Noun phrase cards

Follow-up

In a subsequent lesson, dictate the verb + adjective combinations you focused on previously. Pause after each one and allow learners to write the first noun / noun phrase that comes to mind:

cause severe ... [pause]   *require further ...* [pause]

Give learners a minute to compare answers in pairs before conducting whole-class feedback. To add interest, you could divide the class into teams: the first team to write an appropriate noun / noun phrase on the board wins a point.

Rationale

The more frequently we hear or see recurring sequences of language, the more entrenched they become in memory and therefore the more readily activated they are in future. Native speakers have a processing advantage: they can access these recurring sequences quickly both when processing input and producing speech in real time. Proficient L2 users can also process recurring sequences in a way similar to native speakers, but less proficient speakers handle them on a word-by-word basis. Exposing learners to common strings of words strengthens their 'primings' and arguably allows them to access such strings faster.

5.9 Confusable pairs

Outline Learners research a pair of near-synonyms and make mini presentations in class, highlighting differences in use.

Level Upper intermediate and above (B2+)

Time Variable

Preparation Make a list of word pairs which learners often find confusing. These can be near-synonyms (e.g. *legal/lawful*) or two English words that have only one equivalent in the students' L1. See suggestions for different levels in Figure 5.13 below.

Procedure

1 Allocate a word pair from your list – see *Preparation* – to each learner. Explain that for homework learners are going to investigate the difference between their two allocated words. They can use a learner's dictionary or online resources (see *Useful resources* on p. 227). They are then going to present their findings in the next lesson.

2 Explain that learners should try to focus on the difference in **use** between the word pairs (collocations and grammatical patterns) rather than just the difference in **meaning** (very often there isn't any). To do this, learners can copy out example sentences from a dictionary or cut and paste example sentences from an internet or corpus search. It's also important that students stick to the assigned parts of speech, for example if the assigned word pair is *job/work*, learners should research *work* as a noun, not a verb.

3 Do one or two example presentations for the class. Try to include a few fully grammaticalized sentences such as *I stayed at home and did nothing / We're moving house* in the example below:

Home	*House*
… is at home	*buy/sell/live in a house*
go/get home	*have a big house*
make yourself at home	*have a party at my/John's house*
I stayed at home and did nothing.	*We're moving house.*

4 You could also use a Venn diagram to demonstrate some differences. These are especially useful for words which are near-synonyms with partially overlapping uses:

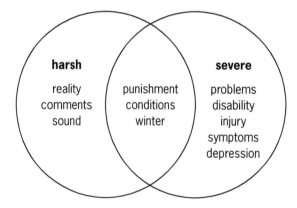

5   In the next lesson, learners present their findings in class. (If possible, try to look at learners' notes before they do their presentations, to help them hone their ideas.)

6   Give each learner a time limit of around five minutes for their presentation.

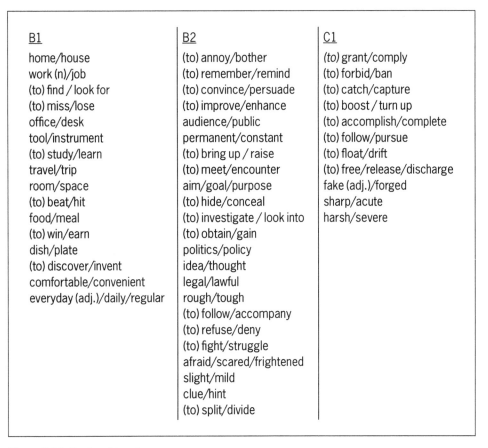

B1	B2	C1
home/house	(to) annoy/bother	*(to)* grant/comply
work (n)/job	(to) remember/remind	(to) forbid/ban
(to) find / look for	(to) convince/persuade	(to) catch/capture
(to) miss/lose	(to) improve/enhance	(to) boost / turn up
office/desk	audience/public	(to) accomplish/complete
tool/instrument	permanent/constant	(to) follow/pursue
(to) study/learn	(to) bring up / raise	(to) float/drift
travel/trip	(to) meet/encounter	(to) free/release/discharge
room/space	aim/goal/purpose	fake (adj.)/forged
(to) beat/hit	(to) hide/conceal	sharp/acute
food/meal	(to) investigate / look into	harsh/severe
(to) win/earn	(to) obtain/gain	
dish/plate	politics/policy	
(to) discover/invent	idea/thought	
comfortable/convenient	legal/lawful	
everyday (adj.)/daily/regular	rough/tough	
	(to) follow/accompany	
	(to) refuse/deny	
	(to) fight/struggle	
	afraid/scared/frightened	
	slight/mild	
	clue/hint	
	(to) split/divide	

Figure 5.13: Confusable pairs

Variation

For lower levels, you can present weekly 'word spots' yourself rather than assigning them to learners.

At higher levels, learners can also be asked to look at the cultural/ideological associations of particular words by making a spidergram of their common collocations. Example word pairs which would benefit from this type of analysis include: *immigrant/refugee, faith/religion, sex/gender, (to) accuse/blame, death/passing.*

Note

Research shows that more than 50% of lexical errors are caused by transfer from L1, therefore the choice of items for the activity will ultimately depend on the learners' L1 and your experience. There are some pairs that learners find confusing regardless of their L1. For example, *study/learn, win/earn, work/job* are known to pose problems for learners of most L1 backgrounds. Other pairs should be determined by the learners' L1.

Usually cases when there is a semantic split (see *Glossary* on p. 223) in English – i.e. where two English words correspond to one L1 equivalent – are good candidates for inclusion. For example, Greek has only one word for *office/desk* and *bother/annoy.* These pairs of English words are, therefore, likely to cause confusion for Greek learners. Similarly, Turkish speakers might confuse *idea/opinion* and *food/meal*, while Russian learners might have problems distinguishing between *comfortable/convenient, suggest/offer* and *decide/solve.*

Although it's generally advisable to stick to one part of speech when comparing word pairs, sometimes looking at different parts of speech can yield interesting results. For example, *travel* is rarely used as a noun on its own; it's usually part of compound nouns or collocations such *business travel* or *travel agency / travel industry. Travel* is often used as a verb (*I want to travel around Europe this summer*) while *trip* is a noun (*go on a trip / day trip / business trip*).

Rationale

Knowing the difference between near-synonyms is often a matter of knowing how each one is used and what it goes with. That's why it is important to move learners away from trying to understand pure denotational meaning and encourage them to explore collocational fields and typical examples of usage of each of the near-synonyms. Definitions from dictionaries aimed at native speakers should be avoided by lower-level learners because they tend to define words using (near-)synonyms and are therefore of limited value.

5.10 Focused grammar tasks

Outline	Learners write sentences with supplied vocabulary items aimed at eliciting target grammatical structures.
Level	Elementary and above (A2+)
Time	Variable
Preparation	None

Procedure

1 Dictate a series of words that are likely to generate a grammar structure you wish to focus on – see some suggestions in Figure 5.14 below.

2 Ask learners to make sentences that incorporate as many of the dictated items as possible. However, do not stipulate which grammatical structures learners should use.

3 Monitor learners as they work, then 'collect' and write on the board any sentences that incorporate the target structure (or that could be re-phrased to incorporate it).

4 Use the sentences on the board to highlight the form and meaning of the target structure. Then elicit further examples using more of the dictated words.

---

comparatives
café/restaurant, pen/pencil, helicopter/plane, city/countryside

***going to* for future plans**
vacation/holiday, ticket, beach, book a hotel, relax, go sightseeing

used to
smoke, cough, quit, anymore, overweight, exercise, car, bike, better

have/get something done
apartment, redecorated, kitchen, painted, carpet, fitted, bathroom, re-tiled

---

Figure 5.14: Grammar structures with suggested prompt words

Rationale

The choice of topic is often a sufficient condition for a target grammatical structure to emerge, for example childhood memories → past forms. But not all grammatical structures can be elicited through a topic alone. This activity shows that carefully chosen vocabulary items can induce the desired grammar output.

The term 'focused task' (see activity title) is borrowed from Ellis (2003), who distinguishes such tasks from situational grammar exercises where learners are informed of the specific grammatical focus in advance. In focused tasks, learners' attention is directed towards the content of the message with only incidental focus on grammar. Here, learners are concerned with using chosen vocabulary items, with a grammar focus only arising out of the writing task.

6   From grammar to words

Throughout this book it has been suggested that grammar and vocabulary go hand in hand and for this reason there should be little difference between a 'grammar' lesson and 'vocabulary' lesson. However, this chapter does have a more grammatical focus. This is because many teachers using the book will be constrained by a syllabus, coursebook or curriculum which specifies certain grammar structures that need to be mastered by a certain level.

This chapter demonstrates that many grammar goals can be reached lexically, either by focusing on vocabulary that is likely to occur with certain grammar patterns or by approaching grammatical structures indirectly, through vocabulary. The chapter contains some generic activities (such as 6.1: *Going over answers: eliciting context* or 6.2: *Going over answers: exploring alternatives*) which can be used for any grammatical structure, as well as some which cover specific grammar points, for example 6.10: *From spoken to written* which focuses on auxiliary verbs. What all the activities in this chapter still have in common is the underlying belief that grammar should be practised in conjunction with vocabulary.

6.1 Going over answers: eliciting context

Outline	Learners add extra sentences to a completed grammar exercise to create more context.
Level	Intermediate and above (B1+)
Time	10 minutes (not including the grammar exercise the activity is based on)
Preparation	None

Procedure

1 After learners have completed a grammar exercise (in class or for homework), give them the correct answers. Then ask them to imagine what another person could say in response to the given sentences or, on the contrary, what questions or comments may have prompted the given sentences. (Alternatively, this could be done while you go over the answers with the class.) See an example in Figure 6.1 below.

2 Conduct whole-class feedback. Write up the most appropriate 'before' or 'after' sentences on the board and discuss them.

3 Ask pairs of learners to do mini role plays / improvisations, where Learner A says the sentence from the exercise, Learner B gives a response and then they continue the dialogue for as long as they can.

Put in *will ('ll)* or *won't*.

1 Can you wait for me? I ___*won't*___ be long.
2 Don't ask Amanda for advice. She _____ know what to do.
3 I'm glad you're coming to see us next week. It _____ be good to see you again.
4 I'm sorry about what happened yesterday. It _____ happen again.
5 You don't need to take an umbrella with you. I don't think it _____ rain.
6 I've got some incredible news! You _____ believe it.

What someone might say in response:

1 Yes, but please hurry up. I'm running late.
2 Why? Last time she was really helpful.
3 Yes, it will be good to meet up again. I'm really looking forward to it.
4 That's what you said last time.
5 Are you sure? I'd rather be safe than sorry.
6 You passed? Really?!

Figure 6.1: Exercise from *English Grammar in Use (Fourth edition)* with suggested responses

Variations

1 You can give specific instructions to learners, for example to use a certain vocabulary item, e.g. *take* (1 *How long will it take you?* 2 *I'll take it anyway.* 3 *I'll get a takeaway.*), or a certain grammatical structure, e.g. past tense (see responses 4 and 6 above).

2 You could ask half the class to write some 'before' sentences and the other half to write some 'after' ones. Then pair up learners to see if their sentences work as mini dialogues.

Rationale

Grammatical competence does not only involve the ability to produce correct discrete sentences, but also the ability to use appropriate grammar at the discourse level, i.e. within more extended conversations and texts. Adding extra turns ('before' or 'after' sentences) shows learners how in conversation both participants contribute to the creation of meaning. Adding more context to grammar exercises also makes them richly situated and therefore more meaningful.

6.2 Going over answers: exploring alternatives

Outline	Learners replace parts of sentences in a grammar exercise.
Level	Elementary and above (A2+)
Time	5 minutes (not including the grammar exercise the activity is based on)
Preparation	None

Procedure

1   After or while checking answers to a grammar exercise, ask learners to replace target words with their own ideas, for example:

I was in a hurry so I <u>didn't have</u> time to call. → *I was in a hurry so I <u>couldn't find</u> time to call.*
It was raining so I took my <u>umbrella</u>. → *It was raining so I took my <u>raincoat</u>.*

2   When learners have finished replacing target words, ask them to replace larger parts of the sentence such as whole clauses, for example:

I was in a hurry so I didn't have time to call. → *I was in a hurry so I left early.*
It was raining so I took my umbrella. → *It was raining so I stayed at home.*

(If necessary, you can prompt learners by asking questions like *What other things can you do when you are in a hurry / it's raining?*)

3   Ask learners to compare their new sentences in groups.

Complete the sentences. Put the verb into the correct form, positive or negative.

1   It was warm, so I ____took____ off my coat.   (take)
2   The film wasn't very good. I ___didn't enjoy___ it much.   (enjoy)
3   I knew Sarah was busy, so I _____ her.   (disturb)
4   We were very tired, so we _____ the party early.   (leave)
5   The bed was very uncomfortable. I _____ well.   (sleep)

Examples of new versions of sentences:

1   It was warm, so I opened the window.
2   The film wasn't very good. I walked out in the middle.
3   I knew Sarah was very busy, so I sent her a text instead of calling her.
4   We were very tired, so we didn't go out.
5   The bed was very uncomfortable. I had a rough night.

Figure 6.2: Exercise from *English Grammar in Use (Fourth edition)* with alternative versions

---

Rationale

The simple techniques outlined in the procedure show how even the most basic grammar exercise can easily be turned into a vehicle for vocabulary work in the classroom.

6.3 Putting irregular verbs to work

Outline An irregular verbs table (which often appears at the end of a coursebook and is mainly used for reference) is turned into an activity.

Level Intermediate and above (B1+)

Time 10 minutes

Preparation Learners will need an irregular verbs table containing three verb forms: infinitive, past simple and past participle. These can usually be found at the end of coursebooks or can be provided in a handout – see Step 1 below. For this activity, the chart should not have more than 70–80 verbs (B1 level).

Procedure

1 Provide the following gapped sentences and make sure learners can see an irregular verbs table – see *Preparation*.
   a *Have you ever _____ it?*
   b *I've never _____ so much.*
   c *I've _____ my keys.*
   d *They've _____ a lot of money.*
   e *It is _____ all over the world.*

2 Tell learners to find past participles which are likely to go into the patterns. They should suggest at least <u>three</u> verbs for each pattern but are not allowed to use any verb more than once.

3 Conduct whole-class feedback by pooling learners' ideas on the board. Possible answers:
   a *seen/heard/eaten*
   b *slept/eaten/run/bought*
   c *lost/found/forgotten*
   d *spent/stolen/found*
   e *spoken/known/grown/sold*

4 In a subsequent lesson, do the same activity with the following patterns. This time <u>two</u> verbs for each pattern will do because the sentences are more context-bound and have fewer possibilities.
   a *The criminal was _____.*
   b *The victim was _____ in the chest.*
   c *The book was _____.*
   d *I've never _____ him.*
   e *Have you _____ to her?*

5 Ask learners to share ideas in small groups. Have group members chosen any of the same verbs? Point out that certain past participles are more likely to go with perfect structures (e.g. *fallen, slept*) than with passive ones. Possible answers:
   a *shot/caught / found (guilty)*
   b *hit/shot*
   c *written/torn/chosen*
   d *met/hurt/seen*
   e *spoken/written*

Classroom management tip

Steps 1 and 4 can be done in the same lesson without breaking the list into two. Give stronger pupils all ten patterns and ask them to find two verbs for each one. Give less able pupils only the first five patterns but ask them to find at least three verbs for each. This way they can focus on fewer patterns for longer and, learn them in more depth.

Variation

This activity is aimed at students who do not know all the irregular forms yet. However, it can also be used with higher-level students who have mastered them. In this case, ask learners to complete the sentences without looking at an irregular verbs table.

Follow-up

Learners are surrounded by past participles, although they may not be aware of it. Ask students to work out where they might see or hear these chunks:

Made in China	(on a product, e.g. item of clothing)
Lost and Found	(at the airport)
Going once, going twice, sold!	(at an auction)
Fallen but not forgotten	(on a war memorial)
English spoken here	(on a shop door)

This doesn't have to be limited to irregular verbs. Some examples with regular verbs are:

Just married	(on the newlyweds' car)
Box office closed	(at a cinema)
Performance cancelled	(at a theatre)
Wanted!	(on a police poster)

To confirm answers, you can use images which illustrate the chunks.

Note

The past participle is sometimes referred to as V3 but a better term for it could be the *-en* form, because almost half of all irregular verbs, e.g. *taken*, *written*, etc., end with *-en*. A further 40% of irregular verbs have matching past and past participle forms, e.g. *teach – taught – taught*, *hit – hit – hit*. Of course, some verbs don't fit into these categories, e.g. *begin – began – begun*, *run – ran – run*, *sink – sank – sunk*.

Rationale

Generally, irregular verbs are something students are expected to memorize without much support or guidance. Activities such as this show learners how certain verbs have certain grammatical preferences, for example that *fallen* or *slept* are more likely to occur in perfect structures than passive ones.

6.4 Life story

Outline Learners describe imaginary life stories using chunks containing dependent prepositions.
Level Intermediate and above (B1+)
Time 20 minutes
Preparation Display on the board or prepare a handout with the following template:

(S)he was born	in _____	
	on _____	
	at _____	
At school, (s)he was	pretty good	at _____
	hopeless	with _____
(S)he	graduated	from _____
	got a degree	in _____
(S)he works	in _____	
	for _____	
(S)he is currently working	on _____	
	with _____	

Procedure

1 Distribute or display your template – see *Preparation*. Look at the first gap and ask for an example sentence, e.g. *She was born in Ireland / She was born in 1979.* Clarify that we can put a place or a year in the first gap.

2 Elicit what kinds of words can go in the other gaps. Complete the gaps in the template as follows:

(S)he was born	in [PLACE/YEAR]	
	on [DATE]	
	at [TIME]	
At school, (s)he was	pretty good	at [SUBJECT]
	hopeless	with [PEOPLE/COMPUTERS]
(S)he	graduated	from [UNIVERSITY]
	got a degree	in [SUBJECT]
(S)he works	in [PLACE/FIELD]	
	for [EMPLOYER]	
(S)he is currently working	on [PROJECT]	
	with [PEOPLE]	

3 In pairs, ask learners to describe the lives of imaginary people using the structures in the template. They should do this orally (written versions can be done for homework – see *Follow-up*). Encourage students to be creative and to use as many patterns as possible. If necessary, do an example life story with the whole class:

> *Peter was born in a small village in the north of England, in 1979. At school, he was hopeless at maths and science, but he was really good at foreign languages. He got a degree in TESOL in 2003. Now he works for International House in Barcelona. He is currently working with a group of children aged 9–10.*

Follow-up

For homework, adult learners can use the same patterns to write about themselves. Teen learners can write about their parents or someone they know.

Note

This activity works best as a review, i.e. if students have already been exposed to the above patterns. Some of the patterns can be taught or practised using Activities 1.3 and 1.4.

Rationale

Prepositions often prove difficult for learners. This is often attributed to their polysemous and arbitrary nature, i.e. they have multiple meanings and, much of the time, the correct preposition cannot be guessed. However, the difficulty may partly stem from the fact that teachers don't always give prepositions as much attention as other more 'concrete' parts of speech: nouns, verbs and adjectives. Teachers also sometimes delay dealing with prepositions until relatively higher levels. One of the ways of dealing with these problems is to teach prepositions as part of the expressions they go with – in other words, as chunks (for example *AT home/school/work, ON Monday/Tuesday*).

6.5 Sentences on strips of paper

Outline	Learners are given prompts containing the same grammatical pattern. They think of a sentence that precedes each prompt and write it on a strip of paper.
Level	Intermediate and above (B1/2+)
Time	10 minutes
Preparation	Prepare some cut-up strips of paper – four strips per small group of learners. Each group will also need a pair of scissors.

Procedure

1   Ask learners to imagine someone is turning the key in a car ignition but the engine is not starting. Show an image, if possible. Elicit the most likely thing the person would say in the situation:

The car doesn't start. (no)
The car is not starting. (possible, but less common)
The car won't start. (most common)

2   Clarify the use of *won't* in the above sentence: *won't = refuse to; doesn't want to.* Stress that it does not refer to the future.

3   Provide the following sentence endings on the board:

… but (s)he won't let me.
… but (s)he won't listen to me.
… but (s)he won't tell me (what it is).
… but (s)he won't answer the phone / any emails.

4   In small groups, ask learners to think of sentence beginnings to go with the endings above. Remind the class that the sentences do not refer to future time. Groups should write a beginning and an ending on each of their four strips of paper – see *Preparation*. Here are some examples:

I asked him if I can borrow his car	but he won't let me.
I've tried talking her out of it	but she won't listen to me.
I can see that something's bothering her	but she won't tell me what it is.
I've tried calling him and sending texts	but he won't answer the phone.

5   Monitor and feed in useful language, as required.

6   When groups finish, ask them to cut or tear their strips in half (just before *but* – see the example above). Each group shuffles their cut-up strips and passes them on to another group. Groups match the shuffled halves they have received.

7   Conduct whole-class feedback and put any particularly interesting sentences on the board.

8   In a subsequent lesson write some of the learners' sentence beginnings on the board. Elicit the endings containing *won't*.

Note
For higher levels you might want to add some more idiomatic endings like these:
… but he won't budge.
… but she wouldn't hear of it.

Variation
This activity can be adapted for use with many other patterns. You can also use whole sentences rather than just beginnings and endings. Here are some examples (with prompts on the right and suggested answers on the left):

Modal verb *can* + verbs of senses

[There's a light flickering there in the distance.]	*Can you see it?*
[There's some strange noise coming from my car.]	*Can you hear it?*
[I'm baking a cake.]	*Can you smell it?*
[There's something magical in the air tonight.]	*Can you feel it?*

once + present perfect for future

[I'll lend you the book]	*… once I've finished with it.*
[I'll send you my address]	*… once I've found a place (to live).*
[You'll be bound by the terms of the contract]	*… once you've signed it.*

Rationale
Although most grammarians today agree that English has two tenses, past and non-past/present, many pedagogical grammars and coursebooks still treat *will* as the future simple tense, which always surprises me. This unfortunate misconception often leads learners to believe that *will* is a neutral default future form in English, devoid of any lexical meaning. This assumption is not true and this activity highlights one of the other meanings of *will*. This meaning is close to its original sense (to wish, to desire something) before it evolved into a modal verb with future reference. The original sense survives today mainly as part of relatively fixed chunks such as *as you will* (e.g. *You may do as you will*), and as the present participle turned adjective *willing*.

6.6 Disappearing chunks

Outline	Students use chunks to respond to prompts, first from a list on the board then from memory.
Level	Intermediate and above (B1+)
Time	6–7 minutes
Preparation	Prepare a list of around ten chunks with a similar pattern. For this activity, chunks with a clear transactional purpose would work best. See examples in Figures 6.3 and 6.4.

Procedure

1 Write up your selected target chunks on the board – see *Preparation* and Figure 6.3.

2 Give learners prompts for each chunk in random order. Learners respond by saying the correct chunk together. Once a chunk has been correctly called out, erase it from the board. Continue until all the chunks have been erased.

3 Repeat without a list of chunks on the board. Can learners recall all the chunks?

Chunks with *'ll*	Prompts
	What do you say when …
I'll get it.	… the phone's ringing.
I'll do my best.	… you promise to help.
I'll give you a call.	… you promise to phone.
I'll see what I can do.	… you want to help but don't want to promise anything.
It'll come to me.	… you don't remember something.
Don't worry I'll make time.	… somebody says that you're always busy.
I'll make a start on the dishes.	… a party is finished and you want to start cleaning up.
That'll do.	… you don't want anymore.

Figure 6.3: Chunks with *'ll* and prompts

Chunks with *could*	Prompts
	What do you say when …
I couldn't afford it.	… you wanted to buy something but it cost too much.
I couldn't possibly.	… someone's giving you an expensive gift.
I couldn't hear myself think.	… it was very noisy.
You could hear a pin drop.	… it was very quiet.
I couldn't agree more.	… you have the same opinion.
I couldn't be bothered.	… you didn't feel like doing something.
I could eat a horse.	… you are very hungry.
I couldn't ask for more.	… you are very happy.

Figure 6.4: Chunks with *could* and prompts

Rationale

Although the examples show chunks with modal verbs (such as *will* or *could*), this activity can also be used for practising other grammatical structures. Just draw up a list of prototypical examples containing the grammar point you want to target.

6.7 Slices of meaning

Outline	Learners focus on some uncountable nouns, such as *advice* and *furniture*, and ways of quantifying them (e.g. *a piece of advice/furniture*).
Level	Intermediate and above (B1+)
Time	15 minutes
Preparation:	Bring the following realia (or images) to class: a fork, a necklace (or another piece of jewellery), a small suitcase, a shirt (or another item of clothing).
	Create handouts – one for each learner – containing the gapfill activity in Figure 6.5.

Procedure

1 Place the realia items (or images) on a table so that all learners can see them. For each item, elicit two names: a specific word for the item and a corresponding mass/group noun. Board the items as follows:

necklace   jewellery
suitcase   luggage
fork   cutlery/silverware
shirt   clothing/clothes

2 Point out that the mass/group nouns on the right are uncountable, i.e. you cannot say *two luggages*, but you can say *a piece of* to quantify them:
a piece of jewellery/luggage/cutlery/clothing (note that *a piece of clothes* is not used).

3 Explain that although *a piece of* is the most common way of quantifying uncountable nouns, it is not the only one. Other, more specific words can be used to describe an amount or an example of something that is uncountable: *a slice of bread, a spoonful of sugar, a cup of coffee, a bar of chocolate, an item of jewellery.*

4 Now students are going to look at some uncountable nouns which often cause problems for learners. Write up these words on the board:

luggage   *furniture*   *accommodation*   *art*

       advice   *equipment*   *research*

5 Provide the handout you prepared beforehand – see *Preparation* and Figure 6.5. Ask learners to complete the sentences. In each case, one gap should be filled with an uncountable noun from the board. The other gap should be completed with a more specific, countable word OR a phrase with *piece*.

6 Take feedback and go over the answers. Sometimes more than one answer is possible – see suggested answers in Figure 6.5.

a i Can I ask you for some _____?

   ii Let me give you a _____: avoid leaving household equipment in stand-by mode.

b After the company took delivery of new _____, one _____ turned out to be faulty and had to be replaced.

c A: Have you done any _____ on this?

   B: No, I haven't, but there was an interesting _____ conducted in Sweden last year that might be relevant.

d A: [At airport check-in] Will you be checking in any _____ today?

   B: How many _____ are we allowed to carry with us on the plane?

e I have a friend, who's been living in the town for some time, who is helping me find _____. Once I've found a(n) _____ I'll send you my address.

f There was a lot of interesting _____ at the exhibition but I particularly liked two _____ on the second floor.

g i We had to buy a bed, a table, chairs and sofa. There was very little _____ when we moved in.

   ii They were so poor when they moved, they didn't have a single _____.

Answers

a i advice
   ii tip / piece of advice (point out that *a word of advice* is usually used when you warn someone)

b equipment
   piece of equipment / machine

c research
   piece of research / study

d luggage
   cases/bags/pieces /items

e accommodation
   place to stay / flat / apartment

f art
   pieces/works

g i furniture
   ii stick of furniture (*piece* would also work, but *stick* is more idiomatic)

Figure 6.5: Gapfill activity for countable and uncountable nouns

Follow-up

In a subsequent lesson, you can give learners sentences with uncountable nouns. Ask them to rewrite the sentences using more specific countable nouns:

Much research has shown that … → Many studies have shown that …
There's a lack of accommodation in the city centre. → There aren't any places to stay in the city centre.

Note

Many online learners' dictionaries provide information about 'measure' words (*item, article*, etc.) which can be used with uncountable nouns. For example, in Longman Dictionary (see *Useful resources* on p. 227), the entries for *jewellery, luggage, clothing* and *chocolate* supply corresponding quantifying words. This information can be found in the Collocations box or Grammar: Countable/Uncountable box.

Rationale

Some uncountable English nouns have countable equivalents in other languages, e.g. *accommodation, advice, furniture, information*, which often leads to errors like *I bought some new furnitures*. This activity shows how this potential grammatical difficulty can be overcome by lexical means – through focus on vocabulary.

6.8 Frames and fillers

Outline Learners predict the most common words (fillers) that occur with certain grammatical patterns (frames), then check their intuitions using a corpus.

Level Intermediate and above (B1+)

Time 5 minutes

Preparation Make sure you have access to the internet and a projector during the session.

Although no preparation as such is necessary, during the session you need to look out for grammatical patterns with variable slots (see p. 14: *Chunks and patterns*) as they come up in class – see examples in Figure 6.7 below.

Procedure

1 When you spot a target pattern in class – see *Preparation* – write it on the board and underline the word which can vary, for example: *Have you ever <u>seen</u> …?*

2 Ask learners to think of other words that can fill the pattern or 'frame'. Learners write down their suggestions or 'fillers'.

3 Use a corpus tool such as COCA (see Activity 1.5) to look up the most frequent fillers, as shown in Figure 6.6. Use your projector so learners can see the results, too.

4 Write the six most frequent fillers on the board:

Have you ever	*been*
	seen
	heard
	had
	thought
	tried

5 Point out that learners' own suggestions may be possible. However, it is important to notice the most common fillers because many grammatical structures occur mostly with just a handful of words/fillers. The six verbs above, for example, account for almost 55% of all occurrences of *Have you ever* in COCA. So if your students remember these, they will be correct more than half the time!

6 Repeat the process when you spot another target frame in class. See examples of possible frames in Figure 6.7.

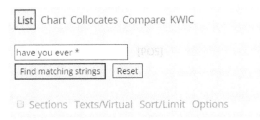

Figure 6.6: Screenshot from COCA

Possible target frames	String to enter into COCA
How long have you <u>lived</u>	how long have you * / how long have you [v?n*]
How long have you been <u>teaching</u>	how long have you been * / how long have you been [v?g*]
I find it <u>difficult</u>	I find it * / I find it [j*]
It doesn't <u>matter</u>	it does n't * / It does n't [v*]
What are you going to <u>wear</u>?	what are you going to * / what are you going to [v*]
you must be <u>joking</u>	you must be [v?g*]
it must have been <u>hard</u>	it must have been [j*] and also: it must 've been [j*]
Is there anything <u>you need</u>	is there anything [pp*] *
What are you <u>waiting for</u>?	what are you [v*] [i*]

Figure 6.7: Frames and strings for COCA search

Note

Many simple searches can be performed using a 'wildcard' query [*], for example:

*Don't you * → think/know/see/remember*

Other corpus tools can be used to find fillers, such as Netspeak or StringNav – see *Useful resources* on p. 227. Even an internet search engine is likely to yield some common patterns.

Follow-up

After you have researched a number of patterns in the way outlined above, write them up on the board. Divide the board into columns with a pattern in each column. Organize the class into teams and assign a pattern to each one. Each team sends a representative to the board to write six frequent fillers. The group to reach six fillers first is the winner – but you might want to check that the words they have written are indeed frequent by repeating Step 3! Extra points can be given to the team that writes the highest number of the most frequent fillers.

Rationale

Certain grammatical structures occur with certain words. The examples below account for 80% of all occurrences of the *How long have you* pattern, which is sometimes considered a troublesome grammatical structure for learners.

How long have you been
How long have you known
How long have you lived
How long have you had
How long have you worked

So if your learners learn these five chunks, they will use *How long have you* correctly very often! Presenting learners with a handful of useful, prototypical examples of a target grammatical structure and getting them to learn these as unanalysed wholes is a worthwhile strategy.

6.9 Lexical snakes

Outline Learners find boundaries between common chunks.

Level Intermediate and above (B1+)

Time 3 minutes

Preparation Collect about ten chunks recently studied in class. For this activity, target chunks should be full sentences, however short (e.g. *Have fun*). Type them up without any boundaries between them, nor spaces between words, and make copies for learners – one per pair. Here is an example containing chunks with *have*:

> ihavetogohaveasafejourneyhaveagood
> dayidon'thavetodoanythingyouhaveto
> doitagainhedoesn'thaveachanceihave
> beenherebeforeyoudon'thavetoworry
> aboutathingihavenoideayouhavebeen
> veryhelpful

Procedure

1 Give copies of the run-together chunks to pairs of learners. Ask pairs to identify the separate chunks and draw lines to indicate the boundaries, as shown below. (For lower levels, you may want to specify how many chunks there are beforehand.) Set a one-minute time limit.

   ihavetogo/haveasafejourney/

2 Do feedback with the whole group. Answers:

   a *I have to go*
   b *Have a safe journey*
   c *Have a good day*
   d *I don't have to do anything*
   e *You have to do it again*

   f *He doesn't have a chance*
   g *I have been here before*
   h *You don't have to worry about a thing*
   i *I have no idea*
   j *You have been very helpful*

3 Spend a couple of minutes analysing any common features of your selected chunks. In the example above, you could ask pairs to sort the chunks into three groups according to these patterns:
   have been
   have to
   have + noun phrase
   You can then discuss some different functions of *have* (as a main verb indicating possession, as a modal verb indicating obligation, as an auxiliary, etc.).

Rationale

Getting students to mark boundaries between chunks is one way of revisiting 'old' chunks. The more firmly the chunk is entrenched in memory, the quicker learners will identify it in a run-together sequence.

6.10 From spoken to written

Outline	In spoken language it is common to omit auxiliaries and subject pronouns at the beginning of a *yes/no* question; this is known as ellipsis. In this activity, learners put the missing words back into questions.
Level	Elementary and above (A2+)
Time	10 minutes
Preparation	None

Procedure

1 Write these questions on the board:

a	*You hungry?*	e	*Ready?*
b	*Want a drink?*	f	*Need a hand?*
c	*Tired?*	g	*Sleep well?*
d	*Fancy an ice-cream?*	h	*He coming?*

2 Tell learners that these are questions you hear in everyday conversations. Ask them to add the missing auxiliaries (and sometimes pronouns) to make the questions 'grammatically correct'. Do the first one together as an example:

You hungry? → *Are you hungry?*

3 After learners have finished, explain that both forms are acceptable but they should be aware of the difference in register (formal or informal): what is acceptable in everyday conversation may not be acceptable in formal writing. Answers:

a	***Are*** *you hungry?*	e	***Are you*** *ready?*
b	***Do you*** *want a drink?*	f	***Do you*** *need a hand?*
c	***Are you*** *tired?*	g	***Did you*** *sleep well?*
d	***Do you*** *fancy an ice-cream?*	h	***Is*** *he coming?*

Variation

For higher levels (B1 +), you can add the following questions. (The missing words are shown in square brackets at the beginning.)

[Have you] Been anywhere nice?
[Is there] Anything decent on? [talking about TV]
[Have you] Got any change? [referring to money]
[Shall we] Meet at the café later?

Note

This activity can be done any time, particularly at the beginning of the year when you want to assess your learners' level of grammar or to supplement any textbook activity focusing on auxiliary verbs.

Rationale

Coursebooks and grammar books tend to focus on auxiliary verbs within the structure they serve, e.g. *do/does* with the present simple and *did* with the past simple. Showing how their behaviour is similar across different grammar patterns is equally important.

7   Problematic structures

Teachers are often concerned about how to deal with some of the trickier structures in English such as the third person singular -*s*, articles *a/the* or the present perfect. These kinds of structures cannot always be explained easily and are often a source of fossilized errors. So can they be taught through lexical chunks? The answer is 'yes'.

This chapter is devoted to practising 'difficult' grammar through patterns. The activities in this chapter are underpinned by the principle that many problems learners have with grammar can be addressed by showing them a handful of prototypical expressions which contain the target grammatical structure. Most of the activities are ready to use, requiring little or no preparation or technology. However, teachers should keep an eye out for grammatical patterns that naturally emerge out of classroom interaction. They can then adapt these activities to work on the patterns they have picked out.

7.1 Does it?

Outline Learners practise asking common questions in the third person singular present simple.
Leve Intermediate and above (B1+)
Time 8–10 minutes
Preparation Prepare a handout with the questions and prompts in Step 1 below (or write them on the board).

Procedure

1   Provide the following questions on the board or in a handout:
   a   *Does it _____? (Is it logical/sensible?)*
   b   *Does it _____? (Is it important?)*
   c   *Does it _____? (Is it written there?)*
   d   *Does it _____? (Do I have to wait a long time?)*
   e   *Does it _____? (Do you feel pain?)*
   f   *Does it _____? (Are you upset/worried because of it?)*
   g   *Does it _____? (Is it expensive?)*
   h   *Does it _____? (Is this something he would say?)*

2   Ask learners to complete Questions a–h using the hints/prompts in brackets. Point out that all the missing words are verbs or verb phrases. Do the first one as an example with the whole class (*Does it make sense?*) to show that more than one word can go into each gap.

3   Tell learners to check answers in pairs then do whole-class feedback. Suggested answers:

a *Does it make sense?*	e *Does it hurt?*
b *Does it matter?*	f *Does it bother you?*
c *Does it say it/that?*	g *Does it cost much?*
d *Does it take long?*	h *Does it sound like him?*

Follow-up

Ask learners to think of contexts for the above questions. They can do one of the following:
EITHER: Write two-line dialogues where the second line is the target question e.g.:
   A: *Children under the age of six are not allowed. Look at the leaflet.*
   B: *Does it say that?*
OR: Learners A says a prompt and Learner B responds with the relevant target question. If the response is correct, learners swap roles. Suggested prompts:
   We will send you the documents once they're ready. (Does it take long?)
   He didn't say that he had a sister. (Does it matter?)
   I fell yesterday. See that bruise on my knee? (Does it hurt?)

Rationale

The third person singular in the present simple is known to be problematic for learners. This activity focuses on some of the most common questions with *Does it* and is underpinned by the assumption that many problematic grammatical structures can be approached lexically – by getting learners to practise, memorize and use common chunks containing the grammar in question.

7.2 It doesn't matter

Outline Learners match sentence halves to contrast *It + be* with *It +* other verbs.
Level Intermediate and above (B1+)
Time 8–10 minutes
Preparation Prepare a two-column handout containing the sentence halves in Figure 7.1 below. Print enough copies for each pair of learners and cut each handout down the middle.

Procedure

1 Divide learners into pairs. Give each pair a cut-up handout so that Learner A has the sentence beginnings and Learner B has the endings. They should not show each other their sheets.

2 Learner A chooses a beginning from their list – in random order – and says it to Learner B. Learner B responds with an appropriate ending.

3 Pair work continues until all the sentences have been matched. To check answers, Learners A and B put their sheets together.

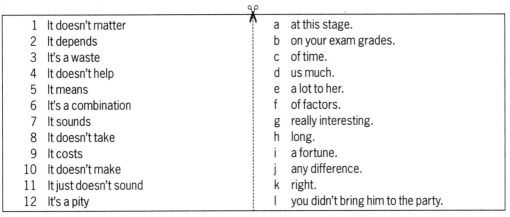

1	It doesn't matter	a	at this stage.
2	It depends	b	on your exam grades.
3	It's a waste	c	of time.
4	It doesn't help	d	us much.
5	It means	e	a lot to her.
6	It's a combination	f	of factors.
7	It sounds	g	really interesting.
8	It doesn't take	h	long.
9	It costs	i	a fortune.
10	It doesn't make	j	any difference.
11	It just doesn't sound	k	right.
12	It's a pity	l	you didn't bring him to the party.

Figure 7.1: Sentence halves

4 Ask pairs what they think *it* could refer to in each sentence, for example in Sentence 9 *it* could refer to a new electronic device – *It costs a fortune.* Encourage learners to justify their suggestions. Agree with the whole class on the best suggestions and make a note of them (you will need these later for the *Follow-up*).

5 Draw attention to Sentence 12. It is not possible to say what *it* refers to because, unlike other examples, it acts here as a 'dummy' subject which is expanded on later in the sentence. Give more examples with *it* in this dummy role:

It's a miracle that he survived.
It's still not known what causes the disease.

Lexical Grammar

6 Write the following patterns on the board and nominate three learners to complete the patterns with words from their handout. They can add a couple of their own examples at the end.

It doesn't ... ⎯⎯⎯ | It ... ⎯⎯⎯ | It's ... ⎯⎯⎯

Answers:

It doesn't ...	matter help take long make any difference sound right	It ...	depends on means sounds costs	It's ...	a waste of time a combination of factors a pity

Follow-up

Read out each suggestion that you collected in Step 4 (the things that *it* might refer to). Learners respond with the appropriate phrase from their handout – first looking at the handout, then without!

Rationale

The third person singular in the present simple is known to be problematic for learners. Even at higher levels, learners who know the rule often forget the *s*. One way of dealing with this fossilized error is to practise several prototypical examples containing this structure. The questions selected for this activity are some of the most common questions starting with *Does it*, according to COCA.

7.3 How long?

Outline	Learners respond to oral prompts to produce and practise *How long have you been* questions (present perfect continuous).
Level	Intermediate and above (B1+)
Time	5 minutes
Preparation	None

Preparation

1   Provide the following example on the board:

Speaker A: *I work as an English teacher at International House.*
Speaker B: *Oh really? How long have you been teaching?*

2   Elicit similar Speaker B responses using the following prompts:

Teacher: *I live in Barcelona*
Learners: *Oh really? How long have you been living here?*

T: *I'm a sales manager with Microsoft.*
L: *Oh really? How long have you been working there?*

T: *I'm studying for a degree in ...*
L: *Oh really? How long have you been studying?*

T: *I do yoga.*
L: *Oh really? How long have you been doing it?*

Follow-up

EITHER: Ask learners to create their own true sentences using *I live ..., I'm -ing ..., I'm a ..., I do ....*
In pairs, they read their sentences to each other, responding with *How long have you been.* Monitor to make sure learners produce the target pattern correctly.

OR: Conduct a milling activity or role play where learners move around as if at a party. They have conversations with each other incorporating the *How long have you been* pattern.

Rationale

How long have you been working/teaching/living can be introduced as a chunk relatively early on. Your learners may even ask you this kind of question in their first lesson! After the chunk has been memorized and practised (see, for example, Activity 6.8: *Frames and fillers*), you can introduce other frequent verbs that go into this pattern.

7.4 Best ever

Outline	Learners complete sentences and do a range of oral drills to practise the present perfect with superlative adjectives.
Level	Intermediate and above (B1+)
Time	Variable
Preparation	Prepare a handout with the sentence beginnings in Step 2 below.

Procedure

1 Write the following pattern on the board and draw attention to the past participle *seen* (see also Activity 6.3: *Putting irregular verbs to work*):

It is the best film I've ever seen.

2 Provide a handout with the following sentence beginnings. Ask learners to complete them with an appropriate verb by looking it up in their irregular verbs table.
 a *It's the best novel I've ever _____.*
 b *It's the best meal I've ever _____.*
 c *It's the worst joke I've ever _____.*
 d *It's the worst pizza I've ever _____.*
 e *It's the best party I've ever _____.*
 f *It's the longest email I've ever _____.*
 g *It's the biggest mistake I've ever _____.*
 h *She's the nicest person I've ever _____.*
 i *It's the longest journey I've ever _____.*
 j *It's the most tiring journey I've ever _____.*
 k *It's the stupidest thing I've ever _____.*

3 Ask learners to compare answers in pairs then do whole-class feedback. Suggested answers:
 a *read* (draw learners' attention to pronunciation)
 b *had* (*eaten* is also possible)
 c *heard*
 d *had* (*tasted* is also possible, although it's not an irregular verb)
 e *been **to***
 f *written*
 g *made*
 h *met*
 i *been **on***
 j *made*
 k *done*

Follow-up

1   After going through the answers or in the following lesson, say the sentence beginnings and ask learners to complete them from memory – either individually or chorally.

Teacher: *It's the worst joke I've ever ...*   Learners: *heard!*

2   Repeat the same drill but vary the adjectives.

It's the most interesting novel ...
It's the worst meal ...
It's the scariest film ...
It's the noisiest party ...

3   Repeat the same drill but this time provide only the adjective + noun collocation. Learners put the adjective in the correct form and add the appropriate verb in the correct form:

Teacher: *interesting book*   Learners: *It's the most interesting book I've ever read.*

Start with longer adjectives (consisting of more than two syllables) as these only require *most* for the superlative form. Then move on to forms with *-est*. Here is a suggested list/order:

exciting journey	*scary movie*
terrible film	*kind person*
funny joke	*crazy thing*
noisy party	*bad song*
tasty meal	*good club*

4   Repeat the same drill but this time provide only nouns. In turn, learners have to come up with entire sentences. However, they cannot repeat the adjectives so when it's their turn to answer, they have to think of a new adjective for each new noun.

Teacher: *book*   Learner: *It's the best book I've ever read.*
Teacher: *party*   Learner: *It's the worst party I've ever been to.*

○ **Classroom management tip**

Parts 1–3 of this follow-up are better suited to weaker learners (or those who are still likely to make mistakes with superlatives, e.g. *the most nice person*). Part 4 is particularly suitable for stronger learners because supplying adjectives no-one has called out before will be fun and challenging for them.

Rationale

The activity can be used whether your learners are already partially familiar with the present perfect or as their first encounter with it. There is no need to delve into a structural analysis at this stage; a simple explanation that we use this structure to talk about experiences in life (without referring to specific times when things happened) should be enough.

7.5 Relay race

Outline	Teams write sentences on the board in a relay race to practise a target pattern.
Level	Intermediate and upper intermediate (B1/B2)
Time	10 minutes
Preparation	Prepare three sets of seven prompt cards. Each card should contain one of the following nouns: *lecture, restaurant, exhibition, hotel, film, weather, her sister.*

Procedure

1   Write the following sentence on the board:

   *The test was **more difficult than I'd expected**.*

2   Divide the class into three teams, with each team standing in line in front of the board. Hand a board pen to the first learner in each line. Place a set of prompts cards face down near the board for each team (make sure learners can't see them until it's their turn to use one).

3   Tell teams they need to come up with other sentences following the pattern on the board. (They can deviate slightly from it if they like, e.g. use *less* instead of *more*.) They should use a new prompt card for each new sentence.

4   When you give a signal, the first learner in each team comes to the board, picks up a prompt card and writes a full sentence using the given noun and their own adjective. The learner then hands the marker to the next teammate in line and goes to the back of the line.

5   The next teammate repeats Step 4 using the noun on their prompt card and their own adjective. Adjectives cannot be repeated.

6   Continue until one of the teams uses up all seven nouns. Learners can then return to their seats.

7   Go through answers eliminating any sentences that are incorrect or which repeat adjectives. Award points. The team with the most points is the winner. Possible answers:

   The lecture was more boring than I'd expected.
   The restaurant was more expensive than I'd expected.
   The exhibition was more interesting than I'd expected.
   The hotel was less luxurious than I'd expected.
   The film was longer than I'd expected.
   The weather turned out to be colder than I'd expected.
   Her sister was taller than I'd expected.

> **Classroom management tip**
>
> If you think some learners might feel anxious about thinking of an adjective on the spot , you could allow teammates help each other, for example by shouting out possible adjectives to the learner at the board. You could also distribute the noun cards in advance so that learners can think of their adjective before they come up to the board.

Follow-up

1   Do a series of oral drills to practise the target structure – see Activity 7.4: *Best ever (Follow-up)*.

2   In a subsequent lesson, display or give learners a worksheet with the following sentences:

The lecture was more boring than I'd expected.
The restaurant was more expensive than I'd expected.
The exhibition was more interesting than I'd expected.
The hotel was less luxurious than I'd expected.
The journey took us longer than we'd hoped for.
The weather turned out to be colder than we'd anticipated.
Her sister was taller than I'd imagined.

Ask learners to split the sentences as follows:

The lecture …. / … was more boring than I'd expected.

Learners should add their own words and phrases to write two new sentences, for example:

The lecture was really tedious. It was more boring than I'd expected.

Very often the language added to the sentences will contain synonyms of the original adjectives *(The restaurant cost a fortune! It was far more expensive than I'd expected)* or antonyms *(The hotel was really dated. It was much less luxurious than I'd expected)*.

Variation
The relay race can also be set up with patterns with two variable slots, for example:

She's not a [nice/easy/pleasant/interesting] person to [live/deal/work/communicate] with.
He's [good/bad/hopeless/lousy] with [people/ money/computers/kids].
At school I was [terrible/hopeless/brilliant] at [maths/science/chemistry/English].

Rationale
Many 'problematic' structures can be first presented to learners as whole chunks and, after being committed to memory, 'unpacked' to create a mental template for producing and practising similar patterns.

7.6 Left hand, right hand

Outline	In this kinaesthetic activity, learners respond to oral prompts to decide whether to use *make* or *do*.
Level	Intermediate and above (B1+)
Time	15 minutes
Preparation	None

Procedure

1   Tell learners you'll be calling out some common words that go with either *do* or *make*. Provide an example on the board, if necessary:

   do + homework
   make + a mistake

2   Call out the items below one by one. If the word you call out collocates with *do*, learners should raise their left hand; if it collocates with *make* they should raise their right hand.

housework	*the cleaning*
a suggestion	*a mess*
the laundry	*some searching on the internet*
a decision	*a fuss*
a statement	*some studying*
a choice	*a fortune*
the ironing	*nothing*
money	*your bed*
homework	*someone a favour*

3   Display the answers on the board or provide a handout:

make	*do*
a suggestion	*housework*
a decision	*the laundry*
a choice	*the ironing*
a mess	*the cleaning*
a fuss	*some studying*
a statement	*some searching on the internet*
a fortune	*nothing*
money	*homework*
the bed	*someone a favour*

Draw attention to how *make* is very often followed by the article *a* and how *do* is often followed by *-ing*: *the ironing, the cleaning, nothing*.

Follow-up
1   Allow learners a couple of minutes to study the collocations on the board, then erase them.
    Provide the prompts below to elicit the appropriate collocation. This can be done chorally with the
    whole class or by calling on individual learners.

I have to complete my school assignments.	*(You have to do some studying.)*
The president gave a speech yesterday.	*(The president made a statement.)*
She put the dirty clothes into the washing machine.	*(She did the laundry.)*
Last weekend I stayed at home and just lazed about.	*(You did nothing at the weekend.)*
He earned a lot of money.	*(He made a fortune.)*
I used Google to find the answer.	*(You did some searching on the internet.)*
He left dirty dishes all over the kitchen.	*(He made a mess.)*

For similar activities aimed at eliciting responses see Activities 2.4: *Prompted recall*,
6.6: *Disappearing chunks*, and other activities in this chapter (e.g. 7.1 or 7.3).

2   Learners take turns asking and answering real questions that recycle the collocations in both the
    question and the answer, for example:

Learner A: *When did you last do the ironing?*
Learner B: *Let me see. I did the ironing a month ago. So when did you last make a suggestion?*
Learner A: *Actually, I made one last night …*

Variation
This activity can be used with other confusable words and structures, for example:
be good at (maths / fixing things)
be good with (people/computers)

there is (no need to worry / plenty of time)
it is (very important / not difficult)

say (a word / what you what)
tell (me/her / the truth)

See also Activity 5.9: *Confusable pairs.*

Rationale

The difference between *make* and *do* is often explained to learners in a conceptual way: use *make* for
things that you can create (e.g. *a cake, a mess*) and *do* for activities (e.g. *the shopping, the washing up*).
However, in order for learners to use the two correctly, it's equally important to show the patterns the
two are likely to occur in.

7.7 I thought you said ...

Outline	Learners use prompt cards to practise irregular verbs and a common reported speech pattern.
Level	Elementary and intermediate (A2/B1)
Time	15 minutes
Preparation	Prepare pairs of cards – one pair for each pair of learners. One card should contain the sentences in the left-hand column in Figure 7.2 below. The other card should contain those in the right-hand column.

Procedure

1   Organize learners into pairs and give them a pair of cards – see *Preparation*.

2   Tell Learner A to say the sentences on their card one by one (each sentence contains a negative verb in the present tense). Learner B responds with *Oh really? I thought you said …* followed by the same verb in the past tense. Provide an example on the board to make sure learners understand:

Learner A: *I don't find English grammar hard.*
Learner B: *Oh really? I thought you said you found it hard!*

3   Learners change roles and repeat Step 2, with Learner B saying their negative statements.

Learner A	Learner B
I don't eat meat.	I don't drink soft drinks.
I never buy flowers.	I don't know Ellen.
I never lend money.	I don't drive.
I never wake up before 8 am.	I never write postcards.
I don't find English grammar hard.	I never sleep in pajamas.
I never forget things.	I don't read print anymore.

Figure 7.2: Prompt cards with negative sentences

Variations

1   To make the activity less mechanical, ask learners to respond with more specific words as follows:

I don't eat meat. → *Oh really? I thought you said you ate chicken.*
I don't drink soft drinks. → *Oh really? I thought you said you drank Sprite.*

2   Instead of *I thought you said*, learners can also be given the following patterns:

Didn't you say you, You told me you, I'm sure you said

Rationale

According to prescriptive grammar, statements in the present tense should change to the past tense in reported speech – sometimes known as the 'backshift' or 'one tense back' rule. However, this isn't just a transformation rule; there is logic behind it. The past tense is often necessary to show that the present situation is somehow different to what was originally claimed. Conversely, we can keep the reported speech verb in the present tense if the situation is still true.

7.8 Charades with prepositions

Outline	Learners mime and guess sentences with *on*.
Level	Elementary and above (A2+)
Time	15 minutes
Preparation	Prepare five cards or strips of paper, each containing one of the following sentences:

I saw a great film on TV last night.
I spoke to her on the phone yesterday.
I usually listen to the news on the radio.
He stayed at home and played on the computer all day.
You can find a lot of funny videos on the internet.

Procedure

1 Divide the class into five groups and give each group a sentence card/strip – see *Preparation*. Groups shouldn't reveal their sentence to anyone else.

2 Tell the groups to take turns miming their sentences for the rest of the class to guess. For each sentence, provide the exact number of words on the board and the word *on* as follows:

_____ _____ _____ _____ _____   ON   _____ _____ _____.

3 One or more of the learners in the group mime the sentence, word by word in front of the class. They don't have to mime the words in order. Other groups have to guess. You can award points for each correctly guessed word to make it more competitive.

4 The teacher or one of the group members fills in the gaps:

__*I*__ __*saw*__ __*a*__ __*great*__ __*film*__ __*ON*__ __*TV*__ __*last*__ __*night*__.

5 Do not erase the completed sentence. Provide the same template for the next sentence underneath so that by the end of the activity there are five full sentences on the board.

6 Draw attention to the noun phrases that appear after *on* and encourage learners to copy the pattern into their notebooks:

> | | |
> |---|---|
> | | *TV* |
> | | *the phone* |
> | *on* | *the radio* |
> | | *the computer* |
> | | *the internet* |

Lexical Grammar

Follow-up

Provide the following sentence beginnings on the board or in a handout:

> *There's not much classical music*
> *What's*
> *She spends too much time*
> *They do all their shopping*
> *You can take the test*

In pairs, tell learners to match these to the endings with *on*. Each beginning should have a different ending, but as some beginnings may take more than one ending a discussion is likely to follow.

There's not much classical music	*on the radio* (*on TV* also possible)
What's	*on TV?* (*on the radio* also possible)
She spends too much time	*on the phone* (*on the computer/internet* also possible)
They do all their shopping	*on the internet*
You can take the test	*on the computer*

Variation

The activity can be used with other 'problematic' prepositions, for example *at*:
I didn't see him at the meeting.
There were many people at the concert.
I met my wife at a friend's wedding.
I'll see you at my birthday party next week.
There were scientists from all over the world at the conference.

Rationale

The preposition *on* tends to collocate with words related to media and *at* with events (*at a wedding/party*, etc.), a fact rarely highlighted in teaching materials.

7.9 Prepositions of time and place

> **Outline** Learners come up with their own noun phrases to go with prepositions of time and place.
> **Level** Intermediate and upper intermediate (B1/B2)
> **Time** 7 minutes
> **Preparation** Prepare a handout with prompts (optional) – see Step 1.

Procedure

1 Provide the following prompts orally (or on a handout if you prefer):

   a *The baby was born on _____.*
   b *Are you free in _____?*
   c *The train leaves at _____.*
   d *The train leaves in _____.*
   e *Christmas is celebrated on _____.*
   f *The museum is closed on _____.*
   g *The baby was born at _____.*
   h *Christmas is celebrated in _____.*
   i *Are you free on _____?*
   j *We're going on holiday in _____.*
   k *Bye-bye, see you in _____.*
   l *Bye-bye, see you on _____.*
   m *The museum is closed in _____.*
   n *The baby was born in _____.*

2 Learners respond – either chorally or individually – with their own ideas. They cannot use the same words more than once. Suggested answers:

   a *The baby was born on <u>Friday</u>.*
   b *Are you free in <u>the afternoon</u>?*
   c *The train leaves at <u>10 am</u>.*
   d *The train leaves in <u>the morning</u> / <u>ten minutes</u>.*
   e *Christmas is celebrated on <u>25th December</u> / <u>December 25th</u>.*
   f *The museum is closed on <u>Tuesday</u>.*
   g *The baby was born at <u>four o'clock</u>.*
   h *Christmas is celebrated in <u>winter</u>.*
   i *Are you free on <u>Thursday</u>?*
   j *We're going on holiday in <u>July</u>.*
   k *Bye-bye, see you in <u>the evening</u>.*
   l *Bye-bye, see you on <u>Monday</u>.*
   m *The museum is closed in <u>August</u>.*
   n *The baby was born in <u>the spring</u>.*

3   Add the examples with *at/in/on* to the board in three columns. Elicit the rules.

at	*in*	*on*
10 am	*the morning*	*Friday*
Five o'clock	*in April*	*25th December*
	in the spring	
SPECIFIC POINT IN	PERIOD OF TIME	DAYS
TIME	MONTHS/SEASONS	DATES

Variation
Instead of responding orally, learners can write down answers then compare with partners.

Follow-up
Although the rules are not as clear-cut as with prepositions of time, the activity can be used for prepositions of place. However, it might help to write the noun phrases on the board. When you say the prompts, learners pick an ending from the board:

> *entrance   office   end   middle of the day   a friend's wedding*
> *birthday party   bed   hospital   work   jail   Heathrow airport   London*

Make sure to include an article *the* or *a(n)* in the prompt, when necessary:
a   *I'll meet you at the (entrance).*
b   *I spent the whole morning lying in (bed).*
c   *We first met at a (friend's wedding).*
d   *I saw her last night at a (birthday party).*
e   *He'll be back home around 7 pm. He's at (work).*
f   *Can you call again next week when she's back in the (office)?*
g   *He's committed a crime. He's now in (jail).*
h   *It was sunny when we arrived at (Heathrow airport).*
i   *It was sunny when we arrived in (London)*
j   *What are you doing here in the (middle of the day)?*
k   *When she sends emails, she always writes 'Hugs and kisses' at (the end).*
l   *He's not feeling well. He's in (bed).*
m   *She's seriously ill. She's in (hospital).* [In American English = *in the hospital*]

Rationale
The following diagram shows how *at* usually refers to a point (in time or space) and *in* to a container or longer period. That's why you arrive *at* an airport (a point) *at* 10 am, but *in* London (container) *in* the afternoon.

7.10 Teacher-led input flooding

Outline	The teacher asks learners a lot of questions containing the same target pattern, in order to provide contextualized repetition.
Level	Any
Time	Variable (depending on size of class)
Preparation	Select a problematic item – this can be a pattern which learners often make mistakes with or find difficult. For some patterns you might have to script some contextualized examples beforehand – see Figure 7.3 below.

Procedure

1   Make sure learners understand the meaning of the target problematic item – see *Preparation*. You can write it on the board (e.g. *be afraid of*) and remind the class that *afraid* is followed by *of* (not *from*).

2   Call on different learners in turn and ask them questions containing the target pattern. Learners may or may not supply the target form in their response. This is what interaction with learners may look like:

Teacher: *Anna, what are you **afraid of**?*
Anna: *Spiders. I hate spiders.*
T: *Anna is **afraid of** spiders. Is anyone else **afraid of** spiders? Hmm? Ben, are you **afraid of** spiders? No? What are you **afraid of**?*
Ben: *I **afraid of** cats.*
T: *You are **afraid of** cats? Really? Ok, Anna is **afraid of** spiders, Ben is **afraid of** cats, let's hear what others are **afraid of**.*

3   Continue asking questions around the class. Make sure you repeat the target pattern as much as possible, both in your questions and when reformulating learners' reponses.

Follow-up
Organize learners into small groups and ask them to practise using the target structure in the same way. Group members can take turns to act as the 'teacher' and lead the conversation.

Note
It may feel unnatural at first to repeat the same structure so many times in such a short period of time. If necessary, you can tell learners before the activity that you are deliberately going to 'flood' the conversation with a particular structure. You could even ask one learner to keep a tally of how many times the structure is said!

<u>difficult for</u>: What's **difficult for** you? Why do you think it is **difficult for** people to learn languages?

<u>want someone to do something</u>: Do you **want me to give** you less homework? Do you **want Anna to help** you with homework? Do you **want Xavi to lend** you his smartwatch?

<u>tell the difference</u>: Can you tell **the difference** between different brands of mineral water? Can you **tell the difference** between an Airbus and Boeing? Can you **tell the difference** between canola oil and soybean oil?

<u>thinking of -ing</u>: What are you **thinking of doing** next weekend? Are you **thinking of going** anywhere next summer? Do you know anyone who's **thinking of quitting** their job?

<u>been to</u>: Have you ever **been to** China? Have you ever **been to** London? Have you ever **been to** a television studio?

<u>good at</u>: What are you **good at**? Are you **good at** maths/science? Is there anything you think you're particularly **good at**? Were you **good at** maths/science at school?

<u>get used to</u>: What things do you find difficult to **get used to**?

Many dependent prepositions are good candidates for input flooding activities:

<u>adjective + dependent preposition</u>:
be/get annoyed with
be/get frustrated with
be satisfied with

<u>verb + dependent preposition</u>:
wait for
rely on
look forward to

Figure 7.3: Structures to use with input flooding

Rationale

During input flooding learners are exposed to massive amounts of input containing the target structure. The technique was originally proposed for teaching grammar. It's relatively easy to devise a text containing numerous examples of regular *-ed* verbs in the past or an artificially increased number of instances of the present progressive, for example, but it would be much harder – and not very natural – to write a text with built-in repetition of the same vocabulary item, whether an individual word or chunk. However, it is not hard to incorporate the target chunk into classroom interaction. Repeated exposure to the same pattern increases the chances of it being noticed (see *Glossary* on p. 223) and becoming intake.

8　Chunks in writing

It is generally believed that there are two main approaches to writing: process-based and product-based. In a process-based approach, learners brainstorm ideas, prepare a draft and then, after feedback given by the teacher or peers, review it and rewrite it (the process can be repeated). A product-based approach starts with looking at the final product: learners study the features of a given piece of writing and then use it as a model to write their own composition. As such, the product-based approach lends itself more to focusing on chunks of language. For example, learners might be asked to look at chunks of language found in a job application covering letter such as *I am writing in response to your advertisement which appeared in / your requirements match my background and qualifications / Attached you will find / Thank you in advance for your consideration*, then use them when writing their own covering letter.

Because ELT coursebooks frequently adopt a product-based approach to writing letters (often including explicit teaching of chunks), this chapter focuses slightly more on expository writing such as essays, articles and reviews. The activities are organized in the order learners would normally go about when writing: starting with brainstorming ideas, developing the ideas into individual paragraphs and moving on to writing a whole composition.

8.1 Key noun spidergrams

Outline	Learners brainstorming suitable chunks of language for an essay.
Level	Upper intermediate and above (B2+)
Time	15 minutes
Preparation	Make sure you and the learners can access an online learner's dictionary in class, or provide a few print dictionaries.

Procedure

1   Elicit three key nouns that relate to the main ideas to be discussed in an essay. These nouns will later form the basis of the essay's paragraphs.

2   For each noun draw a word map (or spidergram) on the board – see Figure 8.1 below.

3   Look up the first key noun in an online learner's dictionary to find its collocates. (If possible, project the search results so the whole class can see them.) Write collocates that occur before the key noun to the left and anything that comes after the noun to the right. Also write one or two whole examples sentences containing the key word.

4   Ask learners to follow the same process for the other two key nouns. You can assign different nouns to different groups. Pool all the results on the board.

5   Learners go on to complete the full writing task, either in class or at home. Encourage them to include chunks from all three word maps in their writing. (They may need to change the form of some of the chunks to do this.) Using the first word map in Figure 8.1, learners could produce a paragraph like this:

   Protection of the environment *is a serious issue. It has been known for some time that CO*^{2} *emissions from vehicles are **harmful to the environment**. Switching to public transport is one way of curbing air pollution and thus reducing the **environmental damage** caused by road transport.*

6   When marking, pay attention not only to the main ideas and how they are developed, but also to how the brainstormed chunks of language have been integrated.

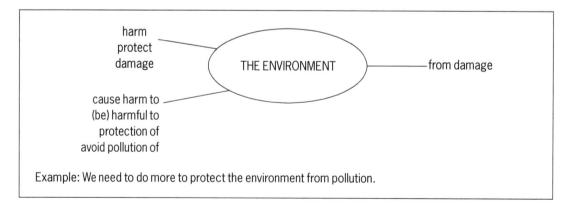

Figure 8.1: (Continued)

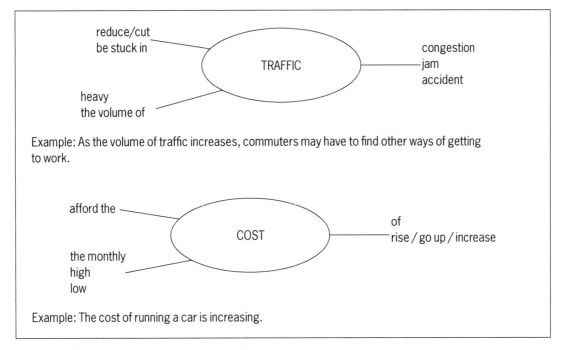

reduce/cut
be stuck in

TRAFFIC

congestion
jam
accident

heavy
the volume of

Example: As the volume of traffic increases, commuters may have to find other ways of getting to work.

afford the

COST

of
rise / go up / increase

the monthly
high
low

Example: The cost of running a car is increasing.

Figure 8.1: Key word maps for an essay about the environment

Variation

You could also ask learners to consult a website like HASK, which displays collocational information visually (see *Useful resources* on p. 227). To produce a pie-chart displaying common collocates in HASK you need to:

- Enter the target word in the search field.
- Choose either verb collocates (**N% collocating with V%s**) or adjective collocates (**N% collocating with AJ%s**).
- When you find the appropriate list of collocations, sort them by **TTest**. (This option sorts collocations according to the strength of the relationship between the collocates rather than by raw frequency, in which common words like *be, have, bad* and *good* usually come out on top.)
- If the list is already arranged by **TTest**, click on the upward arrow and then the downward arrow in order to refresh it. (Toggling the arrows is important to get the Visualization right). After rearranging the list, click on **Visualization** on the right to get frequent collocations displayed graphically – see Figure 8.2.

Collocates of career

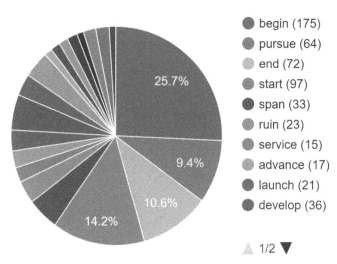

Figure 8.2: Screenshot from HASK (pie-chart for verb collocates with *career*)

Note
This activity is adapted from Michael Lewis's *Teaching Collocation* (2000).

Rationale
One objection learners might have to this kind of activity – especially in exam preparation classes – is that under real exam conditions they don't have access to dictionaries or collocation tools like HASK. Make it clear that an important part of exam preparation is enlarging learners' vocabulary and, specifically, improving their collocational competence. Also, as Michael Lewis (2000) noted, difficulties students may experience with generating ideas for an essay often stem from deficiencies in their phrasal lexicon. Looking up key nouns not only equips learners with chunks they can use in writing but ideas often emerge in the process of exploring collocations. For example, you may not have thought of traffic accidents as relevant to the issue until looking up *traffic* in the dictionary.

8.2 Cause and effect

Outline Learners use chunks to write sentences describing cause and effect relationships.
Level Intermediate / Upper intermediate (B1/B2)
Time 15–20 minutes (longer if there is a debate involved)
Preparation Draw up a list of some social problems and their possible causes. These could be topics you've discussed in class or your own ideas. Prepare a handout with problems in the left-hand column and their causes in the right-hand column – see Figure 8.3 below. Just before the lesson, write up a list of chunks related to cause and effect on the board – see suggestions in Step 3 below.

Procedure

1 Give out the handouts containing problems and causes – see *Preparation* and Figure 8.3. Ask learners to match the problems with potential causes. Clarify that there are several possible answers and some causes may fit more than one problem.

2 Go through learners' ideas and if they disagree, facilitate a brief discussion (there is another opportunity for discussion in Step 4).

3 In pairs, learners choose five cause and effect relationships from their handouts. Ask them to write a sentence for each one and include a chunk from the board – see *Preparation* – in each sentence.

<u>B2/C1</u>
can be the consequence of
is often the result of
stems from
The principal cause of … is
is at fault / to blame
can be attributed to

<u>B1</u>
may cause
can lead to
can result in
can give rise to

4 Learners read out their sentences. If classmates disagree on a particular sentence, it can be used as a basis for an impromptu class debate.

Problems	Causes
poor grades	poor parenting
social problems teenagers have	corruption in the government
violent behaviour	CO_2 emissions
children's obesity	deforestation
economic instability	inadequate access to education
climate change	smoking / alcohol abuse
health problems	lack of exercise
poverty	poor diet
	childhood trauma
	big families

Figure 8.3: Social problems and potential causes

Follow-up

Ask learners to come up with their own cause and effect relationships and write sentences using the chunks on the board. They can develop their sentence into a paragraph by adding one or two lines suggesting what can be done about the problems.

 Cultural awareness tip

Select the problems and causes you'd like to focus on carefully before the lesson. In some contexts, it may be insensitive or inappropriate to bring up issues like childhood trauma, government corruption or alcohol abuse, for example. It is a good idea to ask local teaching colleagues which issues to focus on.

Rationale

We often teach learners to signal cause and effect relationships with conjunctions like *because*, *since*, *therefore*, *consequently*, *as a result*, *therefore*, etc. But cause and effect relationships can also be expressed with lexical chunks such as the ones which appear in this activity.

8.3 Forced choice writing

Outline	Learners include an entire bank of chunks in a piece of writing – without being told the topic.
Level	Upper intermediate and above (B2+)
Time	20 minutes
Preparation	Make a list of at least eight chunks around a topic you want learners to write about. Scanning a couple of articles or coursebook texts on the chosen topic will usually throw up several relevant chunks. See Figure 8.4 below for examples.

Procedure

1   Give learners the selected chunks – see *Preparation* and Figure 8.4. Clarify meanings.

2   Tell learners they need to produce a short essay (two or three paragraphs) using ALL the chunks. Don't tell students the topic or the essay question – it is up to them to decide.

3   When learners finish their writing, get them to compare their work in small groups. Did they write about the same topic? How many learners wrote about the topic you originally had in mind?

B2/C1	B1/B2
when disaster strikes provide humanitarian aid to rely on foreign aid in need of urgent assistance remote areas devastated by an earthquake alleviate suffering	harmful effect research has shown that cause serious harm to a step in the right direction according to several studies live a healthy lifestyle recommended daily limit
Possible topic: humanitarian aid Possible essay question: Should countries spend money on foreign aid?	Possible topic: health and diet Possible essay question: Should sugary foods be banned from schools and hospitals?

Figure 8.4: Chunks for forced choice writing

Variation

If it's the first time you are doing this activity, you could ask learners to find and discuss connections between the chunks before they write. Display the chunks in a scattered manner (like in Activity 2.3: *Memory quiz*) and elicit associations between chunks and some example sentences:
When disaster strikes, *many communities have no choice but to* **rely on foreign aid**.
Eating more than the **recommended daily limit** *of sugar can have* **harmful effects** *on children's health.*
The example sentences can then be used as a basis for paragraphs in the main writing stage.

Rationale

Preparation for writing activities usually starts with brainstorming. Once learners have formulated their ideas (often in L1), they are often faced with a lack of linguistic resources to express their ideas in English. This activity reverses the process by focusing on the language learners need as a starting point. Equipped with a few lexical chunks related to the chosen topic, learners go on to develop their ideas.

8.4 Odd one out

Outline	Learners decide which chunks belong to particular genres of writing.
Level	Upper intermediate and above (B2+)
Time	10 minutes
Preparation	Prepare a handout containing chunks which learners might need for different writing genres during their course. You can include genres like these, depending on your learners' needs: essay, review, report, formal letter, informal letter, story, article. Arrange the chunks into a table with each genre in a separate row BUT make sure one chunk in each row is in the wrong place – see examples in Figure 8.5 below.

Procedure

1   Hand a copy of your table of chunks – see *Preparation* and Figure 8.5 – to each pair of learners.

2   Tell learners that one chunk in each row doesn't fit the genre in the left-hand column – it's the 'odd one out'.

3   In their pairs, learners look at the chunks for each genre and decide which is the odd one out.

4   Conduct feedback with the whole group. Elicit which genre each odd chunk should belong to.

Answers:
a   *I'm looking forward to seeing you* (Letter to a friend)
b   *to curb the rising air pollution* (Essay about the environment)
c   *your prompt attention to the matter will be appreciated* (Letter of complaint)
d   *develop a sense of responsibility* (Article about education/careers)
e   *I remember we always used to* (Story about a childhood memory)
f   *lots of twists and turns* (TV show review)
g   *tackle the problem of obesity* (Report about leisure facilities in town)

> ○ **Classroom management tip**
>
> Give stronger learners the table of chunks without specifying the genres (if you use the example table above, fold over or cut off the left-hand column). Ask learners to identify each genre before identifying the odd chunks.

a **Essay about the environment**	has risen dramatically	I'm looking forward to seeing you	reduce traffic congestion	cause serious problems
b **Report about leisure facilities in a town**	cater for adults and children alike	offers a wide range of activities	provides plenty of opportunities	to curb the rising air pollution
c **Letter to a friend**	haven't heard from you for ages	some exciting news to tell you	your prompt attention to the matter will be appreciated	do drop me a line
d **Letter of complaint**	develop a sense of responsibility	your prompt response will be appreciated	tried a few times to no avail	always been happy with the service provided
e **TV show review**	glued to the edge of your seat	enjoyed every minute of it	I remember we always used to	brilliant acting
f **Article about education/ careers**	has become increasingly common	place too much emphasis on	lots of twists and turns	is not without its disadvantages
g **Story about a childhood memory**	the funniest thing that's ever happened to me	I learned my lesson well	tackle the problem of obesity	while I was staying in/with

Figure 8.5: 'Odd one out' writing chunks

Rationale

Even if you have an excellent control of grammar and can construct syntactically complex sentences, it does not mean you can produce a piece of writing in a genre you are not familiar with. Suppose your boss asked you to write a memo: if you hadn't written one before, you would probably want to look at examples of previous memos. Likewise, if you're applying for a job for the first time you will probably look at examples of cover letters and CVs online before writing your own. If very competent language users often refer to sample writing to orientate themselves to a new genre, that is all the more reason to get learners to familiarize themselves with the linguistic conventions of a genre before writing in L2. Looking at useful chunks from sample writing is an essential part of genre orientation.

8.5 ... which was nice

Outline	Learners write main clauses for prompts containing relative clauses taken from travel reviews.
Level	Intermediate / Upper intermediate (B1/B2)
Time	6–7 minutes
Preparation	None

Procedure

1 Write the following chunks / relative clauses on the board. Tell learners they are all taken from online travel reviews and are related to hotel amenities.

which was nice and

relaxing.
spacious.
shady.
peaceful.
comfortable.
modern.
sunny.

2 Elicit what each chunk could refer to, for example a room, suite, terrace, pool area, spa, balcony, restaurant, garden, lobby, etc.

3 Tell learners to work in pairs and write a main clause to go with each relative clause.

4 To compare learners' ideas with those of real online reviewers, you can simply insert the target chunks into a search engine like Google. Put double inverted commas on both sides of the chunk like this: *"which was nice and relaxing"*. Possible answers:

We spent a lot of time by the pool, which was nice and relaxing.

We stayed in a double room with a sea view, which was nice and spacious.

We had breakfast on the terrace, which was nice and shady.

The hotel was situated off the main road, which was nice and peaceful.

There is free WiFi in the lobby, which was nice and comfortable.

What I really liked about the room is the bathroom, which was nice and modern.

Our suite had a pretty balcony, which was nice and sunny.

Follow-up

In a subsequent lesson, give learners the main clauses (either the ones they wrote themselves, the ones they found online or the example ones above). This time students should add their own relative clauses to the sentences.

Variation

The writing activity can be combined with a speaking activity, in which learners rehearse and perform short dialogues about recent activities. They can insert *which was nice and X* whenever appropriate:

A: *What did you do at the weekend?*
B: *I went to the beach, which was nice and relaxing.*

A: *Where did you go on your last holiday?*
B: *To a cottage in Scotland, which was nice and cosy.*

Note

For more activities using search engines like Google to find chunks or confirm likelihood of certain sequences of words, see Activities 8.9: *Very predictable chunks* and 8.10: *Upgrading a text using Google.*

Rationale

Relative clauses can be tricky to teach. This activity provides a way into this 'problematic' area of English grammar by way of familiar online travel reviews.

8.6 Writing frame

Outline	Learners answer prompt questions to activate target chunks, which are then incorporated into a piece of writing.
Level	Intermediate and above (B1+)
Time	6–7 mins
Preparation	This activity will work well with writing tasks with predictable outcomes, such as writing task 1 in the Cambridge First (FCE) or Advanced (CAE) exams. Put together a list of chunks your learners have recently studied. Then find or create a suitable writing task that could incorporate the chunks. Draw up a writing frame for the task, containing questions aimed at eliciting the target chunks – see an example in Figure 8.6.

Procedure

1 Provide learners with the writing task and the accompanying writing frame you created – see *Preparation* and Figure 8.6. (Note that Figure 8.6 includes example target chunks for reference. Your task will not include any chunks unless you use the *Variation* below.)

2 Ask learners to go through the questions in the frame, using as many recently studied chunks as possible when answering them. They can do this in pairs orally, but should make notes.

3 For homework learners can complete the full writing task, incorporating the notes they made in class.

4 When marking learners' writing, award points for the appropriate use of target chunks as well as the quantity of chunks used.

Variation

If learners need more support or are less familiar with the target chunks, include a 'chunk bank' with the frame, for example:

Essay question about a film called *Blue Jasmine*:
Describe Jasmine's relationship with her ex-husband and their son.

- How did Hal treat Jasmine?
- How did Hal get away with his financial schemes?
- Did Jasmine suspect anything?
- Did his son talk highly of him at the college?
- What did Hal's son do after his father's arrest?

*look the other way   shower someone with gifts   smooth talker   drop out of college
squander his opportunity   slick operator   doesn't know the first thing about
brag about   spoil someone rotten*

Note

Encourage students to use the chunks even if they do not seem immediately relevant to their piece of writing. For example, if one of the target chunks is *spectacular visual effects* and students choose to describe a film without these, they can still incorporate the chunk using a negative sentence:

*Although it doesn't have the **spectacular visual effects** that you normally find in **Hollywood blockbusters**, I'd recommend the film for its **brilliant acting** and **stellar cast**.*

Essay question
Describe a big city you know or have been to.

Writing frame

- How big is it?
- What can visitors see in the city?
- How busy is the city?
- Is the transport system good?
- What problems affect the city?

Target chunks

with a population of	fancy designer boutiques
is famous for	on the outskirts
is home to	residential area
has developed/grown rapidly	jazz /music/art scene
tourist attraction	run-down building
historical site	rough area
places of interest	dimly-lit street
there's a lot going on	noise pollution

Figure 8.6: Writing task with writing frame

Rationale

It has been shown that few L2 writers are willing to take risks and incorporate new lexis into their writing, instead opting to 'play it safe' and stick to relatively familiar language which they are comfortable with. Consequently, a lot of vocabulary items learners can recognize when reading remain passive. To activate these items, it is a good idea to explicitly discuss and draw learners' attention to vocabulary which is relevant to the writing task in hand. Reviewing vocabulary related to the topic – words and lexical chunks – results in transfer of receptive knowledge into productive use. This is supported by an experiment conducted on secondary school L2 learners in Canada (Lee and Muncie, 2006).

8.7 Writing skeleton

Outline	Learners identify the functions of different chunks in a text, then use the chunks as a skeleton to write their own text.
Level	Upper intermediate and above (B2+)
Time	6–7 minutes for Steps 1 and 2; Step 3 can be done as homework
Preparation	Find a text which can serve as a model for the writing task you want learners to do. Identify useful chunks and pick out each type of chunk in the text using different colours or fonts – see examples in Figure 8.7, Key. For the purposes of this activity, the text organization and cohesion is more important than the content.

Procedure

1   Give learners a copy of the model text with chunks shown in different colours, styles or fonts – see *Preparation* and Figure 8.7.

2   Students read the model text and identify the functions of the chunks shown in different colours/fonts/styles.

3   After confirming answers and clarifying the various functions of the chunks, learners write their own texts using the highlighted chunks. If possible, provide a skeleton text like the one in Figure 8.8. Learners can vary the order of the chunks slightly or replace some words but, on the whole, their piece of writing should follow the skeleton as closely as possible.

Traffic congestion has reached unprecedented levels in many cities around the world. **There are two main approaches** the government can adopt to tackle this issue.

One obvious solution is to issue penalties. <u>This implies</u> both levying higher taxes on private cars, particularly heavy vehicles, and increasing the petrol price. <u>Furthermore</u>, punitive measures <u>can include</u> tolls for entering certain restricted zones. Indeed, many cities around the world have introduced congestion charges to ease traffic gridlock in city centres. However, it is important to bear in mind that cities that have opted for this approach, SUCH AS London, are cities with highly efficient transportation systems.

Another possible course of action is to make public transport more appealing <u>so that</u> car drivers have a reason to get out of their cars and take the bus or tram. <u>This can be achieved</u>, FOR EXAMPLE, by offering reduced tickets for using a city's transit system, SUCH AS park and ride schemes which have been implemented in many urban centres. Naturally, this solution depends on having a well-developed transportation network in place, which requires financial investment.

To sum up, although penalties may seem like a more economically viable option, the problem can be solved by rewarding people rather than punishing them. **In my view**, the government should invest in developing and upgrading public transit systems, and offer incentives to use them before adopting the 'big stick' approach IN THE FORM OF taxes and tolls.

Key: **bold**: chunks for introducing different sections, e.g. introduction, body paragraph or conclusion
       <u>underlined</u>: elaborating on / extending the main idea
       DIFFERENT FONT: examples or supporting details that illustrate the main idea
       highlighted: concessions or counter-arguments

Figure 8.7: Model text with chunks in different fonts

There are two main approaches _____.

One obvious solution is _____.

This implies _____.

Furthermore, _____ can include _____.

However, it is important to bear in mind _____, such as _____,

_____.

Another possible course of action is to _____

so that _____. This can be achieved, for example, _____

_____,

such as _____.

Naturally, _____.

To sum up, although _____ may seem like _____

_____.

In my view, _____

in the form of _____.

Figure 8.8: Writing skeleton with target chunks

Variation

Hand out the text without any highlighting. Learners themselves can highlight chunks that serve different functions (see Key in Figure 8.7).

Alternatively, learners can underline ALL chunks in the text, then sort them into generic chunks which can be used for a particular writing genre or a specific topic.

Rationale

Like Activity 8.4: *Odd one out*, this activity is underpinned by the belief that learners should be explicitly aware of the conventions of a given genre before writing, rather than arriving at their goal by experimenting (Hyland, 2003). One of the most important features of such genre-based writing instruction is teaching learners about how target texts are structured and focusing on genre-specific lexical chunks. Although a model may seem rigid, there is still plenty of room for learners' expression and creativity within a (semi-)prescribed structure.

8.8 Learners' own corpus

Outline	Learners build their own corpus then run it through a concordancer to find frequent patterns.
Level	Upper intermediate and above (B2+)
Time	Variable
Preparation	Learners will need a computer with internet access and word processing software.

Procedure

1   Over a period of a few days or weeks, get learners to copy and paste texts belonging to a specific genre into a single new document. Depending on your teaching contexts, these can be abstracts of research papers, plot summaries, travel reviews, restaurant reviews, etc. Learners should be able to find most texts they need via simple internet searches.

2   After they have accumulated enough texts – at least 20,000 words, which can be checked using the document's word count function – explain that you are going to run the document through a concordancer (see *Glossary* on p. 223).

3   Go to LexTutor (http://lextutor.ca/n_gram) and paste the whole of the document into the large text window. Next to **Choose max string**, select five words. Then click on the **Submit_Window** button. You will see lists of patterns extracted from the learners' corpus – see an example in Figure 8.10, from a small corpus of business emails.

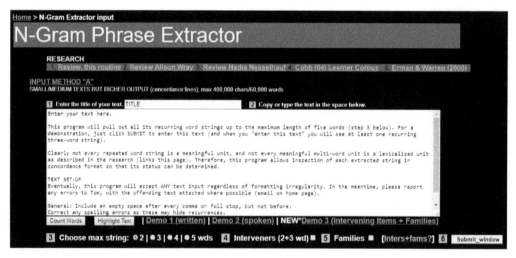

Figure 8.9: Screenshot from LexTutor

```
1334  e delegated. in the weeks ahead we look FORWARD TO receiving comments from campus renaissance a
1335  the area in question. we therefore look FORWARD TO using their input to develop a comprehensive
1336  he first three chapters of each. i look FORWARD TO hearing from you and hope that we may have t
1337  ur account with you. we will be looking FORWARD TO your orders and to the opportunity of servin
1338  contact for further information. i look FORWARD TO hearing from you soon. i may be reached at m
1339  n the agreement. we are eagerly looking FORWARD TO this project and are happy to have the oppor
1340  nfidence that you placed in us and look FORWARD TO a continuing relationship which will prove b
1341  nd organizations to do the same. i look FORWARD TO seeing you at the mayor's special thank you
1342  ies from the conversational style often FOUND IN email messages to the more formal legalistic s
1343  ges to the more formal legalistic style FOUND IN contracts. a style between these two extremes
1344   fancy explanatory texts but instead we FOUND THAT black and white photos had been included in
1345  here at inter-office on august 14 20xx. FRED JOHNSON of your crm group is to act as the meeting
1346  e seeks. the second letter sample #2 is FROM A college senior who does not specify where she le
1347  s required in many different situations FROM APPLYING for a job to requesting or delivering inf
1348  d we look forward to receiving comments FROM CAMPUS renaissance and the community at large abou
1349  chelor of science degree in engineering FROM NORTH carolina state university in june and by tha
1350  roposed garden project as you are aware FROM OUR last meeting the hogarth tenants' association
1351  volunteers in many different capacities FROM SERVING meals to the homeless to entertaining seni
1352  you. sincerely john parker. you can see FROM THE attached document the shipment was in fact dis
1353  t was in fact dispatched as you can see FROM THE attached emails below i have in fact raised th
1354  stance would it be possible for someone FROM THE parks department to attend our next meeting to
1355  ss' which can only be improved by input FROM THE various stakeholders who care the most about t
1356  should respond. business writing varies FROM THE conversational style often found in email mess
```

Figure 8.10: Concordance results from LexTutor

Note

Searching a vast amount of text can take a while – be patient! If the operation times out, click on the Back button on your browser and repeat the process. Alternatively, you could upload your corpus document in txt. format, which has no formatting and therefore has a much smaller file size.

Variation

Instead of LexTutor, you could use AntConc to extract the patterns. AntConc can be downloaded from www.laurenceanthony.net/software/antconc/ and the same page also contains user guides and tutorials. See also this guide by Mura Nava: http://bit.ly/antconcexplore

Rationale

Although there are plenty of corpora available online today, you do not need to limit yourself to existing sources. Learners can compile their own genre- or discipline-specific corpora. Such personalized corpora are particularly suitable for EAP contexts where students come from different academic fields. This also fosters learner-centredness and promotes learner autonomy.

8.9 Very predictable chunks

Outline	Using a search engine or the predictive text function on their smartphones, learners find out which words complete frequent sequences of words.
Level	Intermediate and above (B1+)
Time	Variable
Preparation	Learners will need a computer or mobile device with internet access – at least one per group. Prepare some collocation forks (see Activity 1.4: *Making mini-stories with collocation forks*) and write them on the board – see examples in Figure 8.12 below.

Procedure

1 Divide the class into groups. Depending on the number of groups, assign each group one or two of the collocation forks on the board – see *Preparation* and Figure 8.12.

2 Groups type in the strings of words in the 'handle' of the fork into a search engine or onto their smartphones. They look at the possible completions provided by the search engine or the predictive text function on their phones, for example:

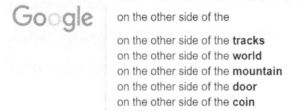

Figure 8.11: Google search results (Google and Google logo are registered trademarks of Google Inc., used with permission.)

3 If one of the results seems strange, encourage students to type/choose the suggested word and see how the suggested string is continued.

4 One representative from each group comes to the board and writes possible completions in their fork.

5 Go over the answers, discussing whether learners were surprised by any of the findings.

6 Erase the strings of words in the handles of the forks. Learners try to remember what they were by looking at the completions they have written. This step can be done at the end of the lesson.

Follow-up
Learners work in groups to write a text which contains at least one combination from each fork.

Note
This search can also be performed using Netspeak – see Activity 3.1.

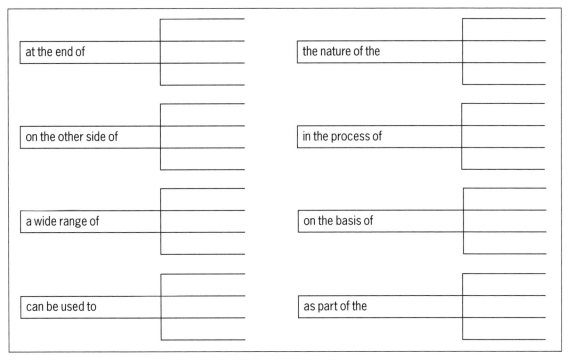

Figure 8.12: Collocation forks with common strings

Variation

The strings in the examples above are suitable for academic writing but the activity can be used for other genres, for example writing emails/letters:

I'm writing to	inform you
	enquire
	complain about

should you require	any
	further
	immediate assistance

look forward to	seeing
	hearing from
	meeting

I'll appreciate your	help
	response
	consideration

Rationale

Predictive text, a common feature in search engines and smartphones, suggests words as you type. In many ways, it is similar to our brain's own built-in predictive function, i.e. our ability to finish off our interlocutors' sentences as well as anticipate upcoming words when reading. Michael Hoey's theory of lexical priming (see p. 4) explains how we become primed to expect certain words in the company of other words. One of the practical implications of the theory is that we should provide learners with opportunities to acquire useful primings, which will allow them to develop fluency, both in language processing and production – and the ability to complete each other's sentences!

8.10 Upgrading a text using Google

Outline	Learners use Google search to find more appropriate or colourful adjectives for a piece of writing.
Level	Upper intermediate and above (B2+)
Time	Variable
Preparation	Learners will need a computer or mobile device with internet access – one per pair. Find and prepare a suitable text in any genre – see examples in Figure 8.15. Replace some adjectives in the text with 'blander' ones such as *good*, *big*, *important*, *nice*, etc. Put the replacement adjectives in **bold** and <u>underline</u> the whole collocation the target adjectives are part of.
	For the purposes of this activity, the adjectives should ideally be part of verb + adjective + noun collocations, such as *achieve our **crucial** goal* and not 'standalone', such as *It is **crucial** that you* – see example in Figure 8.13 below.

Procedure

1 Distribute copies of the modified text – see *Preparation* – to learners.

2 In pairs, learners upgrade the text by replacing the bold adjectives with more suitable ones. To do this, they enter the entire underlined string of words into the Google search bar, using double inverted commas and replacing the bold adjective with an asterisk, as follows:

Figure 8.13: Google search query (Google and Google logo are registered trademarks of Google Inc., used with permission.)

(Inverted commas are necessary to find the exact string rather than individual words in the string. The asterisk * indicates a wildcard query and tells Google to 'fill in the blank'.)

The above search will yield results like these:
achieve our annual/long-term/main / most important goal

3 Make sure learners scroll down through the search results and then onto the following pages (by default, Google only displays ten results per page).

Figure 8.14: Google search results page indicator (Google and Google logo are registered trademarks of Google Inc., used with permission.)

4   If the underlined collocation (search string) contains articles *a/an*, learners should repeat the search to allow for both possibilities.

5   After selecting a few options (for example *to a large/great/significant/considerable extent)* learners Google each suggestion separately – still with inverted commas around the search phrase but without an asterisk – to see how frequent each one is. For example, *to a large extent* returned 10 million hits, followed by *to a great extent* with about 7.5 million. *To a significant extent* and *to a considerable extent* have about half a million occurrences each.

6   Pool learners' findings. After they have shared their results, put the best alternatives for all the 'bland' adjectives on the board – see suggested answers in Figure 8.15 below.

Academic article

Healthy diet defines, to a **big** extent, growth and development during childhood and adolescence, and plays an **important** role in promoting health and longevity in adulthood.

Research indicates that junk food has a **negative** effect on your health and increases the risk of developing certain diseases. It has also been shown that health problems caused by unhealthy diet, such as excess weight, heart problems and certain types of cancer, place a **big** burden on individuals, their families and society at large. Therefore, educating children on healthy eating is a matter of **great** importance.

Suggested replacements

to a great/large/considerable extent
plays a key/crucial/major/vital role
has an adverse/damaging/devastating effect
place a heavy/huge burden
a matter of the utmost / vital/public importance

Cover letter

Having worked for a number of leading IT companies, I have **a lot of** experience in project management with a **good** track record of delivering projects on time. I am highly skilled at establishing and maintaining **good** working relationships with customers and vendors. Therefore, I firmly believe that my qualifications, education and professional experience would make me a **good** candidate for the position, and that I can be a **great** asset to your company.

Suggested replacements

have extensive/vast / many years of experience
with a proven/solid track record
maintaining effective/strong/solid working relationships
make me a strong/perfect/suitable/prime candidate
be a major/valuable/tremendous asset to

Figure 8.15: Texts with bland adjectives and suggested replacements

Variation

The above searches can be also performed using corpus-lite tools such as Netspeak – see *Useful resources* on p. 227 and Activity 4.1 – or on a proper corpus. A search on COCA is done in a similar way to one on Google, with an asterisk * used as a wildcard, for example: [place] a * burden. Square brackets have been put around [place] to include all forms of the verb: *place, places, placed, placing*. See also Activity 1.5.

Rationale

Google is a very accessible and easy-to-use tool for quickly checking language intuitions. It is important, however, to relay to students that Google picks up everything that is out there on the web, including forum postings or blog posts written by learners of English which may contain mistakes. For a more rigorous analysis, their search can be limited to Google Books, which will result in fewer hits but of better quality.

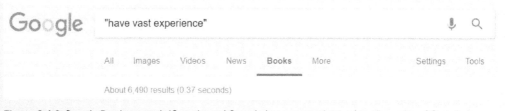

Figure 8.16: Google Books search (Google and Google logo are registered trademarks of Google Inc., used with permission.)

8.11 Live writing

Outline	Learners ask the teacher questions about a recent event, then use the teacher's lexically enriched responses to construct an account of the event.
Level	Intermediate and above (B1+)
Time	30–45 mins
Preparation	None

Procedure

1 Tell learners they are going to write a short report about a recent event in your life. Introduce the event, for example:

Last month I went abroad …
or
On Sunday I went to a party …

In order to find out the details of the event, students need to ask you questions in writing.

2 Divide the class into small groups. Give each group around ten slips of paper to write questions on. (It helps if each group has different coloured paper or pens.)

3 Each group decides on a question they want to ask, writes it on a slip of paper and sends a 'messenger' to deliver the question to the teacher. If the question is well-formed (and relevant), the teacher writes the answer on the back of the slip of paper including at least one chunk, for example:

(PARTY) *Did you go alone?* → No, I **brought a friend along.**
(TRIP ABROAD) *Did you like the food at the hotel?* → *Yes, the food was excellent but the service* **left a lot to be desired.**

4 The messenger then returns to the group where the answer is shared. A new question is formulated and delivered to the teacher. The process is repeated until the group has gathered enough information for their report. The report should be written in the third person and should contain all the chunks you have supplied.

5 If a question is not correctly formed, the teacher sends it back with some notes about how to improve it.

6 When the reports have been written, each group passes their text to the group on their right. The texts are read, and then passed on to the next group. Because the questions that each group asked will be different, each group's text will also be different.

7 Conduct feedback, asking students to comment on the most interesting/useful/unusual chunks.

Lexical Grammar

Variation

To help lower-level learners, you could write some key words and chunks related to the event on the board. These example chunks would be suitable for a story about a day on the beach:

towel   *my beach stuff*   *crowd*   *covered in sand*
                     sunscreen   *shoulders are still sore*

Note

This activity is adapted from an activity called 'Paper interviews' in *Teaching Unplugged: Dogme in English Language Teaching*, by Scott Thornbury and Luke Meddings (2009).

Rationale

This is similar to the two live listening activities in Chapter 3: the teacher deliberately 'plants' as many appropriate lexical chunks as possible and encourages learners to integrate the chunks into their production, in this case, their written work.

---

9 Adapting old classics

Shifting focus from vocabulary and grammar to lexical grammar doesn't have to involve a major upheaval in your teaching. Very often it comes down to changing the focus of your activities rather than how you run them. Many activities that are part of your classroom arsenal can be adapted or slightly modified to provide more focus on chunks. This chapter shows how some 'traditional' classroom activities can easily be given a lexico-grammatical twist.

9.1 Chunks as a way into a song activity

Outline	Learners listen to a song and tick the chunks they hear.
Level	Elementary and above (A2+)
Time	15 mins
Preparation	Choose a song and find the lyrics (there are many useful sites online for this such as genius.com or lyrics.com, or you can just look up the song in a search engine). Choose around ten chunks to focus on. Prepare a worksheet containing selected chunks and some distractors, i.e. chunks that could appear in the song (but don't), or chunks that sound similar to the chunks in the song, or chunks that contain some of the words from the song. See an example in Figure 9.1.

Procedure

1 Hand out the worksheet with the list of selected chunks and distractors from your chosen song – see *Preparation* and Figure 9.1.

2 Play the song. Learners listen and tick the chunks they hear.

3 Ask pairs to compare answers.

4 Go over the answers or hand out the complete lyrics. Play the song again so that learners can listen and read.

5 Conduct a comprehension check, discussion or any other activities you would normally use for teaching songs.

Follow-up

Students create a dialogue incorporating as many of the target chunks as possible. They can first rehearse the dialogue in pairs before acting out in front of the whole class. For example,

A: *She's very house-proud, that's why her house is always spotlessly clean.*
B: *House-proud? I'd say she's a neat freak!*

Note

This activity tends to work well with songs that tell a clear story or ones which describe people and relationships.

'Our House' by Madness

Listen to the song. Tick (✓) the expressions and phrases you hear.

wears his Sunday best   she needs a break   she needs a rest

a date to keep   can't stay long   can't hang around

there's always something happening   things always go wrong   warm and cosy

she's a neat freak   she's so house-proud   nothing ever slows her down

spotlessly clean   gets up late for work   sees them off with a small kiss

waves the boys goodbye   never a dull moment

such a good time   nothing would come between us   we'll never be apart

Answers

wears his Sunday best ✓   she needs a break   she needs a rest ✓

a date to keep ✓   can't stay long   can't hang around ✓

there's always something happening ✓   things always go wrong   warm and cosy

she's a neat freak   she's so house-proud ✓   nothing ever slows her down ✓

spotlessly clean   gets up late for work ✓   sees them off with a small kiss ✓

waves the boys goodbye   never a dull moment

such a good time   nothing would come between us ✓   we'll never be apart

Figure 9.1: Chunks from 'Our House' by Madness

Rationale

Pop songs are naturally rich in lexical chunks. Their inherent repetitiveness and, very often, catchiness make them prime candidates for chunk learning.

9.2 Find someone who

Outline	Learners mingle and use target chunks to find out about their classmates.
Level	Elementary and above (A2+)
Time	15 minutes
Preparation	Prepare a handout of statements describing people that learners need to find in class. Ensure that each statement contains a useful lexico-grammatical chunk – see examples in **bold** in Figure 9.2 below.

Procedure

1 Distribute the handout – see *Preparation* – and tell learners to look through the statements and ask you any questions they might have.

2 When you give a cue, learners get up and start mingling around the room and talking to classmates. When they find another learner who fits the statement in the list, they note down their name and move on to other learners.

3 Depending on the size of the class (and the number of statements) you may want to restrict the number of times learners can note down the same name.

4 You can also encourage students to ask follow-up questions, for example *What kind of coffee do you like? Instant or espresso?*

A2

Find someone who …
… **has been to** China.
… **has coffee** in the morning.
… **switches off their smartphone** when they **go to bed**.
… **was born in** a small town.
… **had their hair cut** last week.
… **is reading** an interesting book **at the moment**.

B1+

Find someone who …
… **is really looking forward to** a vacation.
… **gave someone a helping hand** recently.
… **makes do with** coffee for breakfast.
… **set out to be a doctor** but ended up doing something else.
… has had **to break bad news to** someone recently.
… has **been up to their ears** in work/studies.
… doesn't **make a fuss** when they have to wait for a long time.
… **talked some sense into** his/her friend recently.

Figure 9.2: Chunks for 'Find someone who'

Classroom management tip

You can use music as a signal for students. When the music starts playing, students should get out of their seats and start mingling.

Follow-up

When the mingling activity has finished, organize learners into small groups to share their finding with each other. Each group can then choose three or four of the most interesting facts about their classmates to report back to you and the other groups.

Rationale

Traditionally, sentences used in 'Find someone who' activities exemplify a particular structure, such as the present simple, in order to generate repetition of the target grammar. In this activity, statements are not restricted to a specific structure; instead, they contain common chunks.

9.3 Signatures

Outline	Learners mingle and use chunks *When did you last* and *It's been a long time since*, as well as common verb + noun collocations.
Level	Elementary and above (A2+)
Time	15–20 minutes
Preparation	Prepare a three-column handout containing statements starting with *It's been a long time since* in the left-hand column – see examples in Figure 9.3 below. The middle and right-hand columns should contain spaces for names and signatures.

Procedure

1 Distribute the handout containing *It's been a long time since* statements – see *Preparation*. Explain to learners that the aim of the activity is to collect as many signatures as they can.

2 Learners mingle and ask each other questions starting with *When did you last*. They complete each question with information from the handout, e.g. *When did you last eat soup? When did you last catch a cold?* (You can write the sentence starter on the board, if necessary.) Remind learners not to show each other their handouts – they can only exchange information orally.

3 When the questioner receives an answer about something that happened a long time ago, they write the responder's name in the middle column and ask them to sign the right-hand column. (It's up to questioners to decide exactly what 'a long time ago' means in this game.)

4 Learners are not allowed to ask someone any more questions once they have got their signature. Instead, they mingle and find somebody else to question, and so on. The idea is to talk to as many people as possible and collect signatures from as many different classmates as they can.

5 Stop the activity after one or two learners have completed the mission, i.e. they have got a signature for each statement.

6 Take feedback, asking learners in turn to report what they found out about their classmates. To do this, they have to say *It's been a long time since* [STUDENT'S NAME] *saw a good film*, then explain exactly when it was.

> **Classroom management tip**
>
> You can give these rules to learners before the mingling activity:
> ✓ Use English!
> ✓ Exchange information by speaking.
> ✗ Do not show each other your worksheets.
> ✓ Ask follow-up questions when you are talking to each other.
> ✗ Do not sign your name if you have not been asked a question!

A2/B1

It's been a long time since I …	Name	Signature
… saw a good film.	– – – – – – – – –	– – – – – – – – –
… saw my parents.	– – – – – – – – –	– – – – – – – – –
… went to the hairdresser's.	– – – – – – – – –	– – – – – – – – –
… went to the cinema.	– – – – – – – – –	– – – – – – – – –
… used a hammer.	– – – – – – – – –	– – – – – – – – –
… visited a museum.	– – – – – – – – –	– – – – – – – – –
… ate soup.	– – – – – – – – –	– – – – – – – – –
… drank cocoa.	– – – – – – – – –	– – – – – – – – –

B1/B2

It's been a long time since I …	Name	Signature
… broke a promise.	– – – – – – – – –	– – – – – – – – –
… had a good laugh.	– – – – – – – – –	– – – – – – – – –
… took a risk.	– – – – – – – – –	– – – – – – – – –
… felt out of my depth.	– – – – – – – – –	– – – – – – – – –
… made an offer.	– – – – – – – – –	– – – – – – – – –
… caught a cold.	– – – – – – – – –	– – – – – – – – –
… attended a wedding/funeral.	– – – – – – – – –	– – – – – – – – –
… put up a friend for the night.	– – – – – – – – –	– – – – – – – – –
… was stood up.	– – – – – – – – –	– – – – – – – – –

Figure 9.3: Questions for Signatures activity

Rationale

This is a variation on the popular classroom activity 'Find someone who' (see Activity 9.2), which I got to know during a drama workshop. I tweaked the focus to gives learners a lot of practice with the patterns *When did you last* and *It's been a long time since,* as well as a handful of verb + noun collocations.

9.4 Spiced-up role play

Outline	A role play is lexically enhanced to get learners to incorporate chunks into their speaking.
Level	Intermediate and above (B1+)
Time	15–20 minutes
Preparation	Choose a role play where each learner's role is written on a separate card. This can be from the resource book accompanying your coursebook or it can be any other role play that fits in with your lesson theme. Think about the chunks learners might need to achieve the communicative goals of the role play, then add a chunk to each role card – see examples in Figure 9.4. For higher levels or stronger learners, you can add more than one chunk.

Procedure

1 Hand out the adapted role cards for your selected role play – see *Preparation*.

2 Make sure learners understand the meaning and use of the chunks you added to their cards. Explain that they should say the chunks at least once during the activity.

3 When you give a cue, learners start the role play.

4 Monitor for appropriate use of the assigned chunks.

5 After the role play, ask students if they noticed their classmates using any interesting chunks of language. Elicit as many as learners can remember.

Chunks for a B2-level role play in *Business Roles* 2 by John Crowther-Alwyn	
President	I don't see how that would be feasible
	without compromising our quality/values/principles
Marketing Manager	keep turning a blind eye to the (figures / falling market share)
	we should be jumping at the opportunity
Head of Quality Control	it would spell disaster for
	that's just shooting ourselves in the foot
Production Manager	can I just come in here
	to maintain a competitive edge
Financial Director	I don't want to take the wind out of your sails but
	sorry, I'm afraid you lost us there
Sales Manager	just hear me out
	do you see what I'm getting at
Head of R&D	a disaster of epic proportions
	you can't get a word in edgeways in here

Figure 9.4: Role cards and chunks

Variations

1   Give each learner a role card with an 'obsession' on it – these can be anything from keeping fit, the Royal Family, star signs, types of chocolate, babies – the more varied and random the better. In groups of four, learners have a conversation about any topic but during the conversation each learner keeps trying to get their 'obsession' into the conversation as often as possible. They should use the chunks below, which you can pre-teach before the activity. After a few minutes, learners change groups and repeat the activity. Chunks to pre-teach:

That reminds me
Funny you should say that
By the way
Incidentally
Speaking of which
Did I mention that

2   Many other role plays can be lexically enriched by pre-teaching chunks. For example, for a role play involving an argument or discussion, you can pre-teach these ways of agreeing and disagreeing:

Absolutely!
I'm not sure I entirely agree.
You may be right, but

Allow students to choose one or two chunks each – preferably ones that they don't already use. They can write them on a piece of paper and when they manage to slip a chunk into their speech, they can turn the paper face down.

Rationale

Some role plays, such as the ones described in *Variations* above, naturally lend themselves to practising certain conversation gambits, e.g. agreeing, interrupting, etc. But chunk practice can be injected into almost any other role play by adding context-specific or role-specific chunks to role cards and thus adding a lexical component to oral fluency practice.

9.5 Matching words and definitions

Outline Learners review vocabulary by matching words with lexically enhanced definitions.
Level Elementary and above (A2+)
Time 15–20 mins
Preparation Prepare several set of cards – one set per small group of learners. Half the cards should contain words you've recently covered in class and the other half their definitions. Each definition should contain a gap for the target word and you should also highlight co-text (see *Glossary* on p. 223), i.e. collocations or grammatical patterns that go with the target word. See examples in Figure 9.5 below.

Procedure

1 Divide the class into groups. Give each group a set of cards – see *Preparation* – and ask them to match the target words and definitions.

2 Early finishers can be asked to turn over the word cards and recall the target words by looking at the definitions.

3 Go over the answers, elaborating on any tricky items. You can also ask learners to make example sentences with the target words (see Activity 9.7).

When you ask many people about their opinions on a topic, you **carry out a** _____.	**survey**
When something is important and necessary, for example a computer, it is an _____ **part of** our lives.	**essential**
When you're looking at the goods in a shop without wanting to buy anything particular, you're just _____ **around the shop**.	**browsing**
When someone receives a lot of public attention and interest, she **is in the** _____.	**spotlight**
When you change **a book** or **novel** in order to make a film, you _____ it.	**adapt**
When you start doing or using something **new**, for example **a method** or **habit**, you _____ it.	**adopt**
When the pain or injury you've had is very bad and serious, you **suffered a** _____ **injury** or **suffer from a** _____ **pain**.	**severe**
A computer, mobile phone and heart monitor are examples of **electronic** _____.	**devices**

Figure 9.5: Cards with definitions and highlighted co-text

Note

Avoid definitions which look too much like native-speaker dictionary entries (see *Rationale* below) such as:

conceal: prevent something from being seen; hide
essential: necessary, vital, basic
survey: an examination of people's opinions made by asking people questions

Learners' dictionaries like Cambridge Dictionary (dictionary.cambridge.org) are better sources of learner-friendly definitions and natural examples – see *Useful resources* on p. 227.

Notice how the example target words are not necessarily provided in the infinitive. Instead they expose learners to a variety of grammatical structures, for example the third person singular -*s* or the continuous form.

Follow-up

1 In a subsequent lesson, give out the definition cards without the target words. Ask learners to see how many target words they can recall.

2 For higher levels (B2+), you can give groups the word cards without the definitions. The cards should be face down in a stack in the middle of the table. Group members take turns to pick a card and give their own definition. They should not use the target word itself, but they should be encouraged to give collocations and examples. The group member who guesses the word first gets to keep the card. The winner is the learner with most cards at the end.

Rationale

Follow-up 2 often proves hard even for advanced level learners. This is because learners tend to give paradigmatic definitions (see *Glossary* on p. 223) by providing antonyms or synonyms, for example: *suffer for a long time, deal with something hard without complaining* (= *endure*). This makes the task of guessing quite daunting. It's generally easier to guess the target word when syntagmatic definitions are used, i.e. ones which contain words/structures that go with the target word, for example: *I couldn't _____ the pain any more so I went to the hospital* (= *endure*).

One way of making students switch from paradigmatic to syntagmatic definitions is to tell them to hum the target word, for example:

If you work in the same job for a long time, it pays you regular money and you don't need to worry about losing it, so you have a <u>hmm-mmm</u> job. (= *steady*)

9.6 Picture this

Outline	Learners draw pictures (or mime) to illustrate chunks.
Level	Upper intermediate and above (B2+)
Time	15–20 mins
Preparation	Prepare a set of cards containing chunks which learners have studied in class and/or which have come up in a reading/listening text. Use the template in Figure 9.6 below to create the cards. Each card should have four or five kinds of chunks: a verb + noun collocation, an adjective + noun collocation and two or three other categories of your choice. Possibilities include: idioms related to a specific theme (e.g. animals, the body); similes; expressions about time; personality adjectives; phrasal verbs with *up*, etc.

Procedure

1 Lay the stack of cards on the table face down. Learners, in turn, come to the front of the class and pick up a card from the stack. They choose a chunk from one of the categories and tell the class which category it is (verb + noun collocation, animal idiom, etc.)

2 The learner then draws a picture on the board representing the chunk. (Alternatively, you can allow learners to choose between drawing and miming the chunk. This way the activity will not unfairly favour more artistically inclined learners.) Classmates call out answers.

3 When learners have gone through the whole pack of cards, start going through the pack again. Learners cannot draw or mime an item on the card that has already been defined and guessed, so it's a good idea to cross out items that have been mimed or drawn.

Variations

1 Organize the class into teams. A member of each team comes to the front and you show all of them a card at the same time, pointing to a specific chunk/category. Members rush back to their team and draw the chunk. The first team to come up with the correct answer gets a point. The game continues with different team members taking turns to go to the front of the class.

2 Rather than having separate categories on the cards, you can embed the options into a constant sentence frame, and perhaps answer a question, such as *How does Nancy feel today?* The options can all fit the frame *She feels*:

> *She feels ...*
>
> *under the weather*
> *down in the dumps*
> *on top of the world*
> *on cloud nine*
> *over the moon*

Note

When it comes to idioms, it is, of course, much easier to illustrate their literal meaning. For example, draw a black horse for *she's a bit of a dark horse*, rather than trying to draw a person who looks secretive.

Some of the items may be very tricky to draw but that is all part of the fun! Because the items are not new to learners, even the simplest drawings or mimes will help learners recall the chunks.

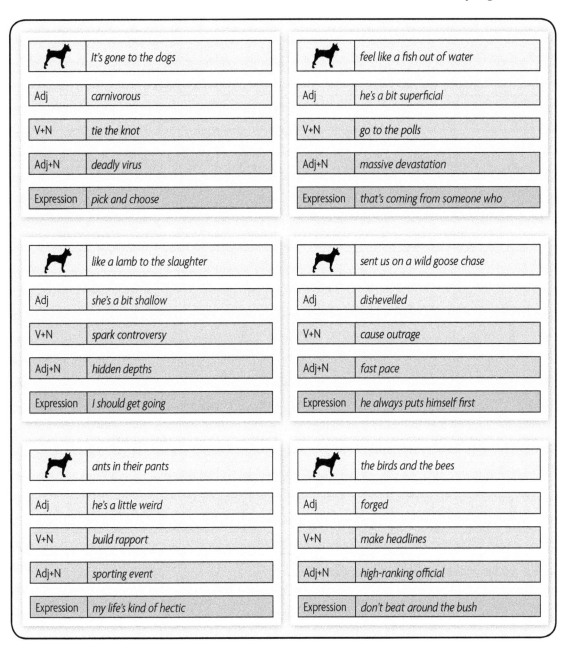

Figure 9.6: Cards and categories for drawing game – Set 1

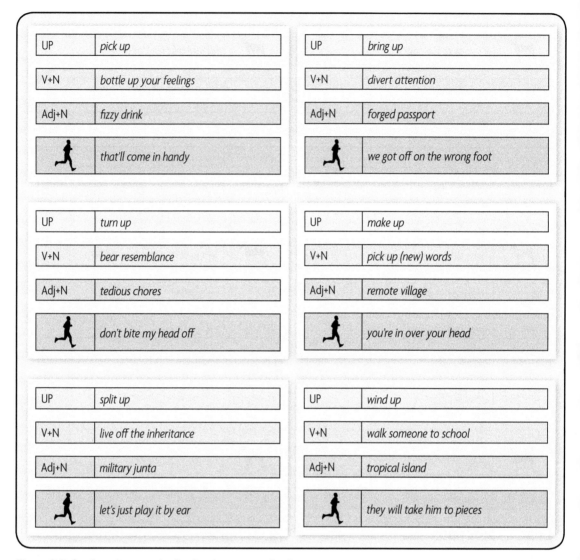

UP	pick up
V+N	bottle up your feelings
Adj+N	fizzy drink
🏃	that'll come in handy

UP	bring up
V+N	divert attention
Adj+N	forged passport
🏃	we got off on the wrong foot

UP	turn up
V+N	bear resemblance
Adj+N	tedious chores
🏃	don't bite my head off

UP	make up
V+N	pick up (new) words
Adj+N	remote village
🏃	you're in over your head

UP	split up
V+N	live off the inheritance
Adj+N	military junta
🏃	let's just play it by ear

UP	wind up
V+N	walk someone to school
Adj+N	tropical island
🏃	they will take him to pieces

Figure 9.7: Cards and categories for drawing game – Set 2

Rationale

The activity is inspired by Pictionary™, a guessing game where players do drawings to help teammates guess words. The game has been adapted to focus on chunks.

9.7 Two sentence contextualization

Outline	Learners contextualize new vocabulary by writing two sentences with a new word.
Level	Pre-intermediate and above (B1+)
Time	Variable
Preparation	None

Procedure

1 Whenever a vocabulary exercise in a coursebook calls for writing example sentences with new words, ask learners to write TWO example sentences. One sentence should include the target word and the other should provide additional context.

2 Do one or two examples with learners such as:

couch potato
*All he does is sit in front of TV all day and eat chips. He is a real **couch potato**.*
(The first sentence provides context; the second uses the target item.)

arrange (to do something)
*We **arranged** to meet at 3pm but she cancelled. It's not easy to make plans with her.*
(The first sentence uses the target item; the second provides additional context.)

Note
This activity is particularly suitable for adjectives. Adding an extra sentence which elaborates on the target word will enable teachers to check learners' understanding, for example:

remote
Single sentence: *It's a remote place.*
Two sentences: *It's a remote place. It takes a long time to get there.*

Rationale
Getting students to make a sentence with a new word is a common way of practising new vocabulary. In this activity, learners are asked to make TWO sentences, which encourages more linguistic output and shifts the focus from pure vocabulary practice to vocabulary + grammar + discourse practice.

9.8 Classroom language posters

Procedure

1 Remove the poster from the wall.

2 Write up some of the chunks from the poster on the board. Categorize the chunks according to their patterns, for example:

Can you repeat that, please? Can you play it again, please?	How do you say ... in English? How do you spell it?
May I come in? May I get some water?	I don't understand.

3 Elicit what each group of chunks has in common. In the examples above:
Can you ...? = request
May I ...? = asking for permission
How do you ...? = general questions

4 Ask learners to add one or two more examples to each category, for example:

Can you repeat that, please? Can you play it again, please? **Can you help me?**	How do you say ... in English? How do you spell it? **How do you pronounce this word?**
May I come in? May I get some water? **May I go to the toilet?**	I don't understand. **I don't know.** **I don't have a pen.**

5 Erase the first two or three words from each pattern and ask learners to complete them. (This can be done in the following lesson.)

_____ repeat that, please? _____ play it again, please? help me?	_____ say ... in English? _____ spell it? pronounce this word?
_____ come in? _____ get some water? go to the toilet?	understand _____ know have a pen.

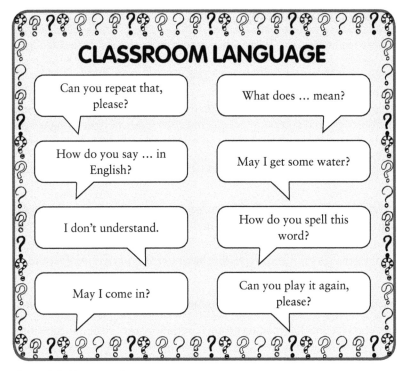

Figure 9.8: Classroom language poster

Variation

Instead of Step 2, give learners the phrases from the poster on separate cards. Learners can sort them into patterns themselves.

Follow-up

Divide the class into four groups and assign one of the target patterns to each group. Groups work together to create a new classroom language poster. Provide the patterns only; students have to recall the rest of the chunks themselves.

 Classroom management tip

For larger classes, divide the class into eight groups with each pattern assigned to two groups. The activity can then be turned into a competition – the best poster gets to be hung up on the wall (or you can hang both posters on different walls).

Rationale

If learners are encouraged to use the language from classroom posters, they will memorize many expressions without focusing on form. This is in line with one of the main principles of this book: memorization precedes analysis. When a few prototypical expressions have been committed to memory, you can move on to unpacking the chunks, extracting the pattern and extending it to other items.

9.9 Thinking synonymously

Outline	As a post-reading activity, learners find synonymous chunks for the highlighted chunks in a text.
Level	Upper intermediate and above (B2+)
Time	15 minutes
Preparation	Use a text in your coursebook or an online article. Some short easily exploitable texts can be found on https://tinytexts.wordpress.com or https://breakingnewsenglish.com
	Underline or highlight the chunks you want learners to find synonyms for – see examples in Figure 9.9 below.

Procedure

1   After reading the text, tell learners to find synonyms for – or paraphrase – the highlighted chunks. Clarify that learners should use multi-word synonyms (i.e. synonyms of chunks rather than synonyms of individual words). With longer chunks (three or more words), learners can keep some of the original words (in the example text below, *ground-breaking TV drama* → *cutting edge TV series*).

2   Allow learners around five minutes to discuss possibilities in groups before taking feedback.

3   Conduct whole-class feedback by asking groups for their paraphrasing suggestions. Board the best ones.

Note

Since the aim of the activity is to replace whole chunks with their alternatives rather than finding synonyms for individual words, it is better to use the word 'paraphrase' when giving instructions, or simply say 'find another way of saying the same thing'.

Review of 'Breaking Bad'

'Breaking Bad' is a ground-breaking TV drama about a terminally ill chemistry teacher who turns to crime in order to cover his medical expenses and provide a nest egg for his family. Throughout its run, the series received wide critical acclaim and numerous awards. The lead actor, Bill Cranston, won three consecutive Emmy Awards for his portrayal of the meek school teacher who slowly evolves into a notorious criminal. After five successful seasons, the series drew to a close in September 2013.

Possible paraphrasing

ground-breaking TV drama = cutting edge TV series
turns to crime = becomes a criminal
cover his medical expenses = pay for his hospital bills
provide a nest egg = save money for a rainy day
received wide critical acclaim = was met with praise by critics
won three consecutive Emmy Awards = received three Emmy Awards in a row
drew to a close = came to an end

Figure 9.9: Text with highlighted chunks and paraphrasing

Classroom management tip

This works well as a digital activity. If learners work with computers and the text is supplied as a digital file, they can use their computer's thesaurus feature to look up synonyms. The thesaurus will yield several suggestions. To choose the best one, learners can look them up in an online learners' dictionary to check their use or find the most appropriate collocation(s) – see *Useful resources* on p. 227.

Follow-up

In a subsequent lesson, write up some of the paraphrased chunks on the board. Ask learners to try and remember what the original corresponding chunks were:

save money for a rainy day = provide a nest egg

Rationale

Many post-reading activities in coursebooks focus on finding single-word synonyms for the words in a text. This activity shifts focus from synonymous words to synonymous chunks.

9.10 From word box to chunk box

Outline	Many teachers keep a 'word box' (or 'word bag') in their classrooms, where new words are written on small cards and added to the box at the end of each lesson. In this activity, learners keep and use a 'chunk box'.
Level	Any
Time	15 minutes
Preparation	You will need a small box and a lot of small pieces of card or paper.

Procedure

1 Whenever a new chunk comes up in class, write it on a card and put it inside the box – see *Preparation*. Alternatively, this can be done by learners: different members of the class can be assigned the task of copying chunks from the board or coursebook at the end of each lesson.

2 Whenever time permits – at the end of a lesson or any time during it – use the day's chunks as the basis for a quick review activity. For example, learners can be asked to translate the chunks or use them in a sentence (or in two sentences – see Activity 9.7: *Two sentence contextualization*).

3 When you have accumulated a large number of chunks – for example, after a few weeks or towards the end of a course – put learners into pairs or groups and give each pair/group a stack of cards. Do one of the following activities:

- **Sorting:** Groups go through their cards and sort them into at least three categories of their choice. Then they explain their choice of categories to the other groups. Possible categories:

    Fridge – I'll be able to use this chunk in my day to day life.
    Freezer – I don't need to use this chunk, but I'll save it for when I do.
    Dustbin – I don't think I'll ever need to use this chunk.

    ✓ – I understand and know how to use it.
    ? – I understand it but not sure how/when I can use it.
    ✗ – I don't understand it.

    Our favourite useful chunks
    Our favourite difficult chunks
    Our favourite fun chunks

- **Creating a context:** Groups work with around five chunks. They write a dialogue which uses all of the items they have picked. Dialogues are then performed or read out to the other groups. Listeners can guess which chunks the speakers had on their cards.

- **Peer-testing:** Cards are placed in the middle face down. Group members take turns picking up the cards and giving their own definitions. Other group members guess and keep the card if they say the chunk correctly (this is similar to Activity 9.5: *Matching words and definitions*).

Variation

You/Learners can record the chunks on the cards in more detailed ways, for example:

1   Use a classic flashcard format, with the target item on one side and its translation into L1 (for monolingual classes) or a definition on the other side.
2   Put just the key word of the chunk on one side and collocations and/or a sample sentence on the other. This format works well with partially known chunks, i.e. when learners know the meaning of the key word but need to work on their depth of knowledge.
3   Put just the key word from the chunk on one side and the rest of the chunk with the key word gapped out on the back.

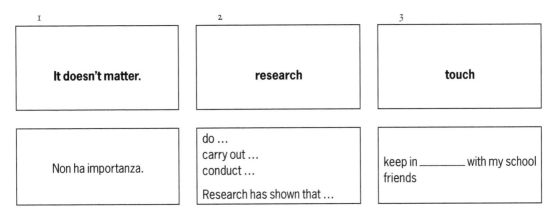

Note

It might take some time before you accumulate enough chunks to do the activities in Step 3. Periodically, you should clear the box of chunks that no longer need recycling.
This activity is adapted from an activity called 'Word bag' in *Memory Activities*, by Nick Bilbrough (2011).

Rationale

The choice of format for your chunk cards will depend on your context: whether you're teaching a monolingual or multilingual class, whether you can speak and write the learners' L1, and the level of learners. Whatever format you choose, it might be a good idea to discuss with the class the importance of recording and revising new/useful language before embarking on the 'chunk box' project.

9.11 Turn word clouds into chunk clouds

Outline	Learners look at a word cloud containing chunks from a reading text and use it to predict the content and themes of the text.
Level	Elementary and above (A2+)
Time	15 minutes
Preparation	Choose a reading text in a digital format, for example an article on the internet. Paste the text into a word processing document and identify useful chunks. Use the tilde key (~) to keep the words in each chunk together like this: *reserve~a~table*. While editing the text, you might also want to eliminate any words which you don't want to appear in the word cloud. You can also repeat some key words or chunks that are particularly important – this will make them bigger in the word cloud.
	When you have finished editing, paste the text into a word cloud generator to make your word cloud – see Figure 9.10 and *Note* below. After it's generated, you can still tweak your word cloud by eliminating words, connecting them with tilde keys or repeating the most useful chunks for impact.

Procedure

1 Display your word cloud – see *Preparation* – or provide it as a handout.

2 If your learners have never seen word clouds, explain that the words and chunks in the cloud are all taken from a text. Bigger words/chunks indicate higher frequency in the text. Ask students to predict in pairs what the text is about.

3 Do feedback with the whole group. Have learners identified similar themes? Can they guess what the reading text title might be?

4 Proceed with reading activities as you would normally do.

Note

A word cloud is an image composed of words (or in this activity, chunks) from a particular text, in which prominence is given to the most frequent words. There are several online word cloud generators, most of which allow you to change the font, layout and colour schemes. You can also duplicate certain words/chunks to make them more prominent in the cloud. In the example cloud, *parents* and *babysitting* were added a couple of extra times to the original text to increase their frequency and make them bigger. It's also possible to use the edit function to ignore certain words. Some generators do not distinguish between capital letters (e.g. *parents* and *Parents*) so the same word might appear twice. It is advisable to save a copy of your original text and the resulting word cloud in a new document as most generators do not keep copies.

Not all word cloud generators support the tilde key (~). Among the ones that do are:
https://worditout.com – This site allows you to easily eliminate words you don't want to appear in the word cloud, but all the words/chunks can only be displayed horizontally.
www.wordclouds.com – There are lots of different options and more control over the shape, size and colour scheme of the word cloud.

The author learned how to turn word clouds into chunk clouds from Hanna Kryszewska, who attributes the idea to Jamie Keddie.

We use apps to order~taxis, reserve~a~room in a hotel or book~flights. But some things must be too important to seek~online, surely? It seems not. These days, many parents are turning~to~the~internet to find~a~babysitter.

Word~of~mouth and notices in community~centres are~being~replaced~by babysitting~apps such as CitySitters or Rockababy, and business~is~booming. The~number~of~people using CitySitters has~grown~by~60% in the last three years.

Bookings are more flexible than ever and can be made with~just~an~hour's~notice. Parents put~in~a~request, the app notifies nearby babysitters and the booking can be confirmed in~a~ matter~of~minutes.

Apps are particularly~popular for late-night requests, but early~morning sitters for parents who want to have~a~lie-in~at~the~weekend are also on~the~up.

Figure 9.10: Reading text with tilde symbols, and corresponding word cloud (generated by worditout.com)

Variations

1 Use only the first paragraph of a reading text to create a word cloud. Get the class to predict the text content from the word cloud.
2 (Learners will need computers with internet access.) Organize the class into groups. Hand out different paragraphs of the text to different groups. Each group creates a word cloud for their paragraph. Explain how parts of chunks can be connected using the tilde key (~) – see *Preparation* – and encourage groups to identify as many chunks as they can. Groups swap their word clouds and predict what each paragraph is about.

Rationale

When learners think of vocabulary of a foreign language, often they think of single words. After all, dictionary entries traditionally consist of single words (although modern learners' dictionaries do also feature chunks as part of the entries – see *Useful resources* on p. 227). This reinforces a belief that single words are what matter most in language learning. However, as you have seen from this and other activities in this chapter, it is relatively easy to shift the focus from individual words to whole chunks of language. This shift shows learners that, for the most part, meaning originates not in words themselves but in the chunks in which the words are found.

10 Loving language

The capacity to appreciate the complexity and subtlety of a language and differences between English and learners' L1 is important from the early stages of language learning. Needless to say, this ability is also a powerful motivator for many language learners. This final chapter includes activities which allow learners to 'play' with language – mainly (but not only) with chunks.

   Some of the activities can be used for introducing new language items, for example 10.4: *Binomials*. Others, such 10.1: *Spoonerisms* and 10.2: *That doesn't sound quite right*, assume that students have already encountered the chunks in focus. What all activities in this chapter have in common is that they seek to make learners aware of the intricacies of the language and to help them appreciate that English may use different linguistic means than L1 to express the same ideas. Although learners may like the safety of rules and the comfort of logic, learning a language is a journey into the unknown – and often into the seemingly illogical! As Michael Lewis (1993) memorably put it, language is an organism, not a mechanism; therefore many things simply cannot be explained because … that's just the way they are!

10.1 Spoonerisms

Outline	The teacher deliberately swaps round the first letter(s) of two words in a chunk. Learners correct the teacher's slips of the tongue.
Level	Upper intermediate and above (B2+)
Time	5–6 minutes
Preparation	Prepare a list of chunks learners have already practised or been exposed to, for example in a reading or listening activity. The activity won't work with every chunk – see some suggestions below.

Procedure

1 Say your chosen sentences – see *Preparation* – at a natural speed, swapping round the first letter(s) of two words in each chunk. Here are some example sentences with deliberate slips:

   a *He didn't study enough, so no wonder he **tailed his fest**. (failed his test)*
   b *I like yoga. I do it on a **baily dasis**. (on a daily basis)*
   c *You're all sweaty. Go and **shake a tower**. (take a shower)*
   d *What are you talking about?! I'm just **shout of the hour**. (out of the shower)*
   e *Take some tissue and **know your blows**. (blow your nose)*
   f *He never says 'Thank you' or 'Sorry'. He has very **mad banners**. (bad manners)*
   g *There was nothing interesting on TV so I was just **chipping through flannels**. (flipping through channels)*
   h *Have you **flopped the moor**? (mopped the floor)*
   i *Before we make a decision we need to weigh all the **cos and prons**. (pros and cons)*
   j *We've searched every **crook and nanny**. (nook and cranny)*

2 Learners correct your slips, either by shouting out the correct chunk or noting it down and then comparing answers with partners.

3 Discuss with students whether they have heard any funny spoonerisms in English or their own language.

Note

A spoonerism is a slip of the tongue in which a speaker accidentally switches the initial sounds (phonemes) of two words in a phrase, as in *You have hissed all my mystery lectures* (*You have missed all my history lectures*). This can be done deliberately to create a humorous effect, as in this activity.

Rationale

Spoonerisms and other verbal blunders are very local in nature, in that they occur within a span of two or three words. In other words, spoonerisms invariably occur inside lexical chunks. In a way, the existence of spoonerisms is further proof that speakers build sentences chunk by chunk rather than on a word-by-word basis.

10.2 That doesn't sound quite right

Outline	Learners identify the wrong words in familiar chunks.
Level	Intermediate and above (B1+)
Time	5–6 minutes
Preparation	Prepare a list of chunks students have already practised or been exposed to. Change one word to introduce a deliberate error into each chunk – see examples below.

Procedure

1　Write your selected chunks with wrong words on the board – see *Preparation*. Here are some examples:

B1

it's up with you	*(it's up TO you)*
every now and that	*(every now and THEN)*
I'm short with money	*(I'm short OF money)*
bear on mind	*(bear IN mind)*
What's up to you?	*(What's up WITH you?)*

B2

once in a black moon	*(once in a BLUE moon)*
more trouble than it's worse	*(more trouble than it's WORTH)*
leaves a lot to do desired	*(leaves a lot to BE desired)*
won't get no for an answer	*(won't TAKE no for an answer)*
to make matters worth	*(to make matters WORSE)*
for years to go	*(for years to COME)*

2　Ask learners to work in pairs to identify a mistake in each chunk.

3　Take feedback with the whole class.

Variation
The activity can also include grammatical mistakes, for example wrong auxiliaries or mistakes with subject–verb agreement:

<u>Do</u> you sure?
It <u>isn't</u> make sense.
I haven't seen him <u>since</u> ages.
<u>I'm agree</u> with you.
I look forward <u>to see</u> you.

Follow-up
Point out that sometimes replacing a word in a chunk would not be considered a mistake. In fact, many proficient speakers take 'poetic licence' with chunks and use them creatively, often for humorous effect. Give the following examples to learners, asking them to figure out what the original chunk was, i.e. which word was replaced:

Let's call it a night. (Let's call it a day.)
come rain or thunder (come rain or shine)
pour money down the toilet (pour money down the drain)
I'm up to my nose with work. (I'm up to my ears/eyes with work.)
You're making a mountain out of an anthill. (You're making a mountain out of a molehill.)

Rationale
The activity is aimed at 'fine-tuning' lexical chunks that learners are familiar with but have not yet fully mastered or committed to memory. Encouraging and actively helping learners to memorize lexical chunks promotes both fluency and accuracy; it enables learners to retrieve whole chunks as single units and produce them accurately. Research shows that learners who explicitly learn lexical chunks come across as more proficient.

10.3 Schlub dub

Outline Learners choose a chunk and repeat it each time they hear a cue from the teacher.
Level Elementary and above (A2+)
Time Whole lesson
Preparation Prepare a list of chunks that have recently come up in class or that contain target grammar structures you have recently covered in class. Display the list on the board. There should be slightly more chunks in the list than the number of learners in the class, i.e. if you have 12 students, provide 14–15 chunks; if you have 30 students, provide 32–33 chunks. See some example chunks in Figure 10.1 below.

Procedure

1 At the beginning of a lesson, call out learners' names followed by the nonsense phrase *schlub dub* (pronounced /ʃlʌb dʌb/). This can be done as you take attendance, for example. Upon hearing their name followed by *schlub dub*, each student should 'adopt' a chunk from the board – see *Preparation* – and say it aloud.

2 To hold learners' attention (and keep the game fun), you can occasionally call out students who have already adopted a chunk. Upon hearing their name followed by *schlub dub*, they should recite their chunk.

3 Cross out the chunks which have been adopted as you go along. Continue until all the chunks have been chosen, focusing on pronunciation as necessary. After that, erase the chunks or hide them from view.

4 Throughout the lesson, add *schlub dub* occasionally when addressing learners. Each time a learner hears their name followed by *schlub dub* they should respond with their chunk.

5 You can also reverse the order by occasionally saying the chunk yourself, followed by *schlub dub*, in which case learners should shout out their name.

I haven't seen him for ages.	He runs his own business.
How long have you been doing this?	I wouldn't recommend it.
Are you done packing?	I agree to a certain extent.
It doesn't matter.	The problem cannot be solved.
It's been almost an hour.	densely populated area
What does it mean?	It's not as hard as it sounds.
What's it supposed to mean?	Now we can sigh with relief.
Have you been to the USA?	cut down on sugar
I didn't find it funny.	Global temperatures have risen since the 1980s.
It leaves a lot to be desired.	The car is the main means of transport.
showed an upward trend	I got you a present.
It's become a thing of the past.	Mind if I look around?

Figure 10.1: Example chunks for *Schlub dub* (level B1/B2)

Note

Depending on the length of the lesson (and the size of the class), you may choose to extend the activity to a series of lessons.

The author was introduced to the single-word version of this activity by Jenny Gordon.

 Classroom management tip

When you select learners to adopt a chunk, start with weaker / less able pupils, who are likely to opt for easier, shorter or more familiar chunks. More challenging chunks will then be left for stronger / more able students to adopt.

Rationale

This fun activity helps learners to review and memorize chunks. It's also a very useful classroom management tool.

10.4 Binomials

Outline	The activity raises awareness of binomial expressions (see *Glossary* on p. 223) such as *dead or alive*, *give and take* and *law and order*.
Level	Upper intermediate and above (B2+)
Time	Variable
Preparation	Create several sets of cards containing halves of binomial chunks – see Figure 10.2 below. Keep the Group A cards and the Group B cards separate. You will need one full set of cards (Group A and B) for approximately every eight learners.

Procedure

1 Write *fish and chips* on the board and point out that the order of the expression cannot be changed (i.e. we can't say *chips and fish*) and that the nouns are connected with the conjunction *and* (not *with*, as may be the case in other languages).

2 Ask learners if they can think of similar expressions in English (you don't have to introduce the term 'binomial'). Elicit *salt and pepper* or *bed and breakfast*.

3 Divide the class into A and B groups, with around four people in each group (make sure you have an even number of groups). Give each Group A a set of the Group A cards and give each Group B a set of the Group B cards – see *Preparation* and Figure 10.2.

4 Ask groups to match their binomial halves. They should put the halves next to each other – and not, for example, on top of each other – so that all words are visible. This way you can monitor and see if they've matched correctly (and it will be necessary for the next step).

5 Ask all A and B groups to exchange places so they can check each other's sets/matchings. Clarify any difficult items.

Group A		Group B	
back and	forth	bigger and	better
blood and	guts	cut and	dried
cut and	paste	dead or	alive
fish and	chips	forgive and	forget
heads or	tails	kiss and	make up
law and	order	loud and	clear
lost and	found	nip and	tuck
now or	never	null and	void
odds and	ends	rise and	shine
sooner or	later	spick and	span
sticks and	stones	toss and	turn

Figure 10.2: Binomial cards

Note

Over 20 binomial pairs may seem too much for one lesson. However, only a handful of these will be genuinely new items: your learners will probably know some of these and will no doubt know the individual words comprising most of them. If you think it's still too many items for one lesson, remove six and give each group eight pairs.

Follow-up

1 To provide contextualized practice, use sentences like the ones below. Note that some expressions in the sentences don't appear in the matching activity. Learners can look up any pairs they don't know using Netspeak (see Activity 4.1: *Are you primed for this?*) or Cambridge Dictionary Online (see *Useful resources* on p. 227), which has an autocomplete function, i.e. if they type *give or* the dictionary will suggest *take*.

   a *This activity should take you three minutes, **give or** _____.* (*take*)
   b *When he's bored he'll start running **back and** _____ along the fence.* (*forth*)
   c *Paul and Nicole often have arguments, but they always **kiss and** _____.* (*make up*)
   d *The government had to call in military forces to maintain **law and** _____.* (*order*)
   e *That actor looks so different – clearly he's had a bit of a **nip and** _____.* (*tuck*)
   f *Sleepless nights and dirty nappies are **part and** _____ of being a parent.* (*parcel*)
   g *We're looking forward to some **peace and** _____ in the countryside after the **hustle and** _____ of the city.* (*quiet, bustle*)
   h *After four hours of cleaning, my house was **spick and** _____ and ready for my mum's arrival.* (*span*)
   i *Grammar rules in English are not as **cut and** _____ as grammar books would have you believe.* (*dried*)

2 To encourage active recall, you can provide sentences like these where the binomial pair has been paraphrased. Get learners to replace the parts in bold with a binomial expression.

   *This activity should take you **approximately** three minutes.* (*more or less*)
   *That actor looks so different – clearly he's had a bit of **plastic surgery**.* (*nip and tuck*)
   *Sleepless nights and dirty nappies are **an essential component** of being a parent.* (*part and parcel*)
   *After four hours of cleaning, my house was **spotless** and ready for my mum's arrival.* (*spick and span*)
   *Grammar rules are not as **clearly defined** as grammar books would have you believe.* (*cut and dried*)

Rationale

Contrary to what some may believe, binomials are not sophisticated expressions that should be reserved for higher levels. Pre-intermediate learners come across such binomials as *sick and tired*, *back and forth* and *ups and downs* relatively early on. Therefore, binomials deserve attention in the classroom from the earliest stages, like many other chunks.

10.5 Alliterative chunks

Outline	The activity draws attention to alliteration (see *Glossary* on p. 223), a common phenomenon in chunks in English.
Level	Any (the example is at B2 level)
Time	6–7 minutes
Preparation	Prepare a handout containing several gapped alliterative chunks – see examples in Figure 10.3 below.

Procedure

1   Elicit a few alliterative chunks by using oral prompts like the ones below. Tell learners that each target chunk consists of two or three words containing repetition of the same sound (the /b/ sound, in the examples below). Oral prompts:

A large increase in the birth rate after the Second World War (*baby boom*)
A sad feeling some people have after giving birth (*baby blues*)
A small hotel where you can have a room and a meal in the morning (*bed and breakfast*)
Someone who spends all their time on the sea shore (*beach bum*)
A large explosion which some believe created the universe (*the Big Bang*)
An underground section in a shop where things are sold at reduced prices (*bargain basement*)
A well-known London landmark with a clock (*Big Ben*)

(For lower-level learners or less familiar chunks, you could give the first word of each chunk, for example you say *The Big* and learners respond with *Bang*.)

2   Point out that English has a lot of alliterative chunks like this, which makes for catchy and memorable expressions. Ask if the learners' own languages have a similar phenomenon. Clarify that very often, word choice in a relatively fixed chunk in English is determined by alliteration. For example, we eat *fast food* and not *quick food* and stay in a hotel on *bed and breakfast* terms, not *room and breakfast*.

3   Elicit whether learners can recall any other alliterative phrases like this.

4   Provide your handout – see *Preparation* and Figure 10.3. Ask learners to complete the missing words starting with the given letters.

5   Tell learners to check answers in pairs, then do feedback with the whole group. Elicit a possible context for each sentence. Answers for sentences in Figure 10.3:
a) *finding my feet*, b) *prim and proper*, c) *unwilling or unable*, d) *bite the bullet*, e) *fish to fry*,
f) *sob story*, g) *beat around the bush*, h) *rave reviews*

---

a I'm new to this job so I'm still finding my f_____.

b Everything has to be by the book with him. He's so prim and pr_____.

c I asked her to help me with the move but she was unwilling or un_____.

d I hate going to the dentist but I suppose I just have to bite the b_____.

e Sorry, I can't drop everything and help you. I have other fish to f_____.

f She told me something about her father losing his job and her mother being ill, but I think it was just another s_____ story.

g You want me to lend you money? Just say so and don't beat around the b_____.

h His latest film has got rave r_____ in the media. Some critics have gone as far as to say that this is the best film of his career.

Figure 10.3: Alliterative chunks gapfill

Note

Notice that the gaps tend to occur towards the end of the sentences. This is much easier than having a sentence start with a gap before the learner has been given any (contextual) clues about the target item. Placing the gap as close to the end as possible provides context (and co-text), which arguably activates schema and aids recall. This process also corresponds with a phenomenon encountered in everyday conversation: people often complete each other's sentences by volunteering the last word, not one at the beginning or in the middle!

The activity can be combined with or done after Activity 10.4: *Binomials*, as many binomial pairs have alliterative patterns. In fact, almost 30% of English binomials alliterate (as in *part and parcel*, *spick and span*) or rhyme (as in *hustle and bustle*) (Boers & Lindstromberg, 2005).

Follow-up

1 In a subsequent lesson, provide the same sentences on the board but with both target words blanked out. Learners try to recall the chunks. Leave the first letter(s) as a clue, as follows:
I'm new to this job so I'm still f_____ my f_____.
Everything has to be by the book with him. He's so pr_____ and pr_____.

Alternatively, provide just the first letter(s) (without context) as follows:
f_____ my f_____
pr_____ and pr_____

Learners recall the chunk and make their own sentences with them.

2 Bring a copy of a historic speech to class (for example the US President John F. Kennedy's inaugural speech, which can be found here: www.bartleby.com/124). Ask learners to identify examples of alliteration (there are 21 examples in Kennedy's speech).

Variation

Every time an alliterative chunk comes up in class, draw attention to the pattern by highlighting the repeated sounds. (Note that it's the sound repetition that constitutes alliteration, so *short and sweet* is not really an alliteration because the words start with different sounds: /ʃ/ and /s/.)

Alternatively, suggest that learners create their own alliterative chunks as mnemonics to help them remember new words (see *Glossary* on p. 223). Bear in mind that all other words in their mnemonics should be known. Here are suggested alliterations, with target words (i.e. the words to be learned) in **bold**.

A2	B1/B2	B2/C1
a **can** of coke	**fossil** fuels	**tuck in** your t-shirt
broke up with her boyfriend	**cure** for cancer	**seek** a solution / settlement
attract a lot of attention	hot and **humid**	food **fads**
drowning in **debt**	**spectacular** special effects	sit and **sulk**
cover their **costs**	certain **circumstances**	tourist **tat**
accompanied by an adult	**fascinating** facts/film	feeling **faint**
noisy neighbours	my cat **cuddled** up to me	**close-knit** community
turn on the TV	**gadget** geek	on the **brink** of bankruptcy
school **subject**	dark and **dimly lit** alley	**brag** about her bracelets / his baby
borrow money from the bank	scared **stiff**	**dutiful** daughter
	comprehensive car insurance is **compulsory**	
	soft furnishings: carpet, curtains, **cushions**	

Figure 10.4: Alliterative chunks used as mnemonics

Rationale

Research shows that learners retain more easily chunks that exhibit an alliterative pattern, so deliberately draw learners' attention to these. If students are encouraged to notice alliteration in chunks, it can also help them avoid errors, for example *make a mistake* (not *do*).

10.6 Seemingly easy verbs

Outline	Learners revisit a delexicalized verb and learn new meanings.
Level	Upper intermediate and above (B2+)
Time	15 minutes
Preparation	Find a dictionary entry (online or paper) for one of the delexicalized verbs such as *get*, *put*, *take* (see *Glossary* on p. 223). Choose around ten example sentences, making sure learners are familiar with all (or most of) the words in them. Create a document containing the example sentences with the target word gapped in each case – see an example for *put* in Step 1 below.

Procedure

1 Display or distribute your gapped example sentences – see *Preparation*. Below are some examples for *put*. Tell learners the same verb is missing from all the sentences.

   a *He _____ salt into the sugar bowl by mistake.*
   b *_____ your address in the top right-hand corner.*
   c *Where have you _____ the keys?*
   d *They've got to _____ an end to their fighting.*
   e *She wanted to tell him the relationship was over, but she didn't know how to _____ it.*
   f *I _____ my arm around him to comfort him.*
   g *Are you prepared to _____ your children at risk?*
   h *This _____s me in a very difficult position.*
   i *What has _____ you in such a bad mood?*
   j *He's _____ting pressure on me to change my mind.*

2 Tell learners to guess the missing verb, then check with a partner.

3 After they've guessed, ask learners which sentences contained the clues that led them to the answer. Also ask which uses of the verb word were new to them.

Note

Make sure that a few of your example sentences contain more or less literal use of the target word (e.g. *put the keys*) as well as some figurative or idiomatic uses (e.g. *she didn't know how to put it*). Present the literal and non-literal examples in a mixed order.

It is also advisable not to include multi-part/phrasal verbs to avoid confusion. For example, if your key verb is *take* do not include sentences with *take off* or *take after* as these are single units of meaning, and learners should be encouraged to see them as such.

Follow-up

1   Learners sort the example sentences into two groups: where the target verb is used in its more literal sense and where the meaning is more figurative. (In the examples for *put* above, Sentences a, c and f have a more literal meaning; the others have a more figurative meaning.) Clarify that in the figurative sentences, *put* often means *cause*:

*Are you prepared to **put** your children **at risk**?* (= cause someone to be at risk)
*This **puts** me **in a very difficult position**.* (= cause someone to be in a bad position)
*What has **put** you in such **a bad mood**?* (= cause someone to be in a bad mood)
*He's **putting pressure** on me **to change my mind*** (= cause someone to so something)

If your class is monolingual, this activity can be done in students' L1. Translations will often correspond to different senses of the word. Results of the sorting activity can also be presented visually as a word web, either on paper or using a mind-mapping tool such as www.coggle.it

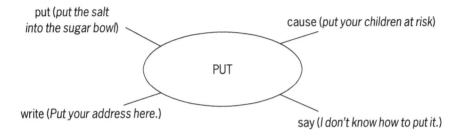

2   If you are using the example sentences for *put* above, you can ask additional questions such as:
   • Why is the present perfect used in Sentences c and i? (= to show the connection with the present – the keys are still lost and the person is still in a good mood)
   • What do you think the situation might be in Sentences g, h and i?

Rationale
On one hand, delexicalized verbs seem easy: they are all words that you encounter at beginner levels. However, because of their polysemous nature and the fact that they are part of many common chunks, they warrant attention at intermediate and advanced levels too. Learners will benefit from frequently revisiting delexicalized verbs and consolidating already known and partially known meanings and uses of these verbs.

   See also Activity 1.5: *Revisiting delexicalized verbs with COCA.*

10.7 Guess the word

Outline	Learners complete sentences with a polysemous word, i.e. a word with many meanings.
Level	Upper intermediate and above (B2+)
Time	15 minutes
Preparation	Find a dictionary entry (online or paper) for a polysemous verb or noun such as *shot* (n.), *acquire* (v.), *way* (n.) (see *Glossary* on p. 223). Choose around ten example sentences, making sure learners are familiar with all (or most of) the words in them. Create a document containing the example sentences with the target word gapped in each case – see examples for *shot* and *acquire* below.

Procedure

1   Display or distribute your gapped example sentences – see *Preparation*. Below are some examples for *shot* (n.) and *acquire* (v.). Tell learners the same noun/verb is missing from all the sentences.

> *shot*
> a   *I've never played golf before so I thought I'd give it a _____.*
> b   *A lot of older people get a flu _____ at the beginning of winter.*
> c   *Ellen took a great _____ of the harbour in the sunset.*
> d   *He fired two _____s from a gun.*
> e   *Wow, great _____! So that's three games to two, my serve.*
> f   *He was a very good _____: he learned how to handle a gun from his father.*
> g   *Just before half time the Frenchman took another _____ at goal.*

> *acquire*
> a   *After a year in Munich, he _____ a good working knowledge of German.*
> b   *The course enabled me to _____ new skills that I could immediately apply in my job.*
> c   *They _____d the firm for £115 million and sold it for £170 million.*
> d   *He quickly _____d a reputation as a dazzling and entertaining performer.*
> e   *The scheme encourages residents to _____ the habit of recycling and sorting waste.*
> f   *I enjoy eating crab but I've never really _____d a taste for mussels.*

2   Tell learners to guess the missing noun/verb, then check with a partner.

3   After they've guessed, ask learners which sentences contained the clues that led them to the answer. Also ask which uses of the noun/verb word were new to them.

Follow-up

After students have guessed the key word, ask them to pick out collocations in each sentence (see the highlighted collocates in the *acquire* examples above). In a subsequent lesson, write brief clues from the example sentences on the board and ask students to recall the collocates, for example:
crab / mussels (= *acquire a taste for*)
course / apply in my job (= *acquire new skills*)
recycling and sorting waste (= *acquire the habit of*)

Note

In the above lists of examples, the least obvious meanings come first. In this way students have to work through most of the sentences before the answer becomes obvious. If you put easier examples at the beginning (e.g. *He fired two _____s from a gun*), learners will guess the answer too quickly and lose motivation to keep reading.

Here are some other words which could be used for this activity:

Verbs

carry	*gain*	*release*
catch	*grip*	*settle*
fit	*pick*	*switch*

Nouns

action	*issue*	*sense*
charge	*matter*	*step(s)*
deal	*mind*	*term*
favour	*point*	*way*

Rationale

The activity focuses on polysemy but indirectly highlights the contextual nature of meaning: to guess a missing word, learners have to look at its co-text (see *Glossary* on p. 223).

10.8 Lost in translation

Outline	Pairs translate sentences into L1 and back into English, then notice differences between their own version and the original.
Level	Upper intermediate and above (B2+)
Time	Variable
Preparation	Prepare around ten sentences in English and write or type each on a separate piece of postcard-sized paper. You will need one set of papers for every four learners. Each sentence should contain a chunk that is either idiomatic or different in some way from the learners' L1, i.e. it cannot be directly translated – see examples in Figure 10.5 below.

Procedure

1 Divide the class into an even number of groups, with four learners in each group. Split each group into two pairs: Pair 1A and 1B; Pair 2A and 2B, etc. (You can allow some groups of three, if necessary.)

2 Give each group a set of papers/sentences – see *Preparation*: half to Pair A, and half to Pair B.

3 Each pair discusses how their sentence can be best translated into L1, then folds their paper into two and writes their translation on top of the folded paper. (Instructing learners to translate may result in a mechanical word-for-word rendition of the target chunk. To prevent this, ask students 'How would you say it in your language?' rather than saying 'Translate it into L1'.)

4 When the translations are ready, each pair swaps papers with the other pair in their group (Pair 1A swaps with Pair 1B, and so on). Pairs should now translate the L1 sentence they have received back into English. They must not unfold the paper and should write their English translation underneath the L1 version.

5 All groups open the folded papers and compare their versions with the originals. Discuss with learners what was 'lost in translation' and reinforce the importance of memorizing whole chunks of language.

The passenger was killed but the driver walked away without a scratch.

How long are you planning on staying?

I should really get going.

You're better off without him.

I haven't seen him for ages.

A: 'I can't find it' B: 'Don't worry, it'll turn up'

Let's talk about it over coffee one day.

My family is scattered all over the place.

I stayed in all day and did nothing.

They stopped playing and exchanged glances as he passed.

Figure 10.5: Possible sentences for back translation

♀ Classroom management tip

If you have a multilingual class, organize groups or pairs of students in such a way that they work opposite another group/pair with the same L1, for example Pairs 1A and 1B – Korean speakers, Pairs 2A and 2B – Russian speakers.

    For larger classes, you could use coloured paper to colour-code groups, for example, Pairs 1A and 1B are blue, Pairs 2A and 2B are pink. When it comes to Step 4, you can tell learners to swap their papers with pairs who have the same colour. This makes the transition between stages much smoother.

Variation

After pairs have translated the sentences into L1, collect the papers. Hand out the L1 translations the following week for students to translate them back into English. (For this variation, you don't need to divide groups into sub-groups/pairs as each group gets their own papers back.)

Rationale

Translating sentences or chunks into L1 and then back to English helps students notice the gap between their knowledge and the target output. Depending on the learners' L1, *planning on staying* might be rendered into the less idiomatic *planning to stay, turn up* is likely to turn into *appear*, and *glances* might become *looks*. Some phrases (such as *You're better off without him*) usually get lost in translation altogether – unless learners know them as chunks, of course!

    Adding the present perfect into this activity adds an interesting twist as in many languages it will have to be translated into either the past or the present, depending whether it relates to an experience or finished action (*I've been there loads of times*) or a continuing situation (*We've known each other for years*). When translating back into English, the present perfect often gets lost. Of course, knowing *We've known each other for ages* or *I've been there* as chunks helps!

10.9 Discourse markers game

Outline	Learners insert as many discourse markers as possible into their conversation.
Level	Upper intermediate and above (B2+)
Time	20–25 minutes
Preparation	Prepare a handout containing sentences with discourse markers (see *Glossary* on p. 223) in **bold**. The sentences should be unfinished – see Figure 10.6 below. Also prepare sets of cards containing discourse markers – see Figure 10.7 below. You will need one set for each group of three or four learners.

Procedure

1 Distribute your handout to pairs of learners – see *Preparation* and Figure 10.6. Pairs complete the sentences with their own ideas.

2 Collect learners' answers and discuss the function of the discourse markers in **bold** (you don't have to introduce the term 'discourse marker'). Suggested answers for the examples in Figure 10.6:

  a *... **but apparently** he's from Canada* (shows the real situation is different; *apparently* has other uses too, e.g. to report what you've read but don't know for sure)

  b *... **just in case** we lose ours* (= a way of protecting against something that might happen)

  c *... **mind you**, it's convenient* (used to say something that makes your previous statement less strong)

  d *... **predictably**, he didn't bother* (= as one would expect)

  e *... **the trouble is** he never accepts any help* (warns the listener that a negative comment is coming)

  f *... **considering** how hard it was to set up* (= when you take something into account)

  g *I wouldn't go there again **though*** (= similar to *but*; only used at the end of a sentence)

  h ***Come to think of it**, I've never used one* (used for adding something you've just remembered)

  i ***In fact**, I haven't seen her since the beginning of the month* (used for adding something surprising to what you've just said)

  j *... **let alone** go to work* (used after a negative statement to say that because the first thing is not possible, the next thing is even less likely)

3 Divide the class into groups of three or four. Give each group a set of discourse marker cards – see *Preparation* and Figure 10.7. (You can exclude any that learners are not familiar with.) The cards should be dealt out so that all group members have the same number.

4 Learners try to get rid of their cards by saying their discourse markers during a group conversation. Every time they use a discourse marker, they put the relevant card on the table. Give groups a topic to talk about, then monitor to ensure learners use the discourse markers correctly.

5 The first group member to get rid of their cards is the winner. Tell learners to shuffle and deal out the cards again to repeat the game. Give groups a new topic to discuss.

a	I thought he was American, but **apparently** _____.
b	We gave a spare key to our neighbour **just in case** _____.
c	Fast food is not good for you. **Mind you,** _____.
d	I asked him to do his homework and **predictably,** _____.
e	I've offered to help him twice before – **the trouble is** _____.
f	All went very well **considering** _____.
g	I had a great time in Thailand. _____ **though**.
h	I'm afraid I know nothing about tablets. **Come to think of it,** _____.
i	I haven't seen her this week. **In fact,** _____.
j	I was so ill I couldn't get out of bed, **let alone** _____.

Figure 10.6: Sentence beginnings with discourse markers

apparently	just in case	mind you	predictably
the trouble is	considering (how)	though	come to think of it
in fact	let alone	frankly	to put it mildly
needless to say	so to speak	incidentally	when it comes to

Figure 10.7: Discourse marker cards

Variations

1   You can also prepare a separate set of cards containing topics for students to discuss, for example: what I did last night, money, homework, a recent trip, an interesting article I read. Learners pick a card from the deck and have a conversation on the given topic.

2   Learners keep their discourse marker cards for the whole lesson and try and use them in any classroom discussions and interactions. The winners are those who have got rid of their cards by the end of the lesson. For this variation, you could deal out a whole set of cards to each learner.

Note

This activity was inspired by *Natural English*, by Ruth Gairns and Stuart Redman.

Rationale

Discourse markers used in speaking are quite different from linking words and phrases used in writing. In my experience, learners find it easier to learn linkers used in written language – such as *furthermore*, *moreover* or *however* – and often overuse them by extending them into their oral production. For this reason, spoken discourse markers deserve explicit attention.

10.10 Memes and memorable movie quotes

Outline Groups use a corpus tool to look up collocations with amplifying adverbs (see *Glossary* on p. 223) such as *highly* and *perfectly*, then find the combinations in film scripts.
Level Upper intermediate and above (B2+)
Time 20–25 mins
Preparation Learners will need a computer with internet access (one per small group).

Procedure

1   Write the following sentence on the board:
    Although he was <u>highly</u> intelligent, he was <u>bitterly</u> unhappy at school.
    Elicit why we use the underlined adverbs (= to amplify or intensify the adjective; to avoid using *very* or *really*).

2   Display the following amplifying adverbs on the board and ask students if they can think of adjectives that often follow them.

perfectly	*abundantly*
deadly	*strikingly*
fundamentally	*incredibly*
fatally	*drop-dead*
strangely	*insanely*
deliriously	*hugely*

3   Divide learners into small groups. Each group looks up the most frequent adjective collocates of a few of the adverbs on the board. To do this, they can use Word Neighbors, COCA or SkELL – see Activites 1.2, 1.5 and 1.8 in Chapter 1. (You could assign different tools to different groups and then compare their findings.)

4   Pool the learners' findings and write them on the board. Try to agree on the three most frequent collocates. Depending on the tools used, you're likely to end up with the following results:

perfectly clear/normal/legal	*abundantly clear*
deadly dull/serious/boring	*strikingly similar/different/handsome/beautiful*
fundamentally different/flawed	*incredibly difficult/important/powerful*
fatally flawed/wounded/injured	*drop-dead gorgeous*
strangely familiar/quiet/silent	*insanely jealous*
deliriously happy	*hugely popular/successful*

5   Point out how *strikingly* tends to go with both *similar* and *different*, and that *different* generally comes up a lot in the results (because it's such a frequent adjective; it's the 237th most common word in English according to COCA). Draw attention to alliteration in *fundamentally flawed*, *fatally flawed*, *strangely silent* and *deadly dull* (see Activity 10.5: *Alliterative chunks*). Contrast *deadly* with *dead* (which can also be used as an adverb but with different collocations: *dead wrong/serious/set/tired*).

6 Using a database of film quotes called www.quodb.com, tell groups to search for the above adverb + adjective collocations in film scripts. In the search bar, they should put double inverted commas around the collocation to find the exact string (as in Activity 8.10: *Upgrading a text using Google*). When they come across a film they know or have seen, they can click on **Context** to see the chunk in context.

7 After rehearsing any extracts they find, groups can act out mini-scenes containing the target chunks in front of the class. (They can add some extra detail and dialogue if they want to.)

Note

Some chunks in this activity are relatively fixed, for example *abundantly* tends to occur with *clear* and *drop-dead* likes the company of *gorgeous*, while others, such as *perfectly*, have wider collocational fields: *perfectly clear/normal/ legal*. This can be turned into a sorting activity – fixed or more restricted chunks (*deliriously happy, abundantly clear, drop-dead gorgeous, insanely jealous*) versus more variable chunks. The latter can be written on the board as collocation forks – see Activity 8.9.

The activity doesn't have to be limited to amplifying adverbs; it will work well with other adverbs of degree. See these examples, with alliterative patterns highlighted:

somewhat (different/similar/surprising)
increasingly (common/popular/important)
poorly (understood/trained/paid/planned)
readily (available)
fully (aware/awake/fledged)
wildly (popular/successful)
largely (responsible)
ridiculously (low/expensive/cheap)
vaguely (familiar)

Variation

An alternative website for this activity is https://getyarn.io where the quote appears within a short clip from a film. The website allows you to turn these clips into memes (see *Glossary* on p. 223) by capturing a still image and adding your own text, which, for the purposes of this activity, will contain the target chunk. After creating memes, students can share them with each other on a social learning platform, such as www.edmodo.com

---

Rationale

Research shows (Granger, 1998) that advanced learners tend to underuse adjective-specific amplifiers such as the ones in this activity. Instead, they fall back on all-round maximizers such as *completely* and *totally*. One of the reasons why learners play safe and rely on these 'default' adverbs is the sheer number of amplifiers to choose from. In order to encourage appropriate use of more specialized amplifying adverbs, start by helping learners establish useful mental links between amplifiers and the adjectives they go with. This can be done through alliteration (*fundamentally flawed*), mnemonic devices (*it was a huge hit; it was hugely popular/successful*) or semantic association (*ridiculously expensive/cheap* – price).

10.11 Learner-created phrasebooks

Outline	Learners create sections of a phrasebook, then test how effective they are by holding mini role plays.
Level	Elementary and above (A2+)
Time	Variable
Preparation	Students will need a computer with internet access. If possible, bring to class a phrasebook for any language.

Procedure

1 Show learners a paper or online phrasebook (there are many on Wikipedia: http://wikitravel.org/en/List_of_phrasebooks). Elicit when you would use it (= when you travel) and what sections it might have (= renting a car, at the hotel, in a restaurant, at the beach, at the doctor's, etc.).

2 Divide the class into pairs. Each pair should choose one phrasebook section and come up with around ten phrases that can go into it. They can do this either on a piece of paper or in a shared online document such as a Google Doc – this way different groups can work on different sections simultaneously and create a phrasebook with several sections by the end of the activity/lesson. Alternatively, phrasebooks can be created using an online publishing tool like https://issuu.com

3 Allow about ten minutes for pairs to discuss what phrases should go into their sections. Monitor and help with language as appropriate.

4 After pairs have finished, they swap sections with other pairs. Pairs use the phrases they have received in a role play, for example between a customer and a clerk (for renting a car) or a customer and a waiter (for a restaurant scene).

5 Conduct feedback at the end. Ask learners whether the phrases they had were useful. How many phrases did they use? What other phrases would they add?

Variation

The activity can be done using www.phraseum.org, an extremely easy-to-use tool which allows you to keep phrasebooks on different topics. You can also browse phrasebooks created by other users and save their phrases to one of your own phrasebooks. See Figure 10.8 for an example.

When entering a new phrase or saving another user's phrase, you can highlight important words to remember, such as prepositions (*Are we on the right road for*), collocations (*Can you take our photo?*) or important bits of grammar (*Can you show me where it is on the map?*). These words will then be blanked out when the **Memorize** button is clicked, so that learners can practise recall in a similar way to Quizlet (see *Useful resources* on p. 227).

Other advantages of Phraseum include the 'clipping button', which you can add to your browser. The button allows you to collect chunks that you find online and save them to one of your phrasebooks, with a link to the original text in which the chunk appeared. Phrasebooks can be made public and shared with others.

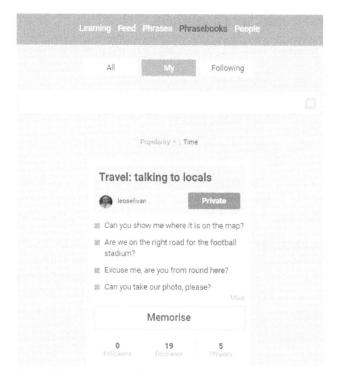

Figure 10.8: Screenshot from www.phraseum.org

Rationale

A quote attributed to Stephen Krashen (as cited in Lewis, 1997) says 'when students travel, they don't carry grammar books, they carry dictionaries'. It would be more accurate to say that they carry phrasebooks – or at least they did until the advent of mobile devices. Although some experts, for example Michael Swan (2006), warn against a 'phrasebook approach' to language learning, in which communication beyond the phrasebook level is not possible, many others, including the author of this book, believe that there is a considerable value in encouraging learners to learn a stock of situation-specific phrases in the initial stages of learning. Of course, these phrases do not have to be limited to travel but as the format of a travel phrasebook will be familiar to many, this topic is a good place to start collecting chunks.

10.12 Chunk chants

Outline	Jazz chants, usually used to practise stress and rhythm, are adapted for practising lexical chunks.
Level	Beginner and above (A1+)
Time	3–4 mins
Preparation	Prepare a chant composed only of lexical chunks – see an example in Figure 10.9 below.

Procedure

1 Display your chant – see *Preparation* and Figure 10.9 – on the board or provide it in a handout. Demonstrate the chant by reading it aloud, with the class repeating it after you chorally.

2 Use a natural rhythm, pace and intonation, and make sure the learners do the same.

3 If the text is written on the board, it can be progressively erased as students become more fluent.

What do you think?
Do you want to go?
If you see what I mean
I mean I don't know

I was going to say
To be honest with you
At the end of the day
I don't know what to do

Thank you very much
And that sort of thing
At the end of the day
I know what you mean

Figure 10.9: Chant composed of lexical chunks

Variation

Chants written in a dialogic form can be chanted by alternating groups. Divide the class into two groups, A and B. Group A reads a line from the left-hand column and Group B replies with the corresponding chunk from the right-hand column. You can also use capital letters to highlight any stressed syllables. See examples in Figure 10.10.

<u>A1/A2</u>

<u>Group A</u>	<u>Group B</u>
Good MORNing.	Good MORNing.
HOW are you FEELing?	I'm FEELing just FINE.
Do you SEE what I MEAN?	No, I DON'T underSTAND.
Do you WANT me to HELP you?	Yes, GIVE me a HAND.
Please COME to my PARTy.	I LOVE a good PARTy.
I HOPE you can MAKE it.	I HOPE I can TOO.

<u>B1</u>

<u>Group A</u>	<u>Group B</u>
TEA or COFFee?	I'M not BOTHered.
MILK or SUGar?	I don't MIND.
HOW would you LIKE it?	HowEVer it COMES.
HERE you GO.	YOU'RE so KIND.
How LONG have YOU been toGETHer?	We've KNOWN each OTHer for EVer.
WHEN was the FIRST time you MET?	So LONG aGO: I forGET.
Would you LIKE it GIFT-wrapped?	Would you BE so KIND?
I'm not SURE I LIKE it.	Well, MAKE up your MIND.
Do you MIND if I GO?	If you FEEL so INCLINED.

Figure 10.10: Dialogue chants

Rationale

Apart from being a fun tool for working on rhythm and connected speech, jazz chants provide a lot of repetition and aid memorization. Memorization and recitation, in turn, improve phonological memory. Many studies have indicated a strong connection between phonological working memory and language learning capacity, including the ability to learn chunks.

See also Activity 4.7: *Rhythmic chunks.*

10.13 The devil's in the detail

Outline	Learners look at pairs of sentences and discuss differences in meaning caused by the addition of one word.
Level	Upper intermediate and above (B2+)
Time	10 minutes
Preparation	Prepare pairs of sentences, where the second sentence in each pair has just one word added or changed. The new word adapts the meaning of the second sentence in some way. See examples in Figure 10.11 below.

Procedure

1   Provide the sentence pairs on the board or in a handout – see *Preparation* and Figure 10.11. Explain that in each pair Sentence b has a single word added or changed, which affects the meaning.

2   Learners discuss the difference in meaning between the sentences in each pair.

3   Take feedback. Here are some suggested answers for the examples in Figure 10.11:

   1   The addition of *do* adds emphasis.

   2   2a means he thought carefully about a decision; 2b means he thought something was finished.

   3   The addition of *'t* (*not*) adds a sense of annoyance; the speaker is irritated because someone is just standing and watching when they could be helping.

   4   *When will you finish?* is a question; *when you finish* is a clause, usually part of a conditional structure, e.g. *Can I borrow it when you finish (reading it)?*

   5   5a implies that Nick is in the photo, while in 5b the photo belongs to Nick (and he may or may not be in it).

   6   In 6a, the speaker is concerned that the person may not have managed to escape; in 6b, the person did escape but the speaker is imagining what things would be like if he hadn't.

   7   In 7a *She's* = *She has* whereas in 7b *She's* = *She is* and *married* is an adjective.

   8   *away* is used to emphasize that the action is continuing for a long of time and/or with enthusiasm, e.g. *She was busy typing away at her laptop and didn't even notice us.*

1a   I like it.
1b   I do like it.

2a   He thought it over.
2b   He thought it was over.

3a   Can you help?
3b   Can't you help?

4a   when you finish
4b   when will you finish

5a   It's a photo of Nick.
5b   It's a photo of Nick's.

6a   What if he didn't escape?
6b   What if he hadn't escaped?

7a   She's married some famous magician.
7b   She's married to some famous magician.

8a   They were chatting like old friends.
8b   They were chatting away like old friends.

Figure 10.11: Sentence pairs with one word added

Rationale

Not only does this activity show how vocabulary and grammar are closely connected, it can also be used – at higher levels – for needs analysis at the beginning of a course. The example pairs of sentences above touch on many grammar points learners are expected to master by B2 level: use of auxiliaries (1), real and unreal conditionals (4 and 6), present perfect (7), etc.

Glossary

Alliteration – A literary device which occurs when a string of words have the same first consonant sound, for example: *born and bred, chalk and cheese, facts and figures, tried and tested, rant and rave.* See Activity 10.5.

Amplifiers / amplifying adverbs – Intensifying adverbs used to emphasize verbs, (gradable) adjectives and other adverbs. Can be divided into two groups: maximizers (e.g. *I was **absolutely** exhausted, The building was **completely** destroyed, It's a **perfectly** simple question*) which denote the highest point on the scale, and boosters (e.g. *She was **bitterly** disappointed, The album was **immensely** popular in the 1990s*) which denote a very high (but not the highest) degree. Adverbs which intensify in the opposite direction, i.e. reduce the force of the word that follows are known as downtoners (e.g. *hardly, barely, slightly, somewhat*). See Activity 10.10.

Binomial – A chunk consisting of two words joined by the conjunction *and, or,* and sometimes *but,* for example: *give and take, law and order, dead or alive, slowly but surely.* They are fixed expressions because the order cannot be reversed, i.e. we can't say *take and give* or *chips and fish.* See Activity 10.4.

Chunk – See p. 13 for a detailed description.

Collocation – A very common kind of chunk consisting of two lexical (content) words that frequently occur together, such as *pursue a career* (verb + noun), *a scenic route* (adjective + noun), *a chance encounter* (noun + noun), *ridiculously expensive* (adverb + adjective), *examine carefully* (verb + adverb) and *the plane took off* (noun + verb).

Concordance / concordance line – A random line of text taken from a **corpus,** which can consist of a full sentence or part of it, showing how a particular word (key word) is used.

Concordancer – A computer program used to extract **concordance lines** from a **corpus.**

Connected speech – A feature of most conversations, where speakers run words together and possibly even pronounce them differently than prescribed in a dictionary.

Corpus (*pl.* **corpora**) – A collection of naturally occurring language samples or whole texts, stored electronically. These samples could be utterances, sentences, conversations, magazines, newspapers and books. The most widely used corpora today are the British National Corpus (BNC) and Corpus of Contemporary American English (COCA), both of which are freely accessible at corpus.byu.edu

Co-text – The linguistic environment of a word. (Not to be confused with **context** which is the surrounding situation or non-verbal environment in which a word is used.) The author of this book takes the view that words cannot be defined without reference to their co-text, i.e. to how words are typically used.

Delexicalized verbs – Verbs with low-semantic content (i.e. without much meaning on their own) and a lot of possible collocates that go with them. Usually the following verbs are considered delexicalized: *do, go, get, look, make, put, set, take*. The only way to master them is to learn them as parts of chunks which contain them, for example: *take place, take part in, take care, take your time, do what it takes*.

See Activities 1.5 and 10.6.

Discourse markers – Words or chunks used to connect, organize and manage conversation or text. They can mark the opening of a new part of a conversation (*so, to begin with …*), the closing of conversations (*Right, fine thanks*), changes in topic (*Anyhow*) and sequencing information (*lastly*). They can also be used to express attitude, in which case they are sometimes referred to as stance adverbials (*Fortunately, Ironically*).

See Activity 10.9.

Ergative verb – A verb that can be either transitive or intransitive, whose direct object when transitive can become the subject of the intransitive form. Examples with *break* and *boil*: *She broke the vase / The vase broke*; *He has boiled the water / The water has boiled*.

See Activity 5.7.

Idiom – A fixed chunk whose meaning is opaque, i.e. it cannot be inferred from the meaning of words it consists of (*be over the moon*). Idioms can be distinguished from fixed chunks with transparent meanings (e.g. *ladies and gentlemen, all expenses paid*).

Meme /miːm/ – A captioned image which symbolizes an idea or depicts a humorous situation, transmitted via social media. Because situations or people in memes should be easily recognizable, images used for memes are often derived from popular films with captions citing memorable movie quotes. Captions very often use the Impact font in white.

Multi-part verbs (MPV) – Verbs consisting of several parts, such as verb + adverbial particle (*look up*, e.g. *look up a word in the dictionary*) or verb + dependent preposition (*look after*, e.g. *look after the children*) or two prepositions (*look forward to*, e.g. *I look forward to seeing you*).

MPVs are often referred to as phrasal verbs in ELT. However, true phrasal verbs are only the first group: verb + adverbial particle constructions, e.g. *look up (a word), take (my shoes) off*. All MPVs are distinguished from verbs followed by prepositional phrases: *climb + up the hill*, where *up* is part of the prepositional phrase *up the hill*, rather than part of the verb.

Mutual Information (MI) – A statistical measurement which shows how much two words in a **collocation** depend on each other. MI takes into account not just frequency but likelihood of the two words occurring together. For example, the word *new* is often found next to furniture (*new furniture*) because *new* is such a frequent word in and of itself, and is 'attracted' to many different nouns. *Antique* and *furniture*, on the other hand, are mutually attracted to each other because *antique* does not have as many partners as *new*. Therefore, *antique furniture* has a higher MI score than *new furniture*. The higher the MI score, the greater the collocality, i.e. the chance of two words being found in each other's company.

Noun phrase (NP) – A word or group of words in a sentence that together behave as a noun. In its simplest form, a noun phrase consists of a single noun, e.g. *I like <u>music</u>*. But the noun can also be accompanied by determiners (e.g. *I like <u>the music</u>*) and modifiers (*I like <u>pop music</u>, I like <u>the music playing on the radio</u>*).

Noticing – The noticing hypothesis, proposed by Richard Schmidt in 1990, states that learners need to consciously register or become aware of linguistic features in the input for input to become intake for language learning. Although noticing does not result in acquisition, it has been argued to be the essential starting point.

Paradigmatic – A paradigmatic relation refers to the relationship between words that are the same parts of speech and which can be substituted for each other in the same position within a given sentence. Synonyms (*<u>old</u> chair – <u>antique</u> chair*), antonyms (*<u>old</u> chair – <u>new</u> chair*) and hyponyms (*<u>chair</u> – <u>table</u>*, i.e. words belonging to the same subcategory of a more general class, in this case furniture) are found in a paradigmatic relation with each other. Contrasts with **syntagmatic** relation.

See Activity 5.4.

Semantic set – A set of words related in meaning and covering the same conceptual domain, for example furniture: *chair, table, sofa, bed*. The words are in a **paradigmatic** relation with each other. Also known as a lexical field.

See Activity 5.3.

Semantic split – When a word in one language can be translated into two different words in another language the word can be said to have a semantic split. For example, Spanish *dedo* corresponds to two English words: *toe* and *finger*.

Syntagmatic – A syntagmatic relation refers to the relationship a word has with other words that surround it, i.e. how a word combines with other words. Syntagmatic relations contrast with and are related to **paradigmatic** relations. For example, the antonym of *old* in *old chair* cannot be *young* because *young* and *chair* are not normally found in a syntagmatic relation with each other. *Young* and *man* or *woman*, on the other hand, are syntagmatically related, i.e. they can occur next to each other.

See Activity 5.4.

Telic verb – A verb that implies a goal or an endpoint, e.g. *arrive*, *drown*, *sing* as in *sing a song* (compare with *sing along* which is not telic).

Transfer – Occurs when learners use their L1 as a resource. Transfer used to be considered something to be avoided (and referred to as 'interference'), but was later recognized as a necessary process for L2 acquisition. All L2 learners apply knowledge from L1, and transfer can occur in any stages of L2 acquisition. It is also sometimes referred to as cross-linguistic influence.

Useful resources

Online learner's dictionaries

Cambridge Dictionaries Online
http://dictionary.cambridge.org

Macmillan Dictionary
www.macmillandictionary.com

The Longman Dictionary of Contemporary English
www.ldoceonline.com

Oxford Learner's Dictionaries
www.oxfordlearnersdictionaries.com

Corpus-'lite' tools

Just-the-word
www.just-the-word.com
A user-friendly visualization tool which enables you to look up the most frequent collocations of a target word, including multi-part verbs.
See Activities 1.3 and 1.4 among others.

HASK collocation browser
http://pelcra.pl/hask_en/browser
Another visualisation tool that illustrates frequency distribution for collocations of a given word. Not as easy to use as just-the-word but it generates colourful pie-charts.
See Activity 8.1.

Phraseup*
www.phraseup.com
A writing assistant which suggests several possible combinations to fill in the words you can't remember. A useful tool for students to use when writing.

Netspeak
www.netspeak.org
Similar to phraseup* in that it helps find missing words. Netspeak will also suggest the most common combinations organized by frequency.
See Activities 4.1 and 5.8.

Lexical Grammar

Fraze.it
http://fraze.it
Another search engine for phrases and sentences on the internet, which comes with an auto-complete function.

StringNet
http://nav.stringnet.org
An archive of multi-word patterns that have been derived from the British National Corpus (BNC). Unlike the tools described above, Stringnet makes it possible to easily navigate from one pattern to other related patterns.

Corpora and concordancing

Lextutor
www.lextutor.ca/concordancers/concord_e.html
A concordancer tool that extracts linguistic data from a corpus. You enter a word and get examples of how it is used, known as concordances or concordance lines – see *Glossary* on p. 223.

BYU corpora
http://corpus.byu.edu/
Mark Davies's website, a home to some of the most popular corpora, including Corpus of Contemporary American English (COCA) and British National Corpus (BNC).

Recording and practising lexis

Quizlet
http://quizlet.com
An indispensable tool for recording and reviewing lexis.

Phrasebot
www.phrasebotapp.com
A website and app with games which allow you to import Quizlet sets for different kinds of practice (particularly suitable for chunks). Navigate to www.phrasebotgames.com and enter your Quizlet set ID, which can be found in the Quizlet URL, for example https://quizlet.com/212931081

Phraseum
www.phraseum.com
A tool for recording lexical chunks which allows you to clip bits of text from online sources
See Activity 10.11.

All of these tools can also be found on the author Leo Selivan's blogsite leoxicon.blogspot.co.uk
Go to the section called Essential Lexical Tools, which is constantly updated: **bit.ly/lextools**

228

References

Aitchison, J. (1994) *Words in the mind: An introduction to the mental lexicon*, Oxford: Blackwell.

Altenberg, B. (1998) 'On the phraseology of spoken English: the evidence of recurrent word-combinations', in A. P. Cowie (Ed.), *Phraseology: theory, analysis and application* (pp. 101–122), Oxford: Oxford University Press.

Boers, F. & Lindstromberg, S. (2005) 'Finding ways to make phrase-learning feasible: The mnemonic effect of alliteration', *System*, 33(2), pp. 225–238.

Bybee, J. (2002) 'Phonological Evidence for Exemplar Storage of Multiword Sequences', *Studies in Second Language Acquisition*, 24(2), pp. 215–221.

Davies, M. (2008) COCA: The Corpus of Contemporary American English (1990–2015), available online at http://corpus.byu.edu/coca

Davis, P. & Kryszewska, H. (2012) *The company words keep: Lexical chunks in language teaching*, Peaslake: Delta Publishing.

Dellar, H. & Walkley, A. (2016) *Teaching Lexically*, Peaslake: Delta Publishing.

Ellis, R (2006) 'Current Issues in the Teaching of Grammar: An SLA Perspective', *TESOL Quarterly*, 40(1), pp. 83–107.

Erman, B. & Warren, B. (2000) 'The idiom principle and the open choice principle', *Text*, 20(1), pp. 29–62.

Folse, K. (2006) 'The effect of type of written exercise on L2 vocabulary retention', *TESOL Journal*, 40, pp. 273–293.

Granger, S. (1998) 'Prefabricated patterns in advanced EFL writing: Collocations and formulae', in A. P. Cowie (Ed.) *Phraseology: Theory, analysis, and applications* (pp. 145–160), Oxford: Oxford University Press.

Hoey, M. (2005) *Lexical priming: A new theory of words and language*, Hove: Psychology Press.

Hyland, K. (2003) *Second language writing*, Cambridge: Cambridge University Press.

Jones, C. (2015) 'In defence of teaching and acquiring formulaic sequences', *ELT Journal*, 69(3), pp. 319–322.

Laufer, B. (1997) 'The lexical plight in second language reading: Words you don't know, words you think you know, and words you can't guess', in Coady, J. & Huckin T. (Eds.), *Second Language Vocabulary Acquisition: A Rationale for Pedagogy* (pp. 20–34), Cambridge: Cambridge University Press.

Lee, S. H. & Muncie, J. (2006) 'From receptive to productive: Improving ESL learners' use of vocabulary in a postreading composition task', *Tesol Quarterly*, 40(2), pp. 295–320.

Lewis, M. (1993) *The Lexical Approach: The State of ELT and a Way Forward*, Hove: Language Teaching Publications.

Lewis, M. (1997) *Implementing the Lexical Approach*, Hove: Language Teaching Publications.

Lewis, M. (2000) *Teaching collocation: Further developments in the Lexical Approach*, Boston: Thomson-Heinle.

Meddings, L. & Thornbury, S. (2009) *Teaching Unplugged: Dogme in English language teaching,* Peaslake: Delta Publishing.

Mondria, J. A. (2003) 'The effects of inferring, verifying, and memorizing on the retention of L2 word meanings: An experimental comparison of the "meaning-inferred method" and the "meaning-given method"', Studies in Second Language Acquisition, 25(4), pp. 473–499.

Myles, F., Hooper J. & Mitchell, R. (1998) 'Rote or rule? Exploring the role of formulaic language in classroom foreign language learning', *Language Learning,* 48(3), pp. 323–363.

Nassaji, H. (2003) 'L2 vocabulary learning from context: Strategies, knowledge sources, and their relationship with success in L2 lexical inferencing', TESOL Quarterly, 37(4), pp. 645–670.

Nattinger, J. & DeCarrico, J. (1989) *Lexical phrases and language teaching,* Oxford: Oxford University Press.

Sinclair, J. (1991) *Corpus Concordance Collocation,* Oxford: Oxford University Press.

Siyanova-Chanturia, A., Conklin, K. & Schmitt, N. (2011) 'Adding more fuel to the fire: An eye-tracking study of idiom processing by native and nonnative speakers', *Second Language Research,* 27(2), pp. 1–22.

Scheffler, P. (2015) 'Lexical priming and explicit grammar in foreign language instruction', *ELT Journal,* 69(1), pp. 93–6.

Swan, M. (2006) 'Chunks in the classroom: Let's not go overboard', *Teacher Trainer,* 20(3), pp. 5–6.

Widdowson, H.G. (1990) *Aspects of Language Teaching,* Oxford: Oxford University Press.

Willis, D. (1990) *The Lexical Syllabus,* London: Collins.

Wood, D. (2015) *Fundamentals of formulaic language: An introduction,* London: Bloomsbury Publishing.

Wray, A. (2008) *Formulaic language: Pushing the boundaries,* Oxford: Oxford University Press.

Index

Activity names are in **bold**.

Milton Keynes UK
Ingram Content Group UK Ltd.
UKHW051524220224
438211UK00015B/32